Hendrik Witt

User Interfaces for Wearable Computers

W0112004

VIEWEG+TEUBNER RESEARCH

Advanced Studies Mobile Research Center Bremen

Herausgeber | Editors:

Prof. Dr. Otthein Herzog
Prof. Dr. Carmelita Görg
Prof. Dr.-Ing. Bernd Scholz-Reiter
Dr. Ulrich Glotzbach

Das Mobile Research Center Bremen (MRC) erforscht, entwickelt und erprobt in enger Zusammenarbeit mit der Wirtschaft mobile Informatik-, Informations- und Kommunikationstechnologien. Als Forschungs- und Transferinstitut des Landes Bremen vernetzt und koordiniert das MRC hochschulübergreifend eine Vielzahl von Arbeitsgruppen, die sich mit der Entwicklung und Anwendung mobiler Lösungen beschäftigen. Die Reihe „Advanced Studies" präsentiert ausgewählte hervorragende Arbeitsergebnisse aus der Forschungstätigkeit der Mitglieder des MRC.

In close collaboration with the industry, the Mobile Research Center Bremen (MRC) investigates, develops and tests mobile computing, information and communication technologies. This research association from the state of Bremen links together and coordinates a multiplicity of research teams from different universities and institutions, which are concerned with the development and application of mobile solutions. The series "Advanced Studies" presents a selection of outstanding results of MRC's research projects.

Hendrik Witt

User Interfaces for Wearable Computers

Development and Evaluation

With a foreword by Prof. Dr. Otthein Herzog

VIEWEG+TEUBNER RESEARCH

Bibliographic information published by Die Deutsche Nationalbibliothek
Die Deutsche Nationalbibliothek lists this publication in the Deutsche Nationalbibliografie;
detailed bibliographic data is available in the Internet at <http://dnb.d-nb.de>.

Dissertation Universität Bremen, 2007

Gedruckt mit freundlicher Unterstützung des
MRC Mobile Research Center der Universität Bremen

Mobile Research Center

Printed with friendly support of
MRC Mobile Research Center, Universität Bremen

1st Edition 2008

All rights reserved
© Vieweg+Teubner Verlag | GWV Fachverlage GmbH, Wiesbaden 2008

Readers: Ute Wrasmann | Anita Wilke

Vieweg+Teubner Verlag is a company of Springer Science+Business Media.
www.viewegteubner.de

No part of this publication may be reproduced, stored in a retrieval system or
transmitted, mechanical, photocopying or otherwise without prior permission
of the copyright holder.

Registered and/or industrial names, trade names, trade descriptions etc. cited in this publication
are part of the law for trade-mark protection and may not be used free in any form or by any
means even if this is not specifically marked.

Cover design: KünkelLopka Medienentwicklung, Heidelberg
Printing company: Strauss Offsetdruck, Mörlenbach
Printed on acid-free paper
Printed in Germany

ISBN 978-3-8351-0256-9

Foreword

Looking at mobile solutions or wearable computing, it immediately becomes apparent that their user interfaces call for different solutions than the desktop paradigm. This is not only due to the very small size of the displays but also predominantly to the need for a much stronger dependency on the applications. In addition, they feature a use of environmental sensors which has never been seen before enabling applications to run in an Ambient Intelligence Environment. This development requires new solutions and constitutes new research questions.

With this book, Dr. Witt contributes to the goal of including mobile and wearable interfaces into a proper development process again: He develops a systematical approach for the development of mobile and wearable user interfaces that can be embedded in standard development processes, and which can also be evaluated during this process. Furthermore, he also describes the architecture and implementation of the WUI, a Wearable User Interface Toolkit, which provides the necessary levels of abstraction to allow the programmers of mobile and wearable solutions to easily implement novel solutions in an almost standardized way.

These results are based on a solid theoretical foundation and thorough state-of-the-art research. The evaluation of mobile and wearable user interfaces which usually combine a primary manual task with computer assistance is developed as an especially clever game-like process: Dr. Witt uses the "hot wire" game to combine all relevant aspects for a proper evaluation.

This book answers a number of research questions in this context:

1. How to evaluate user interface components and interaction concepts for the support of manual tasks,

2. the influence of different work process interruptions by different interaction devices (sound, visual interaction, and gestures),

3. the influence of mobility, posture, and manual actions on the use of interaction and the interruptability of mobile workers, as well as

4. a model-based approach for the development of mobile and wearable user interfaces.

Therefore, this book is a must for everybody who is concerned with the upcoming field of mobile and wearable solutions: Finally, there is a well-founded methodology to develop mobile and wearable user interfaces making them part of the mainstream of software development.

Dr. Otthein Herzog

Preface

First of all, I would like to express my sincerest gratitude and thanks to my adviser, Prof. Dr. Otthein Herzog, who provided me with the opportunity to carry out my research. His constant support and the fruitful discussions we had throughout the years have strengthened me as a researcher. I am also very grateful for the extent of freedom he gave me for conducting my research and the financial funding he supplied me with to travel to various international conferences all around the world.

Secondly, my gratitude goes to my research committee, Prof. Dr. Thad E. Starner, Prof. Dr. Andreas Breiter, and Prof. Dr. Michael Lawo, for their time, support, and encouragement. I am very proud of winning Thad E. Starner, one of the pioneers of wearable computing, for my research committee. His enthusiasm about wearable computers and his great experience in that field have motivated and helped me a lot in making my research more concise. Also, I am very thankful to Andreas Breiter and Michael Lawo for their continuous feedback and tips in revising my papers and suggesting ways to tackle problems. My special thanks go again to Michael Lawo who taught me, with his great experience in management, an efficient way to deal with all kinds of problems.

I like to thank my research colleagues, Tom Nicolai, Christian Dils, and Stéphane Beauregard, for their help and the possibility to discuss problems whenever needed. I also thank Dr. Holger Kenn, the scientific leader of our wearable computing laboratory. He criticized my work, helped me with technical problems, and especially with his tremendous knowledge of all things not related to computer science.

Very special thanks go to Dr. Mikael Drugge with whom I worked together during and after his three months' stay at our research group. I am very grateful for his feedback on my work and the inspiring discussions we had even when he got his Ph.D. and already worked in industry.

My research was partly funded by the European Commission through IST project "wearIT@work: Empowering the Mobile Worker by Wearable Computing" (No. IP 004216-2004). My gratitude and appreciation go to all the 36 wearIT@work project partners for their fruitful work and contribution to my research.

My deepest gratitude goes to my parents, Artur and Ramona Witt, for their love and support. They created the environment I needed to concentrate on my research. Without their support and help over nearly three decades, I would neither have studied at a university nor had I ever tried to apply for a Ph.D.

Finally, I am also very much indebted to my partner, Anna Griesing, for all her help, love, and patience throughout the long time of being a student. She kept everyday things away from me whenever I needed time to work on my thesis. Particularly, I would like to express my deepest gratitude to her for the support during the last months of my Ph.D. work when I was handicapped with a broken leg.

Without you all this thesis would never have been possible. Thank you!

Hendrik Witt

Abstract

Over the last decades desktop computers for professional and consumer applications have become a quasi standard, both in owning them and being able to use them for various applications. Recent years are, however, dominated by a new trend in computing: The mobile use of computers.

The research presented in this thesis examines user interfaces for wearable computers. Wearable computers are a special kind of mobile computers that can be worn on the body. Furthermore, they integrate themselves even more seamlessly into different activities than a mobile phone or a personal digital assistant can.

The thesis investigates the development and evaluation of user interfaces for wearable computers. In particular, it presents fundamental research results as well as supporting software tools for wearable user interface development. The main contributions of the thesis are a new evaluation method for user interfaces of wearable computers and a model-driven software toolkit to ease interface development for application developers with limited human-computer interaction knowledge.

Besides presenting a prototypical implementation of the so-called WUI-Toolkit (Wearable User Interface Toolkit), empirical results of three experiments conducted to study the management of interruptions with gesture and speech input in wearable computing are discussed. Study results allow for deriving design guidelines for forthcoming interface designs. Both, the toolkit and the evaluation method, are essential parts of a generic user interface development approach proposed in the thesis.

Summing up, the research presented motivates and validates the research hypothesis that user interfaces for wearable computers are inherently different to stationary desktop interfaces as well as mobile computer interfaces and, therefore, have to be designed differently to make them usable without being a burden for humans. In connection with this, the thesis provides new contributions for the design and evaluation of wearable user interfaces, mainly in respect to a proper interruption management.

Contents

V Conclusion   219

List of Figures

List of Tables

Chapter 1

Introduction

1.1 Motivation

Over the last decades desktop computers for professional and consumer applications have become a quasi standard, both in owning them and being able to use them for various applications. Recent years are, however, dominated by a new trend in computing: The mobile use of computers.

Nowadays, the use of mobile technology, such as a Blackberry™ or a Personal Digital Assistant (PDA), is a standard for most professionals. Mobile technology has increased productivity and changed work processes even though the use of mobile applications is sometimes still a burden. User interfaces for mobile applications are often designed like ordinary desktop applications. Desktop applications are usually complex, stuffed with many features, and rather general purpose than specific for a single application. Mobile devices differ from desktop systems though. A proper mobile application design requires reflecting its context of use. That is, its mobility and use in many different places and in many different situations.

When considering a special kind of mobile computers that can be used and integrated even more seamlessly into different activities than a mobile phone or PDA, neglecting the context of use is fatal. With the possibility to integrate such computers into clothing, they are highly interesting for industrial application domains such as maintenance or assembly. There, workers have to carry out complex activities on real world objects while being forced to consult instructional material in parallel. Computers supporting workers during such physical activities are called wearable computers. They offer portability during operation, enable hands-free or hands-limited use, can sense the user or environment context, and run continuously.

To let users take advantage of wearable computing technology during their primary activities in the field, a thorough design of the human-computer interface is needed, reflecting its new and unique context of use of being involved in a mobile dual-task situation. Minimized cognitive load and the possibility to let users divide their attention between both tasks as easy and efficiently as possible are crucial design issues of user interfaces for wearable computers. An always limited computational power, restricted interaction possibilities, and constraint mental capacities of users are further properties of the wearable computing paradigm that make solutions challenging that overcome those user interface limitations.

1.2   Wearable User Interfaces

Compared to other software applications, the user interface is also a central part of wearable computing applications. User interfaces for wearable computers (henceforth also called wearable user interfaces) have to reach beyond today's best practice interface designs and classical human-computer interaction (HCI) knowledge to provide an optimal solution for dual-task situations their users are often involved in [Wit07a].

The special input and output devices used for interaction or presentation in wearable computing, such as head-up displays or data glove devices, strongly vary from those devices used in desktop or mobile computing applications where WIMP (Windows Icons Menus Pointing) interfaces similar to Microsoft Windows dominate. Moreover, when operating a wearable application only as a secondary task with most attention paid on a primary physical task, the proper management of interaction like the handling of interruptions originated from the wearable computer is essential but different from desktop and mobile applications where multitasking of users is typically not considered [DWPS06]. Although the primary and the secondary computer task could be serialized by a user, for example, by first stopping one task and then performing the other, the most efficient way to handle both tasks would be to perform both simultaneously. As a consequence, known design guidelines, usability constraints, and available user interface development libraries for desktop and mobile applications are almost not applicable: The desktop metaphor is "dead" for wearable computing [Cla00].

Today, almost no guidelines or standards for wearable user interface design exist [KNW+07]. Instead, special purpose interfaces were designed that require special I/O devices. Such individually designed interfaces have the drawback that they are not easily reusable in different configurations. They cannot be used to reduce implementation efforts for wearable user interfaces by setting up special user interface libraries or interface component repositories as are available for desktop or mobile applications.

Hence, a systematic approach for the design, implementation, and evaluation of wearable user interfaces is needed. Processes have to be established that allow for sustainable interface designs with special evaluation methods to judge their appropriateness for wearable computing. This also includes mechanisms to build reusable repositories or interface libraries that enable application developers to implement adequate user interfaces for their wearable computing applications. This thesis takes up these issues and provides an initial approach to support the design, implementation, and evaluation of wearable user interfaces for mobile dual-task environments where wearable computers support a primary physical task in the real world.

1.3 Research Question and Methodology

The objective of this thesis is twofold. One objective is to investigate the fundamentals of human-computer interaction for wearable computers used in dual-task situations. This enables the design of better user interfaces that adhere to a wearables context of use. To make wearable computers easier to use for humans, a systematic approach to investigate their properties is needed. It should not only allow for research of fundamental issues but also support developers with tools and guidelines needed to implement wearable applications. This is the second objective of the thesis.

The two objectives of the thesis span the entire range of systematic user interface development for wearable computers, i.e., their design, implementation, and evaluation. The thesis is mainly concerned with the following research questions:

- **How to evaluate interface components and interaction concepts for wearable computing applications used in dual-task situations?**
  Classical HCI has proposed many evaluation methods for desktop applications. Only few methods are available that target the evaluation of mobile applications [KG03]. Because wearable computing is different from desktop computing and even mobile computing, new evaluation methods are needed for this paradigm. In particular, methods that allow for an evaluation of user interfaces when users are involved in a dual-task situation with a primary physical task are of interest in many applications.

- **How to appropriately handle interruptions in wearable computing? How do interaction devices impact interruption handling?**
  An inappropriate management of interruptions in a multitasking situation can decrease user performance [ML02]. Because wearable computing takes place in a rather dynamic environment, context changes may impose constraints on users that in turn

may limit them in handling interruptions. Under such constraints, different interaction devices and their characteristics are likely to improve or impair a user's ability to handle interruptions.

- **What is the impact of mobility, postures, and manual actions on interaction device usage and a user's interruptability?**
  Working not only on a single task with the computer, but on multiple tasks with the computer task being only the secondary one, user activity likely means additional load for a user of a wearable system. There may be limits that prevent the use of a certain interaction device or make an interruption impossible to handle in a certain moment. In particular, "users may have trouble moving in a fixed, absolute coordinate frame" [HPGK94] that forces them to always translate frame of reference coordinates between their own dynamic orientation and the frame of reference of an interaction device which is usually fixed.

- **Is there a systematic approach for the development of wearable user interfaces? What special tools are needed to support such an approach?**
  User interfaces for desktop applications have been and are still extensively studied. With the acquired knowledge, tools, guidelines, and processes were created that allowed for the smooth integration of interface development in existing software development processes. With the still young wearable computing paradigm, this situation has not been achieved yet. A systematic approach for the design and development of user interfaces as well as the availability of facilitating development tools is, however, essential for the quality of wearable applications and may raise user acceptance for this new computing paradigm. Here, special software tools will probably make it easier to apply such an approach by application developers.

- **Can model-based approaches facilitate user interface development for wearable computers? Is there a way to build these interfaces with limited or even without expert knowledge?**
  Model-based software development is used to design software on a high level of abstraction. It offers the possibility to abstract low-level details and can, in turn, be automatically interpreted and transformed, for example, based on expert knowledge. Because expert knowledge on wearable computers is not widespread yet, a model-driven development can provide an approach to fill this current gap once available knowledge is integrated in reasoning processes that interpret models to generate user interfaces.

The work presented in this thesis has the ambition to solve real world problems while contributing also to basic research. To accomplish this and to answer posed research questions, a user-driven research methodology was applied. End user demands were the bottom line for both, fundamental research and practical questions. Therefore, all work in the research projects, especially in the EU funded wearIT@work project [Wea04], was conducted with participants from industry and academia. Industry representatives are typically concerned with cost and want to create products based on research results, whereas representatives from academia typically do not care about cost but are concerned with solving rather theoretical problems and building prototypes. To satisfy both groups, an experimental research methodology was used throughout the thesis to examine fundamental research question with user studies in a controlled environment and a more practical methodology for practical and rather industry related questions like the actual implementation of a wearable user interface.

1.4 Scope and Limitation of the Thesis

It has to be noted that, even though different user interfaces often share a common background, their particular design and function always depends on the application domain. Each application domain has unique characteristics with different functional requirements based on their context of use. Providing solutions for all kind of wearable user interfaces in a variety of application domains is not feasible within the scope of this thesis. However, the generic approach for their design, development, and evaluation proposed throughout the thesis, remains applicable for all application domains.

The application domain for this thesis is limited to maintenance and assembly, represented by aircraft maintenance. In aircraft maintenance complex and safety-critical maintenance procedures are carried out on aircrafts in the field. A maintainer's work is dominated by manual actions. In maintenance procedures workers are forced to exactly follow step by step task descriptions for regulatory reasons. Today, these descriptions are still paper-based. Due to this, maintainers are often involved in a dual-task situation with the primary task being the inspection or manipulation of real world objects such as, for example, a turbine or a landing gear, and the secondary task being the reading of task instructions.

The goal of the thesis is to provide a systematic approach for the design, development, and evaluation of a wearable user interface. It is, however, not the goal to develop an in-depth software engineering process model. Instead, considerations emphasize two important aspects of the process: interface evaluation and a software tool concept to facilitate interface development.

Because human-computer interaction covers a large number of aspects, the thesis can only address an in-depth analysis of a subset of encountered user interface challenges in aircraft maintenance. In particular, it focuses on the evaluation of interaction in terms of interruption handling in combination with different wearable interaction devices. Fundamental results and approaches can then be reused or adapted by further research on other application domains. Although long term evaluations are always desired for daily use scenarios, they are beyond the scope of this thesis. Instead the thesis focuses on establishing fundamental results in laboratory experiments to get an initial understanding of coherences between interaction and interruption in a kind of worst case scenario like the one suggested by Sacher and Bubb [SB06]. That is, simulations are used to gather information about a system's usability by novices instead of expert users. Only then the findings can be reasonably validated in long term experiments with novices becoming experts over the course of long term experiments.

Software development tools can be very complex. The prototypical implementation of the software development tool proposed for wearable user interfaces aims to highlight the principle idea and feasibility of the concept for typical step-by-step oriented maintenance applications. It is not the goal to support an unlimited applicability for arbitrary complex application requirements. This is left to future research that concentrates only on software engineering aspects of wearable applications. Also, an in-depth evaluation of the development tool including a concise evaluation of benefits and drawbacks of the chosen architecture design for application developers as well as a qualitative evaluation of its generated user interfaces are not part of this thesis. Instead, an informal evaluation of technical aspects is given, that presents developed applications and first experiences of developers.

1.5   Thesis Organization

The remainder of this thesis is structured in five parts. An overview of its general structure is given in figure 1.1.

Part I builds the fundamental framework of the thesis and describes related work. It consists of four chapters. The first chapter (chapter 2) of part I introduces the basic terminology in wearable computing, and establishes a common understanding of used terms. Additionally, research areas that contribute to the design, development, and evaluation of user interfaces for wearable computers are identified. The remaining chapters 3 - 5 describe the actual framework of this thesis and discuss fundamental concepts and related work for the design and evaluation of wearable user interfaces. Each chapter covers a certain topic:

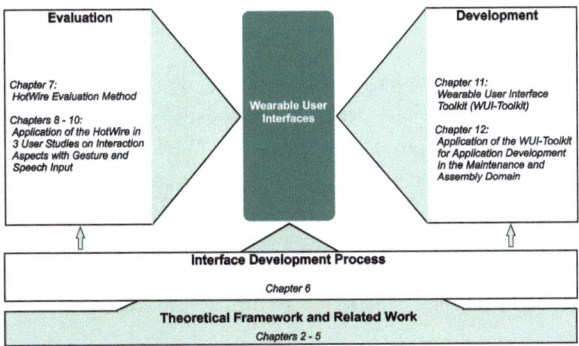

Figure 1.1: Overview of the general structure of the thesis including its two main topics, the evaluation and development of wearable user interfaces.

- **Chapter 3** presents related work by introducing basic principles and important findings from the fields of sensation, perception, and cognition to understand fundamental concepts of interest for user interface design and development throughout the thesis.

- **Chapter 4** builds upon the preceding chapter and discusses the specific aspects and challenges of human-computer interaction with respect to user interfaces for wearable computers. After an introduction of human-computer interaction and user interfaces in general, it focuses on the specific issues of wearable computers. Starting with a discussion of available input and output technologies for wearable computers, the reader's attention is drawn to the properties of interaction and interface evaluation in wearable computing and its difference to traditional desktop devices.

- **Chapter 5** presents related work and especially architectural principles of existing work on the use of context information in user interfaces. Here, adaptive user interfaces are analyzed and discussed with respect to context-based adaptation and used techniques to automatically maintain usability of an interface in different situations.

Part II consists only of chapter 6, where a design and development process is proposed, tailored to meet the special needs of wearable user interfaces, their developers, and researchers. This process is used as an outline in the following two parts of the thesis to systematically design and evaluate new user interface components for wearable computers with the proposed evaluation method and to prototypically implement and use the proposed software toolkit to develop wearable user interfaces with a model-driven approach.

Part III contains four chapters dealing with the design and evaluation of different user interface components and interruption methods according to the previously proposed component evaluation process in chapter 6. While chapter 7 introduces a new evaluation method for wearable user interfaces in dual-task environments, the remaining three chapters discuss specific interface evaluations using the new evaluation method:

- **Chapter 8** studies the impact of different interruption methods on user performance in a wearable computing dual-task setup when gesture-based interaction with a data glove is used.

- **Chapter 9** examines the use of speech input to handle interruptions in a dual-task situation. By basically repeating the experiment described in chapter 8 and replacing gesture interaction with speech interaction conclusions are drawn with respect to the properties of both interaction techniques for interruption handling.

- **Chapter 10** builds on findings of chapter 8. It explores the impact of visual feedback and different frames of reference on gesture-based interruption handling in order to find ways to optimize user performance in wearable computing when using gestures and visual displays.

Part IV deals with the actual development of user interfaces for wearable computers and takes up the user interface development process described in chapter 6:

- **Chapter 11** discusses the prototypical implementation of the proposed model-driven WUI-Toolkit. The architecture of the implemented system as well as its underlying framework is described in this chapter.

- **Chapter 12** presents applications that were developed with the current prototypical implementation of the WUI-Toolkit to show the toolkit's ability to produce working and usable user interfaces that meet end user requirements. Thus, it acts as a first informal evaluation of the toolkit.

Finally, **part V** completes the thesis with chapter 13 that reflects the contributions of the thesis by concluding remarks and an outlook that points out future work and open research questions.

Part I

Theoretical Framework and Related Work

Chapter 2

Interdisciplinary Foundations

The design of wearable user interfaces is an interdisciplinary task. Results from different scientific disciplines have to be taken into account to develop useful and usable user interfaces for wearable computing applications. In particular, fields of research such as graphical design, psychology of perception and cognition, human-computer interaction, and Artificial Intelligence provide important basics and methods.

This chapter establishes a common understanding of wearable computing and its associated research questions by presenting definitions and current research directions.

2.1 What is a Wearable Computer?

In general, the term "Wearable Computer" covers a broad range of devices and concepts of use. It can include "real" computers with standard I/O capabilities that are worn to some extent on the body as well as small embedded devices with very limited capabilities. Hence, wearable computers are not described by a fixed definition, but by different attributes that characterize them.

One of the first notions of a wearable computer goes back to a technical report authored by Thad Starner in 1995 called "The Cyborgs are coming" [Sta95]. There, the author suggested that a wearable computer interface has mainly two characteristic: persistence and constancy. Persistence describes that the wearable computer interface is "persistent" as it is constantly available and being used concurrently with other tasks. Constancy describes the property that the same wearable computer interface is used in every situation. Obviously, this definition is directed more towards a wearable computer being fully integrated into every days live of its user and reminds on Cyborgs. The term "Cyborg" was originally coined by Manfred Clynes and Nathan Kline in 1960. In [CK60] they described a cyborg as a combination of a human and a machine where the interface has become a "natural" extension and does not require continuous attention to control it. Although Clynes and Kline targeted astronauts in their work, it can also be used in wearable computing as a metaphor to express that a seamless integration of users and interfaces is wanted.

In 1997, Rhodes [Rho97] took up this approach and defined that a wearable computer has five properties: It

1. is portable while in operation,

2. enables hands-free or hand-limited use,

3. can get the users attention even if not in use,

4. is always "on",

5. and attempts to sense the user's context for better serving him.

Kortuem et al. [KSB98] introduced almost the same properties as Rhodes did, but under the term of "augmented reality". In particular, they concentrated on the user interface technique that should be able to focus on the user's attention and to present information unobtrusively and context dependent.

Also in 1997, Steve Mann, another pioneer in wearable computing, has defined his wearable system that he called "WearComp" with three attributes [Man97]: A wearable computer is an "eudaemonic criterion", i.e. the computational apparatus has to be situated in a way that it makes it part of the mobile wearer and is, for example, not connected to any stationary power supply that would restrict the way of using the apparatus. The system is also an "existential criterion" whereas its computational capabilities are controllable by the user but "need not require conscious thought or effort, but the locus of control must be such that it is within the user's domain" (p. 66). Finally, Mann's wearable system is an "ephemeral criterion", i.e., delays caused by interaction or operation are nonexistent, as the wearable computer "is constant in both its operation and its potential for interaction with the user" (p. 66). Here, "operational constancy" means that the system is always active while being worn. It may have power saving modes, but is always able to wake itself up. In doing so, the system can take notice of environmental conditions by using an existing sensors subsystem. "Interactional constancy", however, is described by Mann as a property where one or more existing output channels, for example, a head-mounted display (HMD) are visible all the time and not only during user interaction. In this way, the mental effort to change between interaction and non interaction mode is nearly zero.

In 2001 Mann [Man01a] refined his definition of wearable computing and introduced the theory of *humanistic intelligence*. Mann defines humanistic intelligence as the "intelligence that arises when a human is part of the feedback loop of a computational process in which the human and computer are inextricably intertwined" (p. 10). A wearable computer that is an embodiment of humanistic intelligence has three fundamental operational modes: *constancy, augmentation,* and *mediation*.

Thad Starner, one of the founders of the first international wearable computing conference, the International Symposium on Wearable Computers (ISWC), is currently one of the persons that has gained many experiences using wearable computers in daily life. He has worn his computer almost constantly over the last 10 years. In several publications (e.g., [Sta02b, Sta02a, Sta02c, Sta01b, Sta01a, Sta99, Sta95]), he addressed and refined the attributes of a wearable computer over the years. In [Sta99], for example, Starner refines his attributes of a wearable computer based on his work in [Sta95]. Although the basic attributes remain the same, such as that a wearable computer "must be constantly with the user, sharing in the experience of the user's life, drawing input from the user's environment, and providing useful and graceful assistance as appropriate" [Sta99, p. 22], he gave more details to these attributes. In particular, he thinks that a wearable computer should persist and provide constant access. Obviously, this includes that the system has to be unobtrusive and mobile to achieve this goal. If necessary, the wearable system is able to interrupt the user. There is little effort to access the system by the user. To provide useful cues in a task, the wearable computer "must try to observe and model the user's environment, the user's physical and mental state, and the wearable's own internal state" [Sta99, p. 23]. Regarding the presented information to the user, the wearable computer augments and mediates information automatically through filtering. Finally, by adapting existing "input and output modalities automatically to those which are most appropriate and socially graceful at the time" [Sta99, p. 23], the wearable system interacts seamlessly. As wearable computers are often used to support real world tasks, the wearable computer should become a secondary task whereas the physical task (i.e. a real world task) is the primary task that needs to be supported with minimal user attention to the system.

Summarizing the above, wearable computers cannot be easily defined within only one short definition. Instead, a definition can summarize fundamental attributes that a system should have to be considered a wearable computer system.

Definition 1 [Wearable Computer System]:
A wearable system consists of the wearable hardware and a software running on the hardware. A system considered to be a wearable computer system typically has the following properties and constraints:

- **Limited Capabilities:** The wearable computer system is often very limited or constrained in terms of available computation power, energy consumption, and available I/O modalities compared to capabilities of stationary computer systems [Sta99].

- **Operation Constancy:** The wearable computer system is always on and provides the user with useful function. Here, the primary task is the focus, requiring the wearable system to be a secondary support in the background [Sta99, Rho97, Man97].

- **Seamless Environment Integration:** The wearable computer system has to be unobtrusive and non-distracting for the user during a primary physical task. Thus, its user interface is tailored to a specific context of use [Sta02a].

- **Context-Awareness:** The wearable computer system senses properties (of the environment or user) that are useful to support the user during a primary task and may be used to optimize interaction [Sta99, KSB98, Rho97].

- **Adapted Interaction:** The wearable computer system may automatically adapt the interaction style and/or interface rendering of a running application in order to make interaction easier and more efficient while minimizing mental effort [Sch02, Sta02a, SGBT00, Sta99, KSB98].

2.2   Research Topics of Wearable Computers

Today, research in wearable computing is mainly dominated by six different areas. They range from hardware-related research typically dominated by scientists from electrical engineering, to user interaction research, and to research concerned with the integration of electronics into textiles to provide smart clothing. By examining the wearable computing research community over the years at the International Symposium on Wearable Computers (ISWC), we have identified the following relevant research topics along with their aims:

1. **Hardware**

   Because wearable computers are different to today's mobile computer hardware in many ways, developers must find answers to significant challenges in building wearable computers that are not awkward to use. Perhaps the most limiting factor of

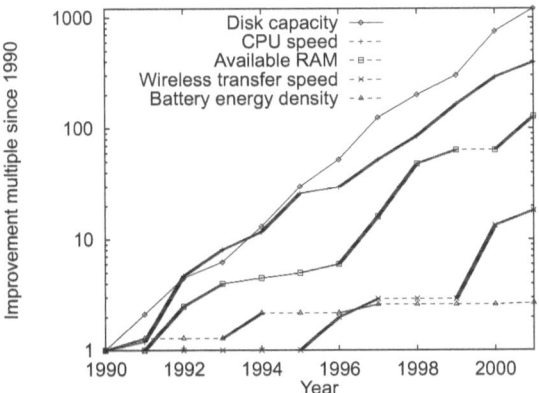

Figure 2.1: Mobile technology improvements since 1990 [Sta02b, p. 1].

all mobile technology is power. Although transistor density has shrunken exponentially over the last years, battery energy density has not, but increased linearly with a shallow slope [Sta01a]. Figure 2.1 shows that battery energy density lags behind other mobile technology improvements. This is why mobile device's weight is often more influenced by its power supply rather than its electronics. Wearable computers weight and form factor are big issues, because the wearable computer is worn over a long period (almost all the time) and should not distract the user, for example, by inappropriate weight or form factor. An accompaniment of power is heat dissipation. Here, the problem is to get rid of the heat caused by processor chips inside the wearable computer. Although the dissipated heat of a mobile computer and its limited computational power does not seem to be an issue, in combination with dissipated heat of the human body it will.

2. **Human-Computer Interaction (HCI)**
   Wearable computers should support their users during a primary task. Therefore, they are only secondary, which distinguishes them from other mobile devices. Not assuming constant attention to the user interface like, for example, in stationary computing, requires new user interfaces and interaction methods that meet these specific requirements. As much as mobile devices need special interfaces [LK93], so do wearable computers. Handling only mobility issues is not enough in wearable computing. The main challenge in wearable HCI is the combination of casual use, environment information, and limited interaction capabilities.

The availability of sensor technology (ranging from temperature sensors to complex acceleration sensors) opens up new opportunities for research in wearable HCI. Among others, implementing context-aware interfaces that automatically adapt to situations or understand the user's intention are envisioned. For this, deeper insight in user interruption, information presentation, and context information processing is needed.

3. **Context Recognition**

Wearable computers are able to collect information from the environment and the user through different sensors. In order to use this information in applications, raw sensor data has to be interpreted and aggregated. Sensor data can range from simple temperature data to data measured by a multitude of complex sensors and makes context recognition challenging.

The goal is to find methods that recognize activities performed by the user or environmental properties. Once a system is able to recognize this information, implicit interaction with the wearable computer could be implemented to significantly reduce interaction. Typically, current recognition methods rely on Artificial Intelligence (AI) machine learning techniques (cf. e.g. [SOJ⁺06, JLT04, LJS⁺04, WBAS03]). Although today's research often uses supervised learning that involves lots of effort on analyzing raw data for feature extraction and preparation of test sets, the envisioned goal is to use unsupervised learning for context recognition. Using unsupervised learning would allow for the development of context recognition methods that could be applied to a broad range of application domains because these methods would be able to learn different contexts autonomously. Ashbrook and Starner [AS03] gave an example for these methods and demonstrated how locations of significance can be automatically learned from GPS data.

4. **Augmented Reality**

Augmented reality is an independent research area. In contrast to Virtual Reality, its goal is not to let the user interact in a virtual world, but to augment the real world with useful information. Typically, augmentation is achieved through overlaying a real world image with computer generated information. Thus, augmented reality often focuses on extending the user interface through sophisticated 3D graphics, but with significant impact on the computational power needed (cf. [BKLP05] for different examples). This is because computer vision techniques are used to analyze a real world camera image for positioning overlay information at the right location on a head-mounted display.

5. **Smart Clothing**

The ultimate wearable computer will be clothing. Users might only wear their daily clothing and glasses and already have access to a complete wearable computing system including a visual display integrated into the glasses. To reach this vision many challenges have to be solved. First of all, flexible circuit boards or micro systems are needed allowing hardware developers to build devices or sensors that can be smoothly integrated into textiles (cf. [Bue06, LKAR05]). To be able to integrate and connect such devices that are potentially distributed over different parts of the garment, conductive yarns and treatment methods for electronic textile materials are needed that allow for an integration into today's textile production. More details on recent technologies can be found, for example, in [BDS07, LKAR05, KX05, MHM05]. Besides these integration-related aspects, there is also research in this area that deals, for example, with expressing the user's current mood through textile accessories that change their appearance accordingly [BC05], or accessories for recharging batteries integrated in smart clothing with special clothes hangers [TTM06].

6. **Applications**

The actual wearable computing applications themselves do not seem to be scientifically challenging, because they are basically concerned with integration issues. Integration, however, is the real challenging aspect. Combining a set of components, for example, interaction devices, computers, etc. and configuring them to work together is engineering. Selecting the right set of components for an application domain is challenging and involves the application of methods and techniques often subsumed under the term "user centered design" [VIR01]. This is, because a wrong selection of components can immediately lead to a loss of unobtrusiveness or usability of the system due to a cyborg look and feel that is likely not to gain much user acceptance. Typically, this includes, to a minor degree, the development of new methods rather than adapting already existing methods to the specific requirements of wearable computing. For example, in 2004 the wearIT@work [Wea04] projected was established to investigate the opportunities of wearable computing applications for industry.

The above identified research areas along with their specific research questions are currently investigated in the wearable computing community. However, there are related research communities that also contribute to similar research questions. Basically, these are the communities of ubiquitous and pervasive computing.

Ubiquitous and Pervasive Computing

The terms "ubiquitous" and "pervasive" are often used equivalently as both deal with information access at any time and any place [BHH+02]. "Ubiquitous computing" was first introduced by Mark Weiser [Wei91] as a future vision of everywhere computing. For him, ubiquitous computing was the "idea of integrating computers seamlessly into the world at large runs counter to a number of present-day trends" (p. 95). His vision was more than just carrying notebooks to different places or using powerful handheld devices. He rather claimed unobtrusive and disappearing computers that are ubiquitously available whether placed in the environment or on the user. Hence, Weiser's definition was more embossed by a theoretical and scientific future perspective than short term implementations.

Hansmann et al. [HMNS01] defined "Pervasive Computing", for example, as the ability of having "convenient access, through a new class of appliances, to relevant information with the ability to easily take action on it when and where you need it". Consequently, "pervasive computing" has almost the same attributes like "ubiquitous computing", but is more concerned with short term realizations using electronic commerce and web technologies [BHH+02].

Although contributions from both research communities often target mobile devices such as mobile phones or PDAs (Personal Digital Assistants), many results can be applied to, or at least are related to wearable computing. In particular, there are many methods, techniques, and architectures that can facilitate the development of mobile applications or handling of context information such as determining, modeling, and processing context information

The research agenda of pervasive computing subsumes that of mobile computing, but additionally includes, according to [Sat01], four more research issues:

1. Invisibility

2. Effective use of smart spaces

3. Localized scalability

4. Masking uneven conditioning

Invisibility is the most self-explanatory research issue mentioned above and basically expresses Weiser's ideal of a completely disappearing technology for the user.

The second issue of an *effective use of smart spaces* is characterized by embedding computing infrastructure into buildings. Once embedded, a smart space is created that enables the control of one world by the other through sensing. For example, heating a room can be automatically adjusted dependent on a current occupancy of people. On the other hand, software applications running on a user's computer may behave differently depending on the user's motion profile.

The issue of *localized scalability* describes the problem that occurs, when highly sophisticated smart spaces are considered. In such spaces the intensity of interaction between a user's computer and her environment will increase along with its complexity. While current web servers are designed to handle as many requests as possible, regardless of the source location of the request, pervasive computing differs. Here, interaction is only wanted in a certain surrounding region of the user or device. Otherwise, it would lead to a multiplicity of distant interactions that would only have little relevance, but could potentially produce high loads on computers.

The fourth issue is the development of *masking uneven conditions* of the environment. In the course of time, pervasive computing technology will be embedded in more and more environments. However, due to different non-technical factors, the specific "smartness" of the environment will vary. Therefore, technologies are wanted that are able to deal with these varying environments while still working. A trivial example might be the capability of a device that is still able to offer its service even though no wireless network connection is available.

2.3   Contributing Research Areas

The previous discussions already showed that wearable computing, although being new, is not a completely independent research area. In fact, research questions to be investigated in wearable computing are related to different disciplines ranging from technical to social sciences. These disciplines can be basically clustered into three groups:

1. Computer Science

2. Electrical Engineering

3. Psychology

When looking at these disciplines on a detailed level (from a perspective of computer science) wearable computing involves mainly Artificial Intelligence (AI), human-computer interaction (HCI), and hardware design. Although all of them are subsets of computer science, none of them is "relatively prime" with one of the two remaining sciences. In fact, HCI, for example, is strongly related to research in sensation, perception, and cognition, which is a branch of psychology. Also, hardware design has its roots in the field of electrical engineering.

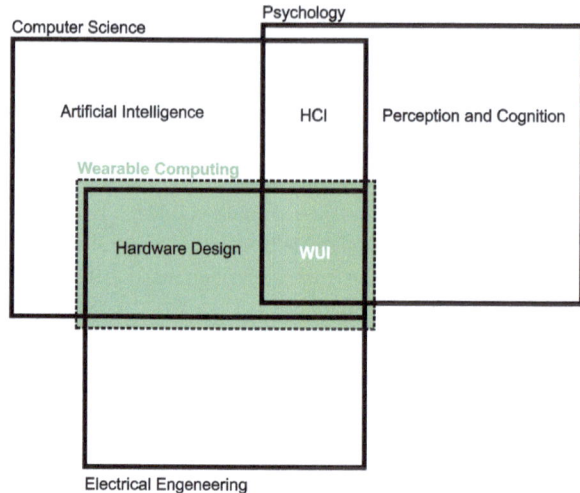

Figure 2.2: Contributing research fields to wearable user interfaces.

When considering wearable user interfaces the identified research areas of wearable computing are still relevant. Wearable user interfaces are, however, particularly related to HCI and psychology rather than electrical engineering. Figure 2.2 illustrates this coherency.

In line with figure 2.2, chapters 3 - 5 will present contributing research to wearable user interfaces that is situated either in the field of computer science, including its subsets AI and HCI, or in psychology. For the latter, the focus will be on perceptual and cognitive aspects of visual and audio data perception. Hardware related aspects beyond interaction devices will be omitted because only very few of them are related to user interfaces.

Chapter 3

Fundamentals of Perception and Cognition

After having provided a common understanding of central terminologies and having identified contributing research areas to the topic of this thesis, this chapter will start to introduce basic principles and related work from the areas of perception and cognition.

Humans and their behavior have been studied already for many years. Cognitive and perceptual psychology have created a huge body of detailed knowledge about humans' cognitive boundaries and their ability to perceive properties of the environment that are important for their survival. Even today new findings are being discovered and this will probably not stop in the foreseeable future due to the incredible complexity of humans.

3.1 Introduction

Researchers in sensation and perception study phenomena that most of us take for granted, such as the ability to safely cross a street or the transcription of sentences from a blackboard to our notes. However, this is only possible if we can use our senses in a normal way. Thus, understanding perception is an important step to help building devices that restore perception to those that have lost it. Understanding perception in order to derive perceptual demands of different activities such as driving a car is also important, for example, to design proper human-computer interfaces for car navigation systems.

Research in sensation and perception is organized around the dynamically and continually changing perceptual process. This process roughly involves pattern recognition, action, transduction, and processing [War04, p. 20]. Each of these steps involves a broad range of questions that can be found in almost every text book on that topic. For more details we recommend reading the text book of Bruce E. Goldstein [Gol02] as a comprehensive source for the current status.

A second important source for the design of proper human-computer interfaces is cognitive psychology. It is concerned with the internal processes of the human brain involved in making sense of the environment [EK05, p. 1]. These processes include attention, learning, memory, language, problem solving, and thinking as well as the overlapping aspects of perception that are particularly investigated in perceptual science. Compared to perceptual science, cognitive psychology is a rather new field started around 1956. In that year, in a meeting at the Massachusetts Institute of Technology (MIT), several researchers presented their work related to cognitive psychology: Noam Chomsky introduced his theory of language, George Miller [Mil56] presented a paper on short term memory, Newell and Simon discussed their model of a General Problem Solver (discussed later in [NS72]), and Bruner et. al [BGA56] found a first systematic approach of concept formation from the perspective of cognitive science. In the same year almost the same researchers founded the field of Artificial Intelligence at the Dartmouth conference. Apparently, this is the reason why cognitive psychology and Artificial Intelligence are tightly related as they use the same model of information processing [EK05, p. 1].

For wearable user interfaces the most valuable findings probably reside in research related to the visual, audio, and tactile senses. Here, graphical user interfaces will benefit the most from findings about how the visual stimulus is constructed and what the cognitive limitations of the human brain are if, for example, monocular head-mounted displays are used as output devices, or users have to simultaneously perform tasks. For wearable audio or tactile interfaces, properties of related senses, needed to operate these interfaces, will provide valuable findings as well.

A detailed analysis of the cutaneous stimulus and implications that could be drawn for tactile wearable user interfaces will be omitted. In section 4.2.3 we give, however, a brief overview of tactile devices developed to control wearable applications.

3.2   The Visual Stimulus

One significant reason for the intelligence of humans is founded in their ability to identify patterns. The visual system is probably the most sophisticated pattern recognition mechanism of humans. More than 70% of our sensory receptors are visual receptors and those engage almost 50% of our cortex [Gol02].

The capacity of our visual system might be the reason why most of today's user interfaces are designed as graphical user interfaces (GUIs). When looking at the evolution of graphical interfaces starting from early text-based interfaces to recent GUIs found in

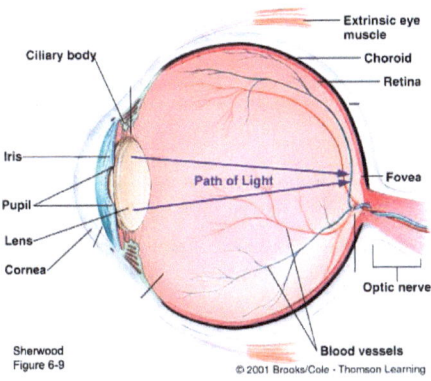

Figure 3.1: The human eye [She06].

applications running on modern operating systems such as Linux or Microsoft Windows, we find that our visual system is still able to maintain these applications although their complexity has dramatically increased over the years. However, when dealing with wearable user interfaces such sophisticated interfaces are hardly imaginable as their complexity would often exceed limitations of the wearable computer or its application domain (cf. section 2.1). In particular, operating these interfaces in mobile environments while being involved at the same time in a real world task, calls for interfaces different to today's standard GUIs [Sta02a, Cla00]. The following discussion will target specific findings in psychology affecting the design of wearable user interfaces.

3.2.1   Light - The Stimulus for Vision

The ability of seeing involves light as the stimulus and the visual system as the mechanism that processes the stimulus. The visible light perceivable by humans has a wave length ranging from 400 to 700 nanometers and is associated with different colors ranging from blue (400 nm) over green (550 nm) to red (700 nm). When the light enters the eye it passes through the eye's focusing elements, the corona and lens. They create a focused image on the retina, where the light of that image stimulates the receptors. The two kinds of visual receptors are rods and cones that trigger an electrical signal forwarded to the optical nerves, which on their part relay them to the cortex. There is a small area on the retina, called *fovea*, that contains only cones and produces the sharpest possible image. The fovea is directly located on the line of sight so that the center of an image

directly falls on the fovea whenever we look directly at an object. Figure 3.1 illustrates
the different parts of the human eye.

3.2.2   Visual Acuity

Many people know a situation where it was difficult to locate their colleagues in the
crowded cafeteria although they knew the area to search in. Unless one of the group
starts to wave her hand or shouts the persons name to get her attention, people tend to
scan systematically all faces in the region until they recognized one of the faces of their
colleagues to find them.

The reason for this scanning behavior is the need to focus the image of a face on the
fovea to see enough details to recognize a known face. Remember, only the fovea has the
ability to see details, because it only consists of cones and thus has the best visual acuity.
All objects in the area around a focused object fall on the rod-rich peripheral retina which
cannot provide the high visual acuity that is necessary for the recognition of an object.
A simple experiment that illustrates the different visual acuity of fovea and peripheral
retina is given in figure 3.2. When looking at the X in the line of letters given in the figure
without moving eyes, one will find that although one can read the letters right next to
the X, one can read only a few of them that are off to the side. This is because the letters
off to the left side fall on the peripheral retina which has only low visual acuity.

$$D \; I \; H \; C \; N \; R \; L \; A \; Z \; I \; F \; W \; N \; S \; M \; Q \; P \; Z \; K \; D \; \mathbf{X}$$

Figure 3.2: Visual perception experiment.

There are different ways to measure visual acuity. The most familiar way to measure
visual acuity uses Herman Snellen letters. Herman Snellen (1834-1908) developed his
method in 1862. The Snellen chart for testing visual acuity usually consists of letters or
numbers printed in lines of decreasing size which a person is asked to read or identify at
a fixed distance. A person achieving "20/20" visual acuity is considered to have "normal"
visual acuity. The person is just able to decipher a letter that subtends a visual angle of
5 minutes of an arc at the eye whereas the distance to the letter is 20 feet. Note that the
visual acuity of a person is better than 20/20 when having, for example, 20/15 acuity and
worse if the achieved acuity is, for example, 20/30. Thus, the lesser the last number in
the visual acuity ratio, the better the acuity; and the greater the last number, the worse
the acuity.

For determining a persons visual acuity we first have to calculate the size of the letters
that a person must be able to decipher. Regarding Snellen's definition the visual angle α

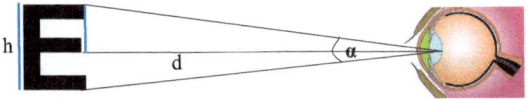

Figure 3.3: Letter size calculation for Snellen's visual acuity test.

is fixed to 5 minutes of arc which is equivalent to 5/60 of a degree (because there are 60 minutes of arc in 1 degree). By using the tangent trigonometry function we are able to calculate the height h of a letter at a certain distance d:

$$
\begin{aligned}
tan(\frac{\alpha}{2}) &= \frac{\frac{h}{2}}{d} \\
h &= 2d \cdot tan(\frac{\alpha}{2}) \\
h &= 2d \cdot tan(\frac{1}{6})
\end{aligned}
\tag{3.1}
$$

Figure 3.3 shows how the tangent is applied. By knowing about the visual acuity of a person we are now able to specify the minimum size of a letter that a person with a certain visual acuity is able to read on a visual output device like an HMD. The only information needed is the perceived distance between the eye and the display that presents a graphical interface to the user to calculate the letter size. Note, visual acuity might be different for the left and right eye. Thus, the minimum letter size also depends on the position, for example, of the used HMD, i.e. whether it is mounted in front of the left or right eye of the wearer.

3.2.3   Perception of Color

The ability to perceive different colors is one of our most important and pervasive qualities. We use colors in various situations in our every day life for interaction such as for traffic lights, daily choice of clothing to be color coordinated, or user interface designs. For describing all colors we can differentiate, we use typically the terms red, yellow, green, blue, and their combination [Hur81]. It was found that when people are asked to describe many different colors with only a subset of these four terms that they cannot describe them properly [Gol02, p. 189]. Therefore, red, yellow, green, and blue, are considered as basic colors by color researchers [War04, p. 101].

Thomas Young (1773-1829) and Herman von Helmholtz (1821-1894) proposed the so called *trichromatic theory* to explain color vision. Their theory states that color vision depends on the activity of three different kinds of cones in the human eye [Gol02, p. 191].

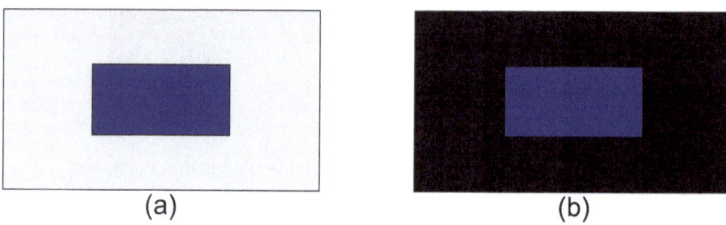

Figure 3.4: Simultaneous color contrast.

For that reason sometimes the colors red, green, and blue are also called basic colors. By changing the color intensity of these three basic colors (almost) all perceivable colors can be mixed. Visual displays, for example, use this three color space (known as RGB color space) for color visualization. Although trichromatic color vision theory is widely accepted and can explain many vision phenomenons, there are some phenomenons that can not be explained properly with the theory, such as afterimages [Her05]. For this, Ewald Hering (1834-1918) proposed the *opponent-process theory* of color vision. It states that color vision is caused by opposing response generated by blue and yellow and by red and green [Gol02, p. 195]. Compare [War04] for a more detailed discussion on this and related issues.

An important phenomenon for user interface design that can be explained with this theory is *simultaneous contrast*. Simultaneous contrast describes the strong dependency of two adjacent colors regarding perception [Dah06, p. 48]. Figure 3.4 illustrates the different perception of the same blue color tone with two different backgrounds. While in figure 3.4(a) blue is perceived as dark and opal, the same blue in figure 3.4(b) is perceived as bright. The surroundings of a color has thus not only an impact on color brightness perception but also on hue. This important property of adjacent colors should be considered in user interface designs and particularly for wearable interfaces where colors could be well used for structuring the typically rather simple interfaces.

As already mentioned above, the stimulus for our vision is light and therefore our perception of colors is also linked to the wavelength of light. When we pick an apple from a tree on a sunny day the color of the apple does not change when we look at it in the evening with artificial light - it is still green. This phenomenon is called *color constancy*. It describes the relatively stability of color perception under changing illuminations [Gol02, p. 207]. One factor for this is *chromatic adaptation*, that is that light sensitivity of color decreases over time [EK05, p. 52]. Hence, chromatic adaptation is responsible for eyes adapting relatively fast when you walk from outside into a room with only pale

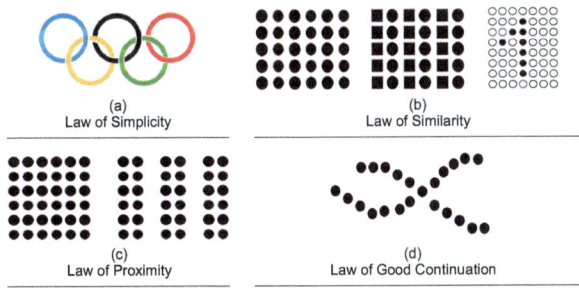

(a)
Law of Simplicity

(b)
Law of Similarity

(c)
Law of Proximity

(d)
Law of Good Continuation

Figure 3.5: Examples of Gestalt Laws.

illumination with decreasing light sensitivity. Another factor for color constancy is color familiarity. People tend to map color to objects independent of illumination. For example, people know that the German postboxes are painted yellow and thus they remain yellow even when they are illuminated by artificial street lamps.

Although color constancy lets us perceive color to be the same at different illuminations, some experiments, however, have shown that under certain circumstances color perception can change (e.g. simultaneous contrast) [BH96, Hur99]. In particular, it was found that color constancy is lower in a laboratory than in real life because some cues (e.g. reflected highlights) are not availably in laboratory. Thus, user interface evaluation of wearable applications should consider real life (physical) simulations for testing instead of virtual ones.

3.2.4   Perceiving Objects

Day by day we are overwhelmed with thousands of visual information of which we make sense usually by identifying, recognizing, and grouping them together. The same holds for visual information that is generated by computers, for example, through graphical user interfaces of applications.

The complex process of perceiving objects has been studied in-depth by research that has looked on the relationship between stimuli and perception [War04, Gol02]. One of the most important contributions to our understanding of how humans perceive objects has been made by the German Gestalt psychologists (including M. Wertheimer, K. Koffka, and I. Kohler) around 1912. They introduced a series of rules, called the *Gestalt Laws of Perceptual Organization* that describe how we organize different small parts into wholes with the basic principle of the Gestalt psychology that *"the whole is different than the sum of its parts"* [Gol02, p. 148]. The six Gestalt laws are:

Law of Prägnanz (Law of Simplicity) *Every stimulus pattern is seen in such a way that the resulting structure is as simple as possible.*
The well known Olympic rings shown in figure 3.5(a) are a good example for the law of simplicity. Instead of perceiving the Olympic rings at their intersections as complex single curved shapes, we see them as five interleaved circles.

Law of Similarity *Similar things appear to be grouped together.*
Grouping can occur because of different kinds of similarity such as shape, lightness, hue, size, or orientation. In figure 3.5(b) most people perceive the first figures as either rows or columns of circles. However, if we replace some of the circles by squares, most people see vertical columns of squares and circles (second figure). The last figure in that row shows the effect of lightness on grouping similar objects. Here, the dark circles are grouped together.

Law of Proximity *Things that are near to each other appear to be grouped together.*
Figure 3.5(c) shows a corresponding example. In the left figure all circles appear to be grouped together as they have all the same proximity to each other. The right figure shows how the grouping changes when we vary the distance between columns.

Law of Good Continuation *Points that, when connected, result in straight or smoothly curving lines are seen as belonging together, and the lines tend to be seen in such a way as to follow the smooth path.*
The two curves in figure 3.5(d) can be still separated and followed easily although they overlap each other.

Law of Common Fate *Things that are moving in the same direction appear to be grouped together.* For instance, on a picture showing tennis balls thrown in the air, they will be perceived as a group of balls even though they are not aligned in any way.

Law of Familiarity *Things that are more likely to form groups if the groups appear familiar or meaningful.* Therefore, humans tend to group things based on experiences gained in other situations.

Although the Gestalt psychologists called their principles of organization "laws", other psychologists rejected the term "laws", because the principles do not make predictions strong enough to qualify as laws [Gol02, p. 153]. Hence, Gestalt principles are more accurately described by heuristics, i.e. rule of thumb solutions that provide a best-guess solution.

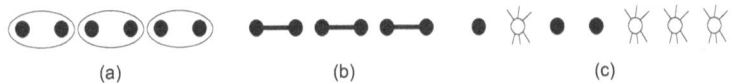

Figure 3.6: Grouping by (a) common region; (b) connectedness; and (c) synchrony. The lines indicate that the circles blink together.

The Gestalt principles reflect basically common regularities that we see in our environment. Things generally tend to be smooth rather than changing abruptly and similar parts tend to be part of the same object. These coherences are also part of some principles of perceptual organization proposed by Stephen Palmer and Irvin Rock [PR94, Pal99]. The proposed three new grouping principles of relevance for user interface design are: the principle of common region, the principle of element connectedness, and the principle of synchrony.

Figure 3.6(a) shows the *principle of common regions*. It states that elements that are in the same region of space are grouped together. This is even true although the circles in the ellipses are farther apart than the circles that are next to each other but in neighboring ellipses. The reason for this is that each ellipse is seen as a separate region of space.

The *principle of element connectedness* is demonstrated in figure 3.6(b). It describes that things that are physically connected are perceived as a unit. Even though the circles that are not connected with a line are closer together, a series of dumbbells is perceived rather than a line of pairs of circles.

Finally, figure 3.6(c) illustrates the *principle of synchrony*. It states that visual events will be perceived as going together if they occur at the same time. The lights that blink at the same time are perceived as belonging together, although not all are spatially grouped together. This is similar to the Gestalt law of common fate. They both describe dynamic phenomenons, but synchrony can occur without movement and does not have to change in the same direction.

The perception of organization is the foundation for all visual information presentation. However, besides perception itself it is also important to know how fast people will be able to extract a certain information out of a perceived object structure. This is particularly important when users are to be supported with task related information through a user interface of an application and cannot permanently maintain focus to it.

The procedure of determining a certain information encoded in a visual display is called *visual search*. Here, an important factor that influences the time of finding an information is the *pop-out* effect. The pop-out effect occurs if elements displayed next to each other either contain different features or have different values for the same features

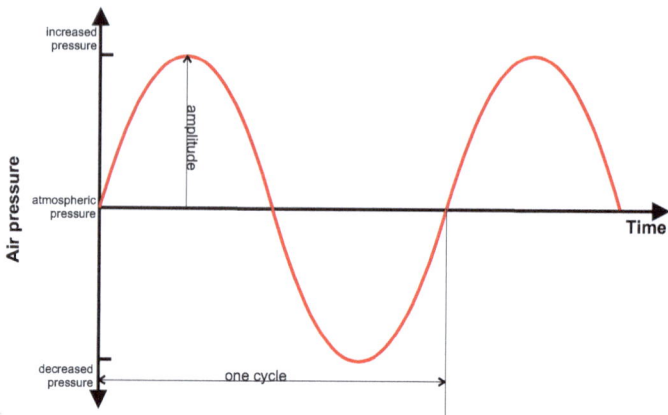

Figure 3.7: Sine wave sound signal.

[War04, p. 151]. For example, searching a single letter "O" merged into a set of "V" letters of arbitrary horizontal orientation will almost instantaneously be found by people, because both letters have different features so that the pop-out effect is caused. Treismann and other researchers ([Tre98, Tre86, Bec82]) have determined which features lead to a pop-out effect. They found curvature, tilt, line ends, movement, color, brightness, and direction of illumination as basic features.

3.3   The Auditory Stimulus

Besides seeing, the ability of humans to hear and speak is very important as it is the foundation for speech-based interaction between humans. Understanding the auditory stimulus can also lead to a better understanding of how humans could use their abilities for interacting with a computer. Hearing allows us to perceive important signals, such as warning sounds of a fire alarm or a cry for help. What we hear is commonly known as *sound* and can be described in two different ways. It can refer to the physical stimulus or the perceptual response [Gol02, p. 334]: In a physical definition sound is pressure changes in the air or other media. In contrast, the perceptual definition of sound is the experience humans have when they hear. Although this section focuses on perceptual foundations, few physical definition of sound are needed to understand the properties of the auditory stimulus.

As already mentioned, sound occurs through the movement or vibration of an object that causes pressure changes in the air, water, or any other elastic medium. Considering loudspeakers, pressure changes are caused by the vibrating speaker diaphragm onto the surrounding air. Because the pattern that is generated by the pressure change can be described by the mathematical sine wave function, it is called *sound wave*. The quality of a sound we hear (basically pitch and loudness) depends on the properties of the sound wave called *frequency* and *amplitude*. As depicted in figure 3.7, the amplitude refers to the magnitude of an oscillation of the sine wave, i.e. it is the distance the diaphragm moves from its rest position to its maximum or minimum. The frequency is the number of times per second that the speaker diaphragm goes through one cycle of moving out, back in, and then out again. The tone frequency is measured in *Hertz (Hz)*, where one Hertz is one circle per second. To describe a sound's amplitude, i.e. change in air pressure, the sound pressure is typically converted into *decibels (dB)*:

$$\text{Number of dB} = 20 \cdot log(\tfrac{p}{p_0})$$

where p stands for the sound pressure and p_0 is the standard sound pressure which is usually set to 20 micropascals.

3.3.1   The Range of Hearing Sounds

As already known from the visual stimulus, we can only see within a certain visible light spectrum (cf. section 3.2.1). The same is true for the auditory stimulus. Humans can only hear within a specific range of frequency that is typically between 20 Hz and 20,000 Hz. However, we are most sensitive to a certain range of frequencies that are shown in the so called *audibility curve* given by figure 3.8. The curve shows how sensitivity changes for different frequencies we hear. Humans are most sensitive within a range of approximately 2,000 and 4,000 Hz. Hence, the threshold for hearing is lowest in this range. Moreover, this range of frequencies is almost the same as for most conventional speech (indicated by the shaded area in figure 3.8). Everything that is above the audible curve lets us hear a tone. However, once we approach the feeling threshold on the very top of the curves the perceived tones become painful and can damage our auditory system. As we have already seen, loudness of sound is closely related to sound pressure. For understanding the dependency between frequency and loudness, figure 3.8 also includes the so called *equal loudness curves*. They indicate the decibels that create the same perception of loudness at different frequencies. For example, the equal loudness curve marked 40 was determined by comparing the loudness of a 1,000 Hz 40dB tone to the loudness of all other tones with different frequencies.

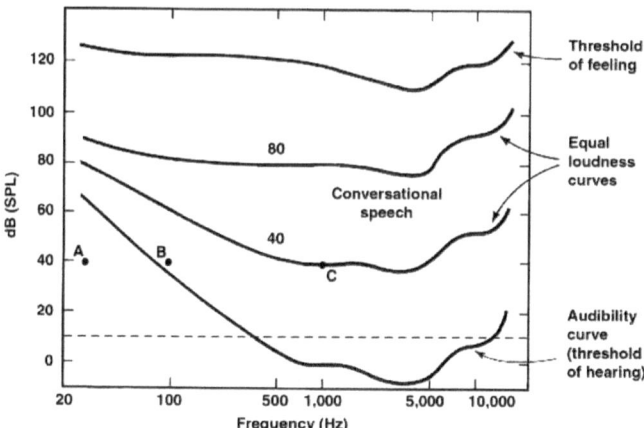

Figure 3.8: The audible curve and the auditory response area. Hearing occurs between feeling and hearing thresholds. Conventional speech is indicated by the shaded area. Figure taken from [Gol02, p. 340].

3.3.2   Speech Perception and its Multimodal Nature

Although speech sound is comparable to other sound, a detailed understanding of all aspects of humans speech perception is still an ongoing task. This is because of the complexity of sound patterns produced by humans while speaking. To underline this, consider the attempts to use computers to recognize speech and the results that have been achieved after decades of research. Only recently there are systems available that allow (after a more or less time consuming training period) the reliable recognition of speech.

What is more important here than understanding speech perception, is to notice its *multimodal* property, meaning that speech perception can be influenced by other senses. There are different methods to distinguish interference between senses, for example, the so called Tadoma method used to describe how speech can be perceived through touch [Gol02, p. 430]. Visual information can also influence the perception of speech. In 1976 McGurk and Mac Donald [MM76], first demonstrated this effect that is today also called the *McGurk effect*. In their experiment they showed subjects a video of a person making the lip movement to the sound "ga-ga", i.e. the voice of this person was omitted. Instead of the original voice, the subjects simultaneously received an audio sound that is usually

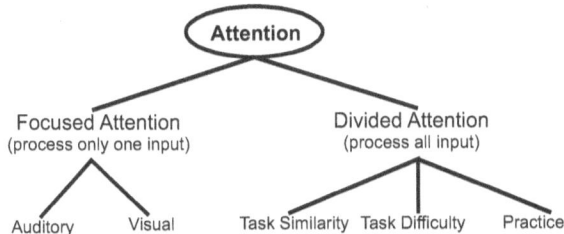

Figure 3.9: Relations between different topics on attention research (adapted from [EK05, p. 142]).

heard as "ba-ba". Surprisingly, the subjects were convinced that they had heard the sound "da-da'. This misperception is an indicator for the influence of the visual stimulus on the auditory stimulus, because when subjects were asked to close their eyes they hear "ba-ba". Once they opened their eyes, they heard again a "da-da" sound.

3.4   Attention and Performance Limitations

Designers of desktop user interfaces can assume that users are solely concentrating on the digital task. When considering user interfaces for wearable computers that typically support a primary task, this is no longer the case. Thus, understanding humans attention and performance limitations is crucial for wearable user interfaces. Particularly, understanding how many different tasks or what kind of tasks can be accomplished by humans at the same time is important.

Attention commonly consists of different but interrelated abilities [Lun01]. There is an important distinction between *focused attention* and *divided attention* (cf. figure 3.9). Focused attention (or selective attention) is the ability to select particular information from a mass of information by responding only to *one* source of information—such as holding a conversation in a noisy environment. Focused attention tells us about the efficiency with which people select certain inputs rather than others [EK05, p. 141]. Focused attention has been mostly studied by either focusing on the auditory or visual sense (cf. [Dri98] for a review).

Although the coordination of two or more modalities at the same time (known as *crossmodal attention*) has great importance for every day life, only little work has be conducted. Driver and Spencer did some studies on crossmodal attention of tactile, audio, and visual modalities [DS98, Dri98]. However, a deep understanding of underlying processes that explain the observed effects in crossmodal attention are still not entirely known [EK05, p. 162].

Divided attention is the ability to select particular information but to respond to *all* sources—such as driving and navigating. Because divided attention is most important for wearable applications, as it involves dual tasks, we will focus on this aspect.

Hampson [Ham89] argued that focused attention and divided attention are more similar than we expect. Factors that aid focused attention in general also aid divided attention. He stated that "anything which minimizes interference between processes, or keep them 'further apart' will allow them to be dealt with more readily either selectively or together". Recently, Strayer and Johnston [SJ01] conducted a study on the ongoing public discussion whether or not mobile phones impair driving performance. In their study they compared the use of hand-held and hands-free mobile phones while driving and found that both impair driving performance, suggesting that all types of mobile phones should be banned while driving.

According to Lund [Lun01] our competence on divided attention is affected by task similarity, task difficulty, and practice. In 1972 D.A. Allport and colleagues conducted key experiments on dual-task performance by studying task similarity [AAR72]. In their study they divided their subjects into three groups and asked them to orally repeat prose (word by word) that was played into one ear of their headphones. In addition to this task, the second task was to learn a list of words. The first group had to listen to the word list played on the second ear of their headphones, the second group attempted to learn the words from a screen presentation, whereas the third group tried to learn the words from pictures representing the words. Allenport at al. found that the group learning from pictures outperformed the other groups. This indicates that listening to a word list or reading it from a screen uses at least some of the same attentional resources as orally repeating prose, i.e. listening and reading words are more similar than interpreting pictures [Sta02a]. Teisman and Davies [TD73] furthermore found that two monitoring tasks interfere with each other much more when both tasks are given in the same modality (audio or visual) rather than different modalities. McLeod [McL77] found that response similarity is also important. In his study he found that task performance is worse when response similarity is high for two response tasks (manual response to both tasks) than with low response similarity (manual response to one task and vocal response to the second task).

Task difficulty also influences the ability to perform dual tasks. There are several studies (e.g. [Sul76]) that support a heuristic that the more difficult the tasks are, the more difficult will it be to perform both tasks simultaneously. However, a definition of "task difficulty" is hard to find. Two tasks performed at the same time might demand the sum of each single task plus some extra overhead caused by coordinating both tasks. Evidence for the extra overhead assumption were, for example, reported by D'Esposito et al. [DDA+95].

Common sense saying suggests that "practice makes perfect". This also seems to be applicable to dual tasks. For example, a beginner in driving a car probably finds it difficult to pay attention to traffic and holding a conversation with a second person, whereas the same person once becoming an expert driver will find it fairly easy. Even though this is a quite intuitive approach, several works support this assumption (cf. e.g. [SHN76, HSR+80]). Because driving a car is a classical dual task, studying attention and performance limitations is of major interest in that field. Although presumably much work has been conducted in that direction by the automotive industry, only little work has been made public, though; likely because study results are seen as advantage in competition. Recently, a special issue edited by Baumann, Leuchter and Urbas [BLU06] on attention and situational awareness in vehicles has discussed some issues with a focus on car driving.

Chapter 4

Human-Computer Interaction

The previous chapter discussed the fundamentals of sensation, perception, and cognition to understand how humans see, hear, think, and why this must be considered in user interface design. This chapter now deals with the specific aspects of the communication between humans and computers.

Following, we introduce the basics of human-computer interaction (HCI) and describe in detail how humans can communicate with computers through a user interface of an application. While doing so, we particularly pay attention to the needed input and output devices that enable interaction with a wearable computer and point out differences and challenges that arise when designing user interfaces for wearable computers compared to traditional desktop systems. Moreover, possibilities to handle interruptions originated from a computer as well as user interface evaluation methods are discussed.

4.1 HCI and Wearable Computers

HCI research combines several disciplines that try to make communication between humans and computers as natural as human-human communication (cf. section 2.3). Diverse ways in natural human communication are used for interaction including speech, gestures, mimicry and voice pitch. Some of these are used for explicit interaction such as speech and gestures. Changing mimicry or different voice pitches, however, are typically used rather implicitly than explicitly in human-human interaction. Implicit interaction basically allows humans "annotating" interaction modalities in a way that might cause the explicit meaning to change. For example, stating a sentence like "You are really looking great in that dress." with a sarcastic voice pitch allows humans to implicitly change the meaning of a spoken sentence without exchanging spoken words.

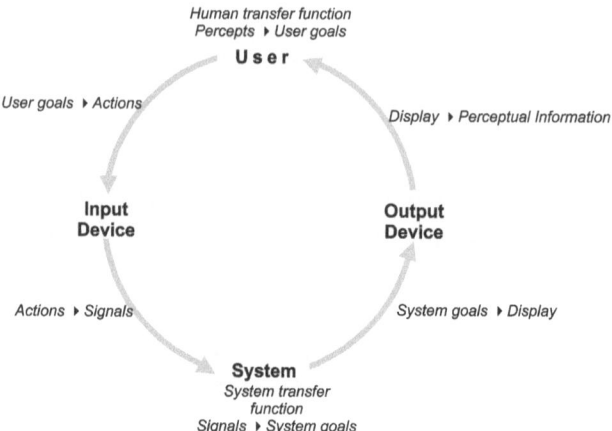

Figure 4.1: Human-computer communication cycle (adapted from [BKLP05, p. 28]).

When considering human-computer communication, communication is much more constrained than human-human communication because the variety of expressions used for communication with the system is limited [Dah06, p. 19]. Users communicate actions, queries, goals, etc. to a computer whereas the computer in turn communicates information about its internal state, query results, etc. to the user [BKLP05, p. 27]. The medium through which this interaction typically takes place is called a user interface. User interfaces translate the user's *input* into a form that is understandable and processable by the computer and that translates the computer's actions back into a human understandable format as *output*, which the user can act upon [HH93]. Bowman et al. [BKLP05, p. 27] describe the transformation of user inputs that generate a corresponding output as a *transfer function*. To communicate with the user, the system translates the information into a digital representation that is then translated by the output device so that it is perceivable by a human stimuli (e.g. vision or sound). Finally, the user interprets the perceptions into meaningful representations. The medium used to communicate either with the human or the system is always a physical hardware device. Figure 4.1 depicts the human-computer interaction cycle of a user interface as a transformation process from user goals to system goals, and to human perceptual information.

Interaction with Wearable Computers

The importance of a good user interface for desktop computers is well known today. It is one of or even the crucial part in the development process of new hardware or software. Over the last decade research has produced lots of results on design principles, interaction styles, interface components, and guidelines for these interfaces that became common knowledge for desktop interface design. Consequently, it can be found in almost every text book on that topic (cf. [Dah06, SP05, Car03, BTT05]). When considering user interfaces for wearable computers, many of these design principles, interface components, or guidelines are, however, inappropriate because they usually do not consider users working or manipulating real world objects. Most existing guidelines and design principles are not designed for nontraditional computing environments. For example, a wearable computer may be used in maintenance where hands-free interaction is needed that makes any keyboard impractical to use. Also, displays used in wearable computing typically have low resolution which makes readability of text more difficult while walking and calls for a redesign of text-intensive interface components. Therefore, wearable computing requires interaction devices and interaction techniques different to those used in today's desktop computing environments.

The remainder of this section will elaborate more on the special output and input hardware, its properties as well as interaction techniques applicable in wearable user interfaces.

4.2 Output Hardware for Wearable Computers

Although figure 4.1 explicitly mentioned only *display devices*, there are more device classes relevant in wearable computing. In general, output devices present information to the user through one or more stimuli that are perceivable through the perceptual system of humans. Typically, these output devices stimulate the visual, auditory, or haptic senses. Recently other output devices were introduced that stimulate, for example, the sense of smell [BMM06, YAM+05].

4.2.1 Wearable Visual Displays

Mobility is one of the key characteristics of a wearable computer user. Stationary displays, such as monitors (that do not move with the user) are of minor interest for wearable user interfaces as they are only usable in selected applications where access to such devices is always possible. More important, however, are all kind of displays that can be mounted to the user's body like, for example, head-mounted or wrist-mounted displays.

	Non See-Through	See-Through
Binocular	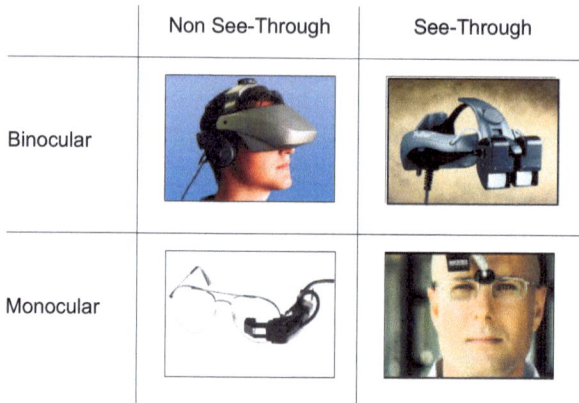	
Monocular		

Figure 4.2: Different types of head-mounted displays.

Head-mounted Displays

A *head-mounted display* (HMD) is a display that is mounted or attached to the wearer's head. Its design requires sophisticated engineering techniques to integrate all required electronics, optics, and mechanical components into a small and lightweight system able to display an image either in front of one or both eyes (for details cf. [Stu01, MM97]). Regardless of a certain design, HMDs offer complete visual immersion, i.e. users can always see the virtual world independent of head position or orientation. Over the last years many different HMDs were developed that all have specific properties. Figure 4.2 shows a selection of HMDs designed for one or two eye usage. HMDs can be divided into different categories that describe their basic characteristics based on the ability whether a user can still see the real world with the eye occupied by a display or not. Displays that allow users to see both real world and virtual world with the same eye are called "*see-through*" HMDs whereas displays that do not offer this possibility are called "*look around*" or "*non see-through*" HMDs [LRO03]. Another category that differentiates HMDs is defined by the number of eyes they occupy. *Binocular* HMDs offer stereoscopic viewing by displaying the image in front of both eyes of the user. *Monocular* HMDs offer monoscopic viewing through only one display presenting an image to one eye only.

Although Steve Mann [Man01b] pointed out the wide range of possibilities of binocular non see-through HMDs that fully block out the real world, they are of minor importance in today's wearable computing research, except for augmented reality applications, because they suffer from different problems [Bab01]. One of the most important problems is that most binocular HMDs do not support different distances between the eyes of different wearers that make stereo viewing problematic for many users [BKLP05, p. 51]. Additionally, studies such as [Pel98] have shown user acceptance problems of binocular HMDs. Recently, Zeiss, a German optics company, introduced a new type of binocular HMD to overcome some of these problems. Their HMD is expected to be used similarly to reading glasses and allows seeing the real world by looking underneath the display that is mounted in the peripheral vision above the eyes of the wearer. To see an image on the display, the wearer has to actively look upward which is, however, deemed to cause fatigue.

Even though some work on overcoming the problems of binocular HMDs is known (e.g. [WFVMP02]), many contemporary wearable computer applications use monocular instead of binocular HMDs for visual output [Bab01]. Compared to binocular HMDs, monocular HMDs obviously provide better attributes in terms of power consumption, weight, and cost. However, they also suffer from different problems. The apparent advantage of covering only one eye, which allows the other (free) eye to look continuously at the real world, has been shown as problematic in terms of sharing attention between the real world and the presented information [NRC97]. The limited field of view (FOV) of monocular displays has also been studied and shown to affect size and space perception [AM90] as well as scanning the environment [SG97]. Peli [Pel98] disproved concerns about potentially harmful effects on the visual system due to the use of (monocular and binocular) HMDs by comparing them with CRT displays. He found no significant visual function differences between HMD and CRT in long-term use but users found HMDs less comfortable than CRTs.

The discussion so far has raised concerns on the usability of both, binocular and monocular HMDs. However, given the popularity of monocular HMDs in today's wearable computing applications, the question is not so much whether they should or should not be used, but how information has to be presented so that it does not interfere with the specific properties of HMDs or other user tasks.

Sampson [Sam93] reported on an experiment where he investigated the use of monocular HMDs while walking around. Subjects were asked to traverse different paths with or without obstacles in their way. At the same time the secondary task was to handle either alphanumeric or spatial information presented in the HMD. It turned out, that subjects performed equally well when standing still or when traversing paths without obstacles in their way. When obstacles were present in their ways, the subject's performance was significantly worse, indicating that maintaining visual attention to presented information on the display and the environment impairs performance. Thus, presented information on HMDs needs to be very limited to ensure their usefulness. In the same experiment

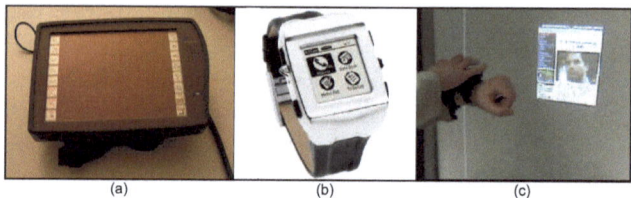

Figure 4.3: (a) Xybernaut wrist-mounted display. (b) Fossil *Wrist PDA* watch. (c) Simulator of a watch-sized wrist projector [BFC05].

Sampson also reported that performance increased when spatial information was presented rather than alphanumeric information. In this context, Barber et al. [Bab01] also found that graphical information led to better performance compared to text information. In addition to these findings, the right structure of presented information that reflects the use of a monocular HMD either on the left or right eye is important [WNK06], suggesting the presentation of important information more towards the focal center of the eye.

Besides these human-computer related properties, McAtamney and Parker [MP06] investigated the effects of monocular HMDs on informal face-to-face communication between humans. They found that monocular HMDs impaired the quality of interaction and affected eye contact when the HMD was displaying information. However, when no information was displayed no effect on the conversation was found. Although all this is already known about HMDs, a detailed understanding of presented information, the design of such information, and the interrelation with task performance is still an unanswered research issue [HB99].

Wrist-mounted Displays

Another (except for sports) rather rarely used kind of wearable display is a *wrist-mounted display* (WMD). These displays are equipped with some mechanism that allows the display to be mounted to the body. Usually, wrist-mounted displays are attached to the forearm or the wrist (cf. figure 4.3). Compared to HMDs, some WMDs offer greater resolution (cf. figure 4.3(a)) and a more familiar usage pattern. Their use reminds of using a standard PDA or a tablet PC. Some WMDs have integrated input devices (e.g. buttons or stylus sensitive displays) for interaction. Examples of such wrist-mounted displays are shown in figures 4.3(a) and 4.3(b). There are also few projector-based WMDs that are not limited to private information access because they can display the image of the WMD on any flat surface in the environment (cf. figure 4.3(c)). With such displays, information sharing is possible [BFC05].

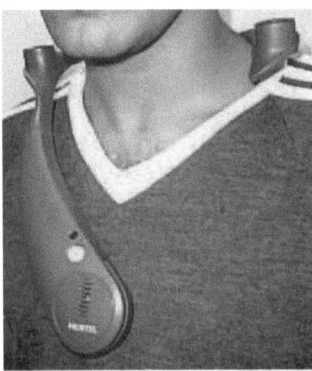

Figure 4.4: The Nomadic Radio device [SS98].

Although WMDs might be easier to use in the beginning, they also have drawbacks. Most obviously, it is not possible to perceive both, the image from a WMD and the real world simultaneously, because of the position of the display. This property makes any instant wearable computer support while performing a primary task difficult. Related to this, WMDs do not support hands-free operation all the time. Their mounting to the forearm may cause usability problems. For instance, the size of the Xybernaut WMD (cf. figure 4.3(a)) might be rather inappropriate in space restricted environments such as the engine compartment of a car.

4.2.2   Wearable Audio Displays

Audio displays are another way to present information to a user with sound. Unlike stimulating a human's visual system that gives detailed information about a small area of focus, audio displays stimulate the auditory system that provides general information and can alert humans to things outside the peripheral vision [Bre03]. For wearable computing this quality is deemed to be well suited to tackle problems occurring, for example, caused by HMDs, multitasking, etc.

Devices used for audio output basically differ on the form factors, their speakers, and the amount of "intelligence" that is integrated to optimize sound quality. In mobile environments audio devices are rather small compared to desktop audio output devices. Also, recent mobile audio devices often avoid the use of cables that can restrict users in their mobility, for example, by Bluetooth communication. Here, *headphones* are the most widespread devices and can be either worn *in-ear* [BH05] or as traditional headphones.

Some headphones like, for instance, the Sennheiser PXC250[1], also offer so called built-in *noise compensation* that records external noise through microphones, inverts it, and plays it back through the headphone, to optimize sound quality by getting rid of environmental noise. Sawhney and Schmandt [SS98] reported on the design and development of a wearable audio device called Nomadic Radio (cf. figure 4.4). Nomadic Radio was designed to deliver information on the move and to reduce interruption effects caused by messages being delivered at the wrong time or in the wrong context such as a ringing telephone during a meeting.

Methods for Using Audio in User Interfaces

There are two different methods of how an audio output can be used in a user interface: First, in a *speech* auditory interface and second in a *non-speech* auditory interface. Speech auditory interfaces use speech (either a computer synthesized voice or a recorded natural human voice) to present information to a user. Examples for such kind of interfaces include automatic computer telephone information systems, car navigation systems, or audio tours in museums. Non-speech auditory interfaces use individual audio tones and combinations of sound and music to present more complex information [RBF03]. For example, digital cameras often play back a special sound to indicate that the trigger was successfully activated and a picture has been made. Of course, both methods have their weaknesses and strengths. Instead of discussing all advantages and disadvantages of both methods, we summarize the most important facts for wearable user interfaces. For a more lengthy discussion on all aspects in a broader context see [Bre03].

The strength of sound is that it can be heard from all around the user, independent of whether its source is above, below, in front, or behind the user [Bre03]. This enables the user to "follow her ears" by turning the view towards the source of an interesting sound to get detailed information. This general behavior leads to the following specific advantages of sound [Bre03]:

Load Reduction on the User's Visual System Today's traditional graphical interfaces are designed rather complex than simple. This results in an intensive utilization of the visual system of a user which may lead to information missing due to visual overload. By also presenting sound, the user's overall load can be shared with the auditory system.

Reduction of Needed Information on a Screen Related to the previous point, mobile screens such as HMDs or WMDs aggravate a visual overload, because they can

---

[1]See http://www.sennheiser.de for more details.

become cluttered very quickly. Therefore, sound can be used to save space on the screen by moving some presented information from the visual to the audio display.

Reduction of Visual Attention Demands Mobile users who are using their devices on the move cannot dedicate all their visual attention to the device. They have to pay visual attention to the real world, for instance, to keep track of ongoing traffic on the highway. In such situations, information on the visual interface can be missed, because the user is not permanently looking at the screen. If some information is displayed in sound, information can be delivered regardless where the user is looking. Car navigation systems are a good example for this.

Sound can grab Attention As discussed in the last point, users can easily choose where to look in a certain situation. However, avoiding hearing something at a certain point in time is more difficult, because of the auditories omni directional property. Therefore, sound can be used to deliver important information and to grab the user's attention.

Although there are quite a lot of advantages for using sound in human-computer interaction, Kramer [Kra94] also pointed out some general problems with sound. Compared to vision, audio has a much lower resolution. By using, for example, different volumes only a few different values can be clearly differentiate [BGB91]. Presenting absolute data like, for example, numbers is difficult using sound. Therefore, interfaces typically present the data in a relative manner by presenting two different tones, indicating an increasing or decreasing of that number. Sound is transient, i.e. once a sound was presented it disappears. This can cause problems if the encoded information is complex and has to be recalled over a longer period, because the user cannot look at the screen again. The approach of continuing to present sound to overcome this problem, directly leads to the next: The potential annoyance of sound. The most common argument against using sound in interfaces is its tendency to be annoying. This important aspect of using sound in HCI has been investigated in many directions. For example, audio feedback in graphical interfaces has been found valuable for novice users, but after a short period it became annoying to them [NDL+05]. Others [BLB+03, LB00, BLC98, RV95, YLM95] investigated the use of sound for presenting menus with audio and recommended its usefulness only for short menus. In connection with this, Yankelovich et al. [YLM95] argued that audio interfaces "are often characterized by a labyrinth of invisible and tedious hierarchies which result when menu options outnumber telephone keys or when choices overload users' short-term memory".

Auditory Icons and Earcons

So far we discussed audio devices to generate sound and the different methods to present sound on an interface. Following, we will complement the discussion by looking at two presentation techniques for non-speech sound that have emerged in HCI: *auditory icons* and *earcons*. The concept of auditory icons was developed by Graver [Gav89] in 1989. He defined them as "everyday sounds mapped to computer events by analogy with everyday sound-producing events. Auditory icons are like sound effects for computers" (p. 69). In his initial work he developed *SonicFinder*, a system that added sound to a Macintosh interface for some specific user action, for example, a dragging sound appeared when files were dragged. Thus, auditory icons are familiar sounds used to represent objects and actions [SP05, p. 383]. The advantage of these auditory icons is that listeners can easily map meaning to them which makes them also easy to learn [Bre03]. However, Gaver et al. reported on problems using auditory icons. For instance, "the bottle braking sound was so compelling semantically and acoustically that partners sometimes rushed to stop the sound without understanding its underlying cause or at the expense of ignoring more serious problems" (p. 89). The question of how auditory icons should be designed has been rarely investigated in formal studies. Mynatt, however, proposed a basic methodology for designing them in [Myn94].

Unlike auditory icons that use familiar sounds, earcons must be learned as they use abstract sounds whose meaning is not always obvious. Earcons were developed by Blattner et al. also in 1989 [BSG89] and are defined as "non-verbal audio messages that are used in the computer/user interface to provide information to the user about some computer object, operation, or action" (p. 13). Earcons typically follow a more musical oriented approach, because they are composed from smaller building blocks such as rhythmics or sequences of pitches [BSG89].

Auditory icons and earcons can both be used to communicate information in sound. More formal research has been accomplished on the design of earcons than on auditory icons. Because of their complex structure, earcons are powerful in situations where no real world sound equivalent exists. Although their drawback is that they have to be learned because of the missing semantical link between object and sound, research has shown that learning can be reduced to a minimum if earcons are designed properly [BM00].

Auditory icons and earcons in their pure form are somehow orthogonal to each other, where auditory icons are characterized as *representational* and earcons as *abstract*. That is, for objects that do not have a real-world sound equivalent, auditory icons have to be designed more abstract so that they move toward the more abstract earcons approach. This also holds for earcons in a reversed situation. Thus, both approaches are not nec-

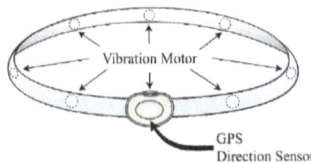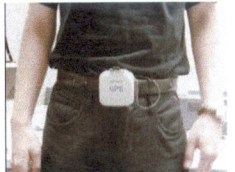

Figure 4.5: Basic concept and first prototype of the ActiveBelt system [TY04].

essarily far apart from each other but can provide very powerful interfaces once they are used in the right mixture. Currently, research on 3D user interfaces frequently investigates the possibility of sound to present information. One of the mayor goals in this direction is the generation and display of spatial 3D sound, enabling the human participant to take advantage of his auditory localization capabilities. For a comprehensive overview on recent 3D user interface techniques we recommend reading [BKLP05].

4.2.3 Haptic Wearable Output Devices

The third type of output displays discussed here are haptic output devices. Haptic devices "generate a feedback to the skin and muscles, including a sense of touch, weight, and rigidity" [Iwa03]. Often, haptic devices are called *tactile devices* since they focus mainly on stimulating the skin. Haptic devices are a major field of research in the area of virtual reality. In wearable computing less research has been documented so far. As haptic interfaces are not considered in this thesis, we will only briefly introduce exemplary work and discuss the most important properties of these devices.

Tan and Pentland [TP97] presented a tactile display for wearable computers called the "rabbit" system. It consisted of an array of flat-panel speakers attached to the wearer's back. By using the speakers, wearers were able to detect motion pulses at different positions to direct them in a certain direction while walking. Often vibration is generated through a small motor with an excenter disk to stimulate the skin similar to most modern mobile phones [LPL+06, HLJ+05, TY04, GOS01]. The biggest advantage of tactile output devices is that they are very unobtrusive and small. They are very discreet because of their seamless integration with most human activities [GOS01]. Because tactile devices stimulate the cutaneous sense, they neither interfere with visual nor audio displays but can encode additional information. Although systems like ActiveBelt [TY04] (cf. figure 4.5) are available, the amount of information tactile displays can encode is limited. When only limited information is needed or already sufficient, for example, to guide firefighters through thick smoke, it is a powerful and unobtrusive output media. In most practical cases, however, a combination with visual or audio displays seems to be advantageous. In line with this Burke et al. [BPG+06] showed that visual-tactile feedback is more effective when multiple tasks are being performed and workload conditions are high compared to visual-auditory or pure visual feedback. A detailed discussion of recent haptic devices is given in [SC03].

4.3   Input Hardware for Wearable Computers

After having discussed wearable output devices, the focus in this section will be on wearable input devices to complete the human-computer communication cycle that described how a user interface is composed (cf. figure 4.1).

Over the last decades input devices were mainly used in desktop environments. Perhaps the most significant input device developed in that period was the mouse pointing device. Since its first version, introduced by Engelbart et al. in 1967 and published in [EEB67], it has revolutionized desktop computing. In wearable computing, however, more "unusual" input devices that are controllable even while being on the move are needed. In this context research has argued that the use of pointing devices is not appropriate or even unusable in most wearable computing applications because keeping track of the pointer requires constant visual attention [Sta02b, Cla00, SGBT00]. Independent from this, some research has evaluated pointing devices for wearable computing anyhow (cf. e.g. [ZTG05, Dav01]).

There are several known input device taxonomies (cf. [CMR91, FWC84, Bux83]). Those taxonomies are often used to determine which devices can be substituted by each other or what type of device is suitable for a certain task. However, in wearable computing rather special purpose devices are used that only take part as a small subset in these general taxonomies. Therefore, we will focus on the very specific properties of wearable input devices that allow us to determine the impact and challenges they impose on wearable user interfaces.

In particular, we will discuss wearable input devices along their "data delivery" property, i.e. whether a device delivers data *continuously* without any need for manual user action or *discrete*, i.e. manually triggered by the user. Others also refer to these properties by the terms *implicit* and *explicit* input or interaction [Sch00]. For instance, Schmidt [Sch02] defined implicit input as "actions and behavior of humans, which are done to achieve a goal and are not primarily regarded as interaction with a computer, but captured, recognized and interpreted by a computer system as input". Hence, implicit input may notably contribute to automatically adapt an interface of a wearable computer where many different sensors are available anyway.

4.3.1   Implicit Wearable Input

To generate implicit input for a wearable computer, input devices are needed that continuously acquire data, for example, about the user, her current behavior, place, or the environment. Such devices are often called *sensors*. A sensor measures a property of the physical world and produces a corresponding signal that can be processed after its digitalization by a computer. There are many different sensors available that allow measuring a large diversity of physical properties. For instance, acceleration sensors measure motion, GPS (Global Positioning System) sensors measure location, and temperature sensors measure arbitrary temperatures.

In ubiquitous and wearable computing, the process of identifying different situations of the user without forcing her to explicitly state her current situation or task but evaluating her implicitly generated sensor data, is called *context recognition*. Although the term *context* is widely used in mobile, ubiquitous, and wearable computing research, its proper meaning and definition often varies between authors. However, in order to use context effectively, understanding what context is and how it can be used is crucial. The first work that introduced the term 'context-aware' was by Schilit and Theimer [ST94]. They addressed context basically as location and relations to nearby objects and people. Dey and Abowd [ADB+99] did an in-depth survey of existing work in context-aware computing and provide definitions and recommendations on what context is without using definitions by example that are sometimes difficult to apply (cf. e.g. [Dey98, BBC97]). According to Dey and Abowed [ADB+99] context is "any information that can be used to characterize the situation of an entity. An entity is a person, place, or object that is considered relevant to the interaction between a user and an application, including the user and applications themselves". Their definition allows context not only to be automatically acquired (implicit) from the user but also to be manually (explicit) entered by the user. As this definition of context does not reduce context to one particular method of acquiring the needed data to determine context, we refer to Dey's and Abowd's definition when considering context.

Definition 2 [Context]:

Context is any information that can be used to characterize the situation of an entity. An entity is a person, place, or object that is considered relevant to the interaction between a user and an application, including the user and application themselves [ADB+99].

Reviewing literature on context leads to the conclusion that past and current researches have focused mainly on implicit context. This is probably because it was deemed more promising to process implicitly acquired data to ease human-computer interaction rather than using context information explicitly provided by the user.

Schmidt [Sch00] proposed that implicit input can offer a way to overcome the trade-off of device qualities (size, energy consumption, weight, etc.) and optimal input and output capabilities to control an application. According to him, implicit input could not solve this problem in general but could help at least to:

- *Adapt the input device to the current situation.*
  For instance, if an environmental noise sensor rates the noise level as too high for speech control the system could automatically switch to another input device.

- *Limit need for input.*
  For instance, sensors could be used to acquire a task context that automatically allows for acquiring certain information already while the user is performing it as system input.

- *Reduce selection space.*
  For instance, based on the current situational context a system could only present information that is appropriate in that situation.

Over the last years, research in wearable computing focused much on how sensors could be applied to recognize different user activities mainly using machine learning techniques. Although many researchers reported successful implementations of context recognition (e.g. [SOJ+06, LG04, LJS+04, HGK+04, JLT04]), one problem is still the effort for selecting and positioning suitable sensors for a certain application and the effort spent on training underlying machine learning systems. Hence, current research in context recognition for wearable computing is task and domain specific rather than general purpose. That is, there is no general notion of using context yet, but useful context information for an application has to be determined based on its domain and purpose. Therefore, general purpose context recognition systems to be used by arbitrary applications are still a challenging research question in the field.

4.3.2   Wearable Text Input

The primary method for textual data entry is still a keyboard [SP05, p. 348]. Different keyboard layouts have been proposed including today's most accepted *QWERTY* layout [LM90] and the less popular *DVORAK* layout. The DVORAK layout has minimized

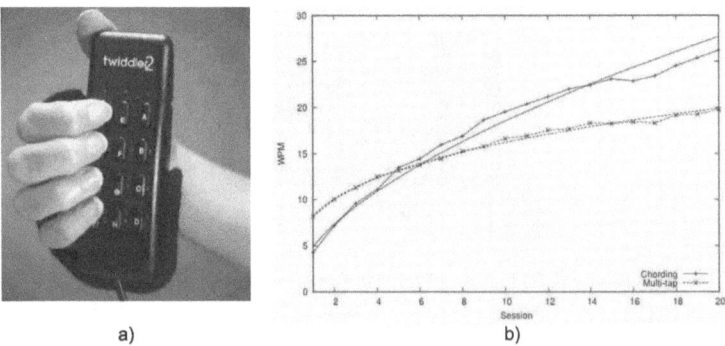

a) b)

Figure 4.6: (a) The Twiddler chording keyboard. (b) Learning curve of the Twiddler in comparison with MultiTap (adapted from [LSP⁺04]).

distances between different keys which can result in higher typing speed. According to [ZSH02], typing speed on DVORAK keyboards is 15% higher than on QWERTY keyboards. However, other work also reports only minor advantages of DVORAK [Wes98]. To be usable in mobile or wearable computing environments, the number of directly accessible characters has to be significantly reduced to save space required by the keyboard. Here, basically two different types are known: *one-handed* and *two-handed*.

The Twiddler is a widely accepted and well researched keyboard in the wearable computing community [CLSC05, LGSC05, LPS04, LSP⁺04]. It is shown in figure 4.6(a). The Twiddler offers one-handed text entry and provides the opportunity to simultaneously type text and manipulate physical objects. In contrast to mobile phones that use Multi-Tap or T9[2] as input method, the Twiddler is based on the *chording* principle to access all available 101 characters with only a limited number of 12 keys. To type, for example, a none directly accessible letter, a combination of different keys has to be pressed at the same time. Although this requires some learning to get used to it, studies have shown that with some training user can achieve high performance peaks because of optimized travel distances among keys [Bux90, Noy83]. For the Twiddler, studies reported on users achieving a word per minute rate (wpm) of up to 22 words (cf. figure 4.6(b)) [LSP⁺04]. In another Twiddler study subjects reached an average of 47 wpm after 400 minutes of training [LPS04].

---

[2]see http://www.t9.com for details on T9

Figure 4.7: The FrogPad "Half-Size" chording keyboard.

The FrogPad[3] is a so called "Half-Size" keyboard. It is also based on the chording method and consists of 15 keys that can be combined as chords to access 101 different characters in total. In principle, it can be used with one hand. However, it has to be placed on a flat surface or can be mounted on the forearm of the user. Although the latter case is suitable for mobile use both hands are occupied while typing; one hand is used for the actual typing and the second hand provides the needed counter pressure for key presses.

A few other devices have also been proposed for text input. Rosenberg and Slater [RS99], for example, presented a chording data glove. The keys were mounted on the fingers of a glove. A chord was made by pressing the fingers against any surface. After 80 minutes of training users achieved approximately 9 wpm and 17 wpn after 10 training sessions of about one hour each.

One of the most natural methods for text entry presumably is speech input. Here, the user has to speak the words or sentences for entering text like in ordinary human-human conversation. The system then translates the recorded audio signal to corresponding characters. Although speech recognition software has made dramatic progress and is commercially available, its successful and reliable implementation in applications is still challenging and sometimes even disillusioning [BM04]. One of its mayor advantages, however, is that it offers users the possibility to enter text or application control commands without using hands, i.e. it provides real hands-free operation [Sta02c]. For a comprehensive interdisciplinary discussion of voice communication including theoretical, technical, and practical views we refer to [Sch94].

In conclusion, although generally possible, mobile text entry is much more challenging compared to text input on standard desktop keyboards and often requires additional learning effort. Systems such as the Twiddler have shown that they can still lead to rea-

---

[3]More information available on product page at http://www.frogpad.com

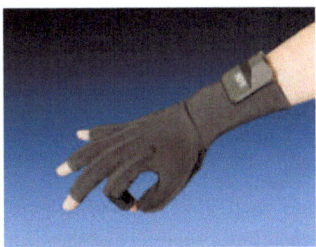

Figure 4.8: Bend-sensing data glove from 5DT.

sonable wpm rates. However, mobile text input is often slower than stationary text entry because of a limited number of keys and the dynamically changing mobile environment that impacts text input.

4.3.3 Wearable Command Input

Besides pure text input, being able to control an application is essential. There are different ways to control an application with an input device. Those ways are often closely related to the interaction style of a user interface. For instance, on *direct-manipulation interfaces* [Shn83], such as Microsoft Windows, actions are directly performed on visible objects using pointing devices that replace typed commands used in command line shells. All of these controls can be abstracted in a way that commands (often also called events) are issued by the input device that in turn are interpreted by the application logic.

As already mentioned, the most natural way for dispatching control commands is probably speech input. Another important method for input in wearable computing are gestures. Initial gesture control was implemented using data gloves often found in virtual reality applications [TP02, SZ94]. Several data gloves using different hardware components have been introduced so far [WLKK06, CWH03, BWCL01, RS99]. Some of them are already commercial products like the data glove shown in figure 4.8 from 5DT[4]. Also, gesture input devices were proposed with form factors different than data gloves. Gesture Pendant [Rek01, SAAG00] is a pendant like input device that recognizes gestures with a camera. Gesture Wrist [Rek01] offers gesture input by using an acceleration sensor and sensor electrodes on the user's wrist. It can recognize several gestures only by wearing it on the wrist. Since Gesture Wrist does not provide a clear mechanism to start and stop gesture recognition, it sometimes suffers from unexpected recognition problems. Ubi-Finger [TY04] is a finger worn gesture input device that allows selecting target appliances

---

[4]http://www.5dt.com

by pointing at them and then controlling the appliances with finger gestures. FreeDigiter [MAS04] is an ear mounted interface for mobile devices which enables rapid entry of digits using simple finger gestures close to the ear. In [DT06], button sized low power cameras that capture black and white images and a distance-sensor have been combined to built the Fingermouse, a wearable mouse input device that is controlled through finger movements in front of the body.

Machine learning techniques such as Hidden-Marcov-Models (HMMs) are frequently used to implement gesture recognition. Toolkits like the Georgia Gesture Toolkit (G^2TK) [WBAS03] or GART (Gesture and Activity Recognition Toolkit) [LBW$^+$07] are available to facilitate development of algorithms. However, unexpected or erroneous recognitions are still a problem in that field. Therefore, gestures for interaction that are easy to differentiate should be chosen not only to ease their recognition but to reduce the learning effort for users [WJ07]. Only a limited number of gestures can be used in an application because users have to remember them without cues while interacting with a system [BKLP05, p. 277].

4.4 Interruption Handling

The more demanding a task to be carried out is, the more affected are humans by interruptions that draw away their attention. Although research has extensively studied interruptions over the last decades, focus was mainly on effects and models of interruption as well as on interruption management including sensing and reasoning systems for interruption handling in stationary environments. Only recently research has moved ahead to study interruptions also in mobile and wearable computing environments.

Interruptions are considered to be, "externally generated, temporary cessations in the current flow of behavior, typically meant for the subject to execute activities that belong to a secondary set of actions" [vdBRZK96, p. 236] or more compact as "the process of coordinating abrupt changes in people's activities." [ML02]. Therefore, interruptions draw attention away from the currently performed activity and force humans to divide their attention in order to engage in a second activity (cf. section 3.4). In the worst case, an interruption is externally triggered with no control of the person being interrupted and consequently often results in human memory failures [Kha06]. Because such failures can decrease task performance and interaction accuracy, interruptions are sill an important issue of human-computer interaction design.

There are two different approaches used by researchers to study interruptions [RPB07]. The first is theory-driven with an interest in cognitive processing. Here, interruptions are used as a tool to study the processes humans get involved in when being interrupted (cf. e.g. [OS04, EC00]). The second approach is practice-driven and uses experiments to explores the effect of interruptions in different situations and environments (cf. e.g. [HJ07, WD06, DWPS06, DNL+04, EMW+03, McF02b, McF99]). Cutrell et al. [CCH01], for example, found in an experiment that even when users try to ignore presented messages, these interruptions still impair task performance. Although both approaches are equal, the practice-driven approach seems to be more frequently applied in the last years, suggesting a trend towards user-centered design by involving end users.

4.4.1 Modeling Interruptions

According to Bailey et al. "a peripheral task causes a greater increase in anxiety when it is presented during a primary task than when it is presented just after the completion of that task" [BKC00]. With respect to mobile and wearable computing environments, where users are involved in real world tasks, this indicates the importance of the right time and way to interrupt a user. In particular in wearable computing, where the computers support the primary task so that interruptions cannot be handled after the completion of a primary task.

Adamczyk and Bailey [AB04], studied the effects of interrupting a user at different moments during task execution in terms of task performance, emotional state, and social attribution. They found that interruptions at different points in time have different impacts on users' emotional state and positive social attribution and argue that a system can reduce the impact of an interruption on the user when designed properly. In line with this, McFarlane [McF02a] suggested and developed a taxonomy of interruption methods. Each method had different properties and impacts on a user being interrupted dependent on the characteristic of the primary task.

Taxonomy of Human Interruption

In [McF99], McFarlane presented the first empirical study examining his taxonomy of approaches to coordinate user interruption in human-computer interaction with multiple tasks. His taxonomy was based on an extensive interdisciplinary body of theory about human interruption and provided a framework for examining user interface design and interaction issues related to the impact of interruptions [McF02a, ML02].

Although there are many different ways to present or represent an interruption, including different visualization strategies such as semi-transparency, spatial location, or selected modality, McFarlane's taxonomy focuses on describing the four primary and fundamental methods for handling and managing interruptions in dual-task situations [ML02]:

1. **Immediate interruption**

   The immediate method interrupts a user at any time in a way that forces the user to immediately stop with the primary task and start to interact with the interruption task.

2. **Negotiated interruption**

   The negotiated method requires a negotiation sequence with the user before it interrupts the user. Here, a system first announces that it needs to interrupt the user but gives control to the user when to deal with the interruption.

3. **Scheduled interruption**

   The scheduled method interrupts the user by a restricted and predefined schedule, for example, once every 5 minutes.

4. **Mediated interruption**

   The mediated method interrupts the user indirectly by taking advantage of additional sources, for example, the current driving speed of a car, that allow determining when and how an interruption should be presented. Hence, it relies on additional context information.

With the definition of these basic methods for handling and managing interruptions, McFarlane created a way to systematically study interruptions in human-computer interaction and to evaluate their impact.

4.4.2 Interruptions in Mobile and Wearable Computing

Handling interruptions in stationary environments is a challenging user interface issue. In mobile environments where users face dynamically changing situations, an improper handling of interruptions may become a safety critical issue, though. For example, when being interrupted at the wrong time or in the wrong way by a car navigation system, a user may spontaneously draw her visual attention towards the navigation display, risking an accident because of not being aware of the ongoing traffic.

Although proper interruption handling in mobile environments is crucial, the availability of context information allows for minimizing the distraction originated by an interruption. Therefore, much research on interruption handling is spent on exploring different implementations of McFarlane's mediated method by using context information as an additional information source. For mobile phones a common approach to minimize interruptions is to use device embedded sensors such as accelerometers, light sensors, or the user's calendar to capture the context of the user and to adjust, for example, the modality of a cell phone for incoming calls (vibration alarm, ringer) accordingly [KC06, HI05, SSF+03, STM00].

Due to the availability of body-worn sensors in wearable computing, fine-grained context information can be obtained to handle interruptions [DWPS06, BVE05, EC00]. In [KASS04, KS03] Kern and Schiele proposed and validated an approach using acceleration, audio, and location sensors to mediate interruptions based on a user's personal and social interruptibility. Unlike in an office environment, users were less receptive for interruptions when being, for instance, in a restaurant.

Instead of focusing only on different ways to use context information to minimize the impact of an interruption, others studied the impact of interruptions with respect to a dual-task involvement of the user. As a continuation of McFarlane's original interruption study [McF02a], a head-mounted display was used by Drugge et al. [DNL+04] to display simple color and shape matching tasks to be answered with an ordinary desktop keyboard. The primary task users had to accomplish was represented by a virtual computer game displayed on a 12.1" screen of a laptop computer. A detailed description of the entire experiment setup can be found in [DNL+04]. Drugge et al. found that the scheduled approach gave the best performance, while using notifications came second although with shorter response times. As wearable computers are closely connected to the user, performance is not the only factor to be considered—the user's preferences on interruption also need to be taken into account. Nilsson et al. [NDL+05] found that audio notification appeared to give slightly better performance although users considered them more stressful, compared to visual signals that on the other hand were more distracting for the primary task. Although this work was already able to relate HCI findings to wearable computing, the conducted experiments only used virtual primary tasks in form of computer games. In [DWPS06] the virtual task was replaced by a more realistic physical task represented by the HotWire apparatus (cf. chapter 7) to study interruptions. While doing so they were able to confirm and complement previous findings on the preferred interruption methods when using gesture interaction, suggesting that a more realistic primary task probably uncovers the real properties of an experiment for wearable computing better than a stationary task would do.

4.5 User Interface Evaluation

There are many approaches in HCI to evaluate a system or its user interface. Most of them have been adapted from social sciences or psychology to meet the constraints of a technology driven process [JM06, p. 196]. There are comprehensive books on different evaluation techniques. Some are more related to HCI, like *Interaction Design* [PPRS06], and others provide a more general perspective on evaluation like *Evaluation: A Systematic Approach* by Rossi et al. [RLF06].

Usually, the goal of a user interface evaluation is to assess its *usability*, i.e. whether the interface is "good" or "bad" and allows users to carry out the required task. Usability is defined in part 11 of ISO 9241 standard as "the extent to which a product can be used by specified users to achieve specified goals with effectiveness, efficiency and satisfaction in a specified context of use" (EN ISO 9241-11, 1998). Stone et al. [SJWM05] defined the three main attributes as follows: *Effectiveness* is "the accuracy and completeness with which specified users can achieve specified goals in particular environments" (p. 6). *Efficiency* deals with "the resources expended in relation to the accuracy and completeness of the goals achieved" (p. 6). Finally, *satisfaction* is defined as "the comfort and acceptability of the work system to its users and other people affected by its use" (p. 6). Note, usability is defined for specified users, not necessarily any user group and neither in any context of use but the specified one it was designed for.

In order to determine to which extent a certain user interface is effective, efficient and satisfactory in an interface evaluation, attributes can be related to data collected during the evaluation. While effectiveness and efficiency can be measured by the accuracy and operational speed with which a user performs a required task without asking the user about her opinion, for example, by examining automatically collected interaction data, a user's satisfaction with the user interface can hardly be determined without asking for her opinion about comfort and acceptability.

Based on the nature of the data collected and processed during an evaluation, methods can be separated into two groups: Quantitative and qualitative evaluation methods.

- **Quantitative Evaluation**
  Quantitative evaluation methods rely on numbers and measurable properties [SJWM05, p. 440]. This can be any data collected from a software system. Examples include error rate or task completion time but may also include data from questionnaires that can be converted to numbers like answers given on a scale of numbers. Quantitative measurements allow applying mathematical calculations and statistics but may also be subject to misinterpretation of values due to a lack of semantics. Moreover, quantitative evaluations often require repeatability which may cause a bias if an experiment is not designed properly.

- **Qualitative Evaluation**
  Unlike quantitative evaluations, qualitative evaluation relies on data that cannot be easily expressed in numbers, i.e. data based on subjective opinions or insights

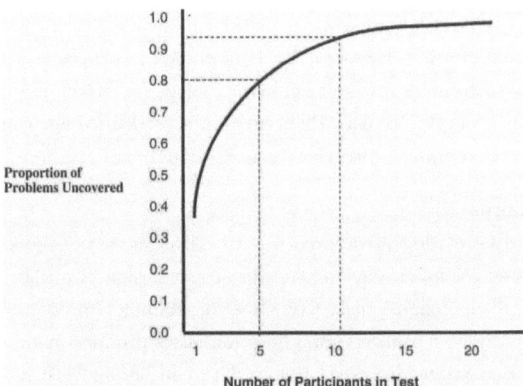

Figure 4.9: Number of participants needed to find various percentages of usability problems [Dum03, p. 1098].

[Dah06, p. 319]. Examples include verbal expressions of feelings, moods, or general descriptions of problems during interaction. Although qualitative data offers the possibility to let users informally describe a situation this leaves space for disagreements during analysis because data has to be interpreted to make use of it.

Independent of the selected method to asses the usability of an interface is the number of participants needed in user-based evaluations to find the various proportions of existing usability problems within the user interface. The "right" number of participants for a user study is still actively and controversially discussed in the research community. Early research in the 1990s argued that almost 90% of existing usability problems can be uncovered with a sample size of 10 participants while others argue that 10 is not enough [Dum03]. Even though there is apparently no consensus about the needed sample size, figure 4.9 suggest that 20 or more participants will likely uncover almost all existing usability problems. However, it has to be emphasized that there may be other factors, like wrong or erroneous metrics, that adversely affect the uncovering process.

4.5.1 Evaluation Methods

Although evaluation methods are manifold, user-based evaluations typically rely on one or a combination of the following three techniques (cf. [PPRS06, Dah06, SJWM05]):

1. **Interviews**
   Interviews are a common technique to let users express experiences in their own

words. This can be either done in a *structured* manner with some predefined sequence of questions and topics or *unstructured*. Gathered information is often videotaped and transcribed to notes for later analysis. Except for closed questions, where users are asked, for example, to place themselves in a predefined age range that can then be translated to numbers, interviews generate qualitative data.

2. **Questionnaires**

   Questionnaires provide a structured way to collect answers to predefined questions. Although often assumed easy to use, the proper design of questionnaires is a time consuming and challenging task. Compare, for example, [SP05] for a brief discussion of that topic. Similar to interviews, questionnaires produce mainly qualitative data unless closed questions are used. Before data can be analyzed it usually has to be cleaned from answers where users misunderstood questions.

3. **Observations**

   Observations can be done in a wide variety, including observation notes, photographies, video and audio recordings, think-aloud protocols, or data-logs. They are often subsumed under the term *contextual design*. Due to the high information density of most of these techniques, data processing efforts are considerably high. For instance, extracting user actions from collected video material of all participants of an experiment may result not only in a huge amount of awkward to handle data files but also requires lots of effort to extract information from those files. To ease life, tools like INTERACT[5] are available. While photography, experiment leader notes, or think-aloud protocols usually result in qualitative data, video recordings and in particular data-logs offer the opportunity to collect quantitative data.

   An important aspect of the observation technique is the location where an evaluation is conducted. In a *field study* an evaluation takes place in the user's own environment, i.e. "in the real world" where an application will later be deployed [JM06]. The disadvantage of a most realistic test environment for a system is the drawback of an uncontrolled environment with many variables that may negatively affect study outcomes.

   Opposite to field studies, *laboratory experiments* take place in a controlled environment set up for the purpose of research [KG03]. That is, laboratory experiments do not necessarily require a real laboratory but can also be conducted, for example, in a specifically prepared office or simulator [SJWM05, p. 470]. Laboratory experiments allow focusing on specific aspects of interest while at the same time offering

---

[5]See http://www.mangold.de for further information on the INTERACT software

a large degree of control of variables before or during an experiment by assigning participants to different groups [KG03]. Furthermore, they offer repeatability and facilitate data collection. The down-side of laboratory experiments is a limited relation to reality and an unknown level of generalizability of findings, which research often tries to overcome with a designed selection of the number of participants for an experiment and statistical methods for analysis.

Beside these three techniques, user interface evaluation, in particular at an early stage in the design or development process of an interface, is often done with expert reviews, also called *heuristic evaluation* (developed by Jacob Nielsen [Nie94]). Here, participants are usually either domain or usability experts that check an interface to conform to existing design guidelines, usability standards, or design principles. Because of the participating user group, heuristic evaluations heavily rely on the ability of inspectors to predict problems with an interface that would occur when end-users experience that interface, which is not always straight forward [SJWM05, p. 529]. One specific form of expert reviews is the *cognitive-walkthrough*. With this technique experts simulate "a user's problem solving process at each step in the human-computer dialog, and check [...] to see how users progress from step to step in these interactions" [PPRS06, p. 592]. Due to its nature, the focus of cognitive-walkthroughs concentrates on evaluating mainly the ease of learning. Taken together, expert tests without end-users are a reasonable approach in the early design phase of an interface that can prevent basic design faults. To uncover more fine grained usability problems, user-tests with a bigger sample size are needed.

4.5.2 Evaluation of Mobile Applications

Mobile devices are usually used on the move rather than stationary. Hence, mobile applications are being used in different situations where context always keeps changing. This includes not only environmental context changes but also social, personal, or technological context changes [JM06, p. 214]. Currently, available evaluation methods for mobile applications cannot uncover usability problems in all possible situations [DThC06]. Although the nature of mobile applications suggests an evaluation right at the place of use, a recent survey by Kjeldskov and Graham [KG03] showed that 71% of all mobile HCI evaluations are done in the laboratory and only few conventional usability tests were modified to meet arising challenges of mobile system evaluations. Lab-based evaluations (e.g. [VPL+06, DNL+04, McF99]) have many advantages such as controllable environment conditions and reproducibility. However, Brewster [Bre02] showed that lab-based experiments can predict performance of an interface being used "in context" but are not a replacement of testing in context because they provide only partial evaluation information. On the other hand, Jones and Marsden [JM06, p. 218] argue that only laboratory testing enable researchers to isolate the effect of different variables on the test subject even for mobile applications. Thus, they suggest first optimizing the design of an interface as much as possible in the lab and only then start the evaluation in the target context.

Because wearable computing is a subset of mobile computing, the above problems can be applied to wearable system evaluations. Compared to mobile systems, wearable system evaluation can, however, be even more challenging because of a tighter physical coupling between the user and the system. For example, if an HMD is mounted very closely to the eye of the user and the display is opaque, the user's perception is that she can see through the HMD, which in turn implies that the perceived visual interface (i.e. an illusion created by the user's mind) can not be captured or observed by a researcher [LS01].

So far, most reported evaluations in wearable HCI rely on laboratory experiments or field studies in restricted areas. Several studies utilize direct observation as their evaluation technique where the user and her performed task are videotaped [LS01, RB00, Esp97]. Although video analysis can yield qualitative as well as quantitative data such as user behavior or number of errors, it does not provide direct insight on interface interaction between the user and the wearable system. Other studies [HJ07, WJ07, VPL+06, BAB06, BAB06, BVE05, BVE05, DNL+04, LSP+04], therefore, use custom tools that do the quantitative data collection of interface interaction. Other qualitative evaluation techniques such as interviews, questionnaires, or think aloud protocols are often used to supplement quantitative techniques (cf. e.g. [NDL+05]). In one of the first reported evaluations of wearable systems, Siegel and Bauer [SB97] used think-aloud protocols to let users report on their interaction with the wearable system during a field study.

Overall, it is worth to mention that mobile computing and in particular wearable computing is a relatively new discipline. As a consequence there is no widely agreed method for conducting interface evaluations of mobile applications yet. That is why many mobile HCI publications are still lacking evaluation components. In a survey carried out by Beck et al. [BCK+03] only 50 out of 114 paper on mobile HCI aspects, published between 1996 and 2002, had some form of evaluation component in them. And even those 50 were mostly using evaluation techniques developed for desktop systems. Hence, "the development of effective methods for testing and evaluating the usage scenarios, enabled by pervasive applications, is an important area that needs more attention from researchers" [BB02].

Chapter 5

Context-Awareness and Adaptive User Interfaces

While the last chapter has reviewed related work for wearable user interfaces from a human-computer interaction perspective, this chapter will elaborate on how user interfaces can be automatically adapted by taking context information into account.

Although having been researched for a long time, adaptive user interface research only rarely yielded results that were satisfactory and is still a topic for controversial discussion [Der06]. There are successful mechanisms that can be indirectly considered an adaptive interface such as operating system algorithms to adaptively swap program files between RAM and hard disk during runtime. The reason for somewhat disappointing results in adaptive user interface research, however, was not caused by lacking technologies, but because of primarily focusing on technological aspects of these interfaces without taking appearing usability problems into account while making user interfaces adaptive [SRC01, SHMK93].

In this chapter, we discuss how adaptive user interfaces are characterized and point out past work including developed frameworks and related concepts that can provide valuable insights for building context-aware user interfaces for wearable computers.

5.1 Definitions

Adaptive user interfaces have been researched since the 1980s. They were not only re-searched under the term *adaptive*, but also under several others including *intelligent*, *context-aware*, or *multiple* user interfaces.

Intelligent user interfaces cover a broader range of "intelligence" and may include other sources for their intelligent behavior than only adaptive characteristics. Dietrich et al.

[DMKSH93] state that "an adaptive user interface either supports users in the adaptation of the interface to their own needs and preferences or performs the adaptation process automatically" (p. 14). Unlike Dietrich et al., who did not differentiate between whether the adaptation process is driven by the user or the system, Thevenin et al. [TCC04] argued in a more recent work that there is a difference. According to them, an interface, as defined by Dietrich et al., is either *adaptable* or *adaptive*: "It is adaptive when the user interface adapts on its own initiative. It is adaptable when it adapts at the user's request, typically by providing preference menus" (p. 35). In line with this definition others [DA04, FDM04, SRC01] also use the term "adaptive" to indicate that the system is automatically adapting the interface.

As already mentioned in the beginning of this section, there are several more context-specific terms that highlight specific aspects of adaptive user interfaces. *Multiple user interfaces* provide different views of the same information on different platforms, i.e. by changing the hardware platform from a desktop computer to a mobile device, while the application content remains the same, but its presentation will automatically adapt to the new device constraints like, for example, a smaller display size [SJ04, p. 4]. *Context-aware user interfaces* refer more to the computer's ability to sense and detect certain context information about the environment, user, or the computer itself. Thus, it is in line with our description of context given in section 4.3.1 and also closely related to the wearable computer platform.

In conclusion, the term "context-aware user interface" and "multiple user interfaces" describe the type of interfaces we are interested in for wearable computers. Context-aware user interfaces can make use of available information gathered by sensors worn on the user's body while multiple user interfaces are related to adapting the interface for different I/O device combinations under certain contexts of use. However, we will use the more self-explanatory term *adaptive user interface* in the following to make the properties of these interfaces more self-contained.

5.2   Design and Architecture Principles

Research on adaptive user interfaces is heading in various directions. Because adaptive user interfaces were introduced by Artificial Intelligence (AI) and especially applied to stationary desktop computer systems, many existing concepts and architectures are based on findings or approaches commonly used in AI. For a detailed overview we recommend reading [MW98] or [SHMK93] as a starting point.

The drawback of that AI bias is that only little specific work can be considered relevant in detail for the envisioned adaptive user interface of a wearable computer. This is mainly because of a wearable computer's specific and very constrained properties (cf. section 2.1) and the often complex methods used in AI. For example, inference systems typically require a stationary hardware infrastructure beyond today's PDA or ultra mobile computer computing power. Even though computationally intensive tasks are offloaded to stationary computers, increased energy consumption due to wireless network activity will impair battery life time and thus autonomy of the wearable system. Nevertheless, concepts and architectures that have a more general scope can still provide useful information on how adaptive user interfaces can be designed and implemented on wearable computers.

5.2.1   Adaptation Goals and Strategies

The main goal of an adaptive user interface is to provide the user with the optimal interface in a certain situation, i.e. an interfaces that is easy, efficient, and effective to use. For instance, an interface automatically reducing the amount of information presented to the user in a certain situation to prevent her from getting lost, might not only ease the use of the interface, but may also speed up task performance. The literature explains many more specific goals a certain adaptive user interface was optimized for (cf. [NCM07, GPZGB05, GW04, BM93]).

Because goals can vary and may be application specific, there are several strategies that can be used to reach a certain goal. One of the most basic but important strategy is *timing*. Rouse [Rou88] defined three different points in time when to adapt an interface:

1. Off-line prior to the actual operation of the interface.

2. On-line in anticipation of changing demands.

3. On-line in response to changing demands.

In [Coc87] only a distinction between off-line and on-line was made. Dietrich et al. [DMKSH93] also distinguish between on- and off-line but added a third point called "between sessions". Their idea is that this enables very complex adaptation strategies that take the entire session of the user into account. The drawback, however, is that preferences etc. might have changed once the user has not used the system for a longer time.

Off-line adaptation provides the opportunity to adapt the interface based on all available context information except that of the user itself. This might include device adaptation, user group adaptation, and—if available—environmental adaptation. For wearable computers that can continuously acquire lots of different context information, off-line adaptation can overcome (to a certain extent) limitations of the computation unit once performed in a boot-strap process.

On-line adaptation is perhaps the more interesting approach for adaptation. It offers a variety of possibilities to adapt the interface because adaptation takes place continuously while the interface is being used. The system is able to instantaneously adapt the interface to optimize its usability for the user, her behavior, and the current situation. A drawback is that users might get confused when the interfaces changes in an unexpected situation [Der06, PLN04]. In connection with this, Browne [BTN90] argued that on-line adaptation can result in a kind of race condition that he called *hunting*: The system tries to adapt the interface to the user and the user in turn tries to adapt to the interface. Such a situation will never reach a stable state.

5.2.2   Architectural Structures

Adaptive user interfaces have to deal with lots of information to implement some kind of intelligent behavior. Therefore, a suitable architecture for such kind of interfaces has to include access to many different information sources (preferably in a modular way). To describe and access needed information, model-based approaches are often used [Nic06, GW04, TCC04, FDM04, Pue97, BM93]. They provide an excellent basis to capture all relevant information about an envisioned user interface in a declarative model [Pue97]. The model can be either *implicitly* contained in the program code or *explicitly* modeled as a knowledge base [DMKSH93]. Because the number of models potentially needed in an adaptive system can be huge, architectures typically include only three main models. Figure 5.1 shows a general architecture presented by Benyon and Murray [BM93] for an adaptive system that is composed of a user model, a domain model, and an interaction model.

The *domain model* contains the application specific knowledge and consists of a task model encoding the user's task as well as a logical and physical model that encodes corresponding knowledge of the application and its runtime environment. The *user model* contains data on the user herself that is typically encoded in the user model, whereas user group information may be encoded in a more general profile model. To enable adaptation to changing environment conditions, an environmental model should be considered in the case of wearable computing. The *interaction model* consists of the interaction knowledge base that holds knowledge on how to adapt and when. Here, the adaptation model encodes adaptation rules that can be evaluated using the inference model. In addition to the interaction knowledge base, the architecture shown in figure 5.1 shows a *dialog record* which records details of an ongoing interaction to compute real time statistics of,

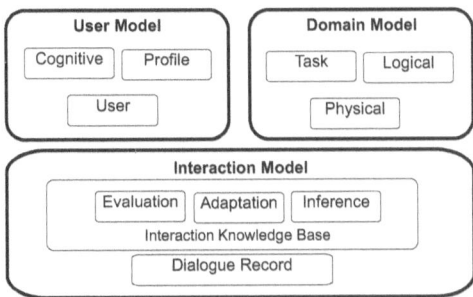

Figure 5.1: General architecture for an adaptive system [BM93]

for example, errors made by the user, or the number of tasks completed that can be used as an additional information source in the adaptation process.

Model-based Development

As the previous example has shown, model-based approaches are widely accepted in the adaptive system development [NCM07, NRCM06, GW04, SJ04, TCC04, FDM04, DMKSH93]. If a system wants to adapt its interface to the user's behavior or task, information needs to be available in a non-static format. Model-based user interface development has the idea of using declarative interface models to represent all relevant aspects of the interface. This is sometimes done using modeling languages. Generally, model-based approaches try to automatically generate a specific user interface instance, i.e. a representation of user interface components a user can interact with, from a generic abstract representation of the user interface [BS98]. The generic abstract representation typically consists of the user, domain, and task model and the generation of the actual interface is done by a mapping from abstract to specific elements. Figure 5.2 illustrates this process of automatically generating a user interface from abstract models and also indicates the mapping procedure. The adaptation procedure is comparable to an iterative user interface generation problem.

Although model-based development techniques, which mainly use task and domain models, seemed promising for the adaptive user interface development, they could not generate high quality interfaces for a long time [SJ04, p. 20]. One reason is the immense complexity of today's graphical interfaces and the difficulty to represent them in models. However, when moving from stationary to mobile devices, the complexity of possible user interfaces reduces, which in turn increases the quality of generated interfaces due to mobile

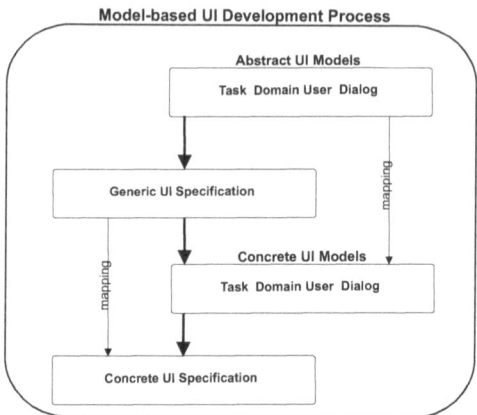

Figure 5.2: Process of generating a specific interface from abstract models.

interface limitations. In fact, recent work by Nichols et. al [NCM07] demonstrated that automatic high quality interface generation is possible for mobile devices.

Gajos and Weld [GW04] have shown with SUPPLE that usable interfaces can be automatically generated in particular for mobile devices. SUPPLE is a system that automatically generates user interfaces for different devices. It can use information from the user model to automatically adapt user interfaces to different tasks and work styles [GCTW06, GCH+05]. For adapting the interface, SUPPLE treats the adaptation process as an optimization problem utilizing constraint satisfaction techniques. It searches for a rendition of the abstract model specification of the envisioned interface that meets the "device's constraints and minimizes the estimated effort for the user's expected interface actions" [GW04]. Thus, SUPPLE warrants usability by defining a special heuristic that encodes the number of interface actions needed by the user for a certain task. Similar techniques were used to automatically generate certain device dependent layouts as comprehensively shown in [Gra97]. The Personal Universal Controller (PUC) is a system developed to improve the interfaces for complex appliances [NMH+02]. It automatically generates high quality graphical or speech interfaces for PDAs or desktop computers, by downloading an abstract description of functions and object dependencies, specified in a special specification language, from the appliances [Nic06]. Unlike the PUC system that generates only interfaces for individual appliances, Huddle [NRCM06] generates PDA interfaces to control all appliances in a multiple appliance system. It is implemented on top of the Personal Universal Controller.

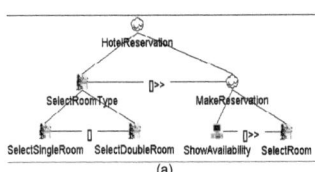 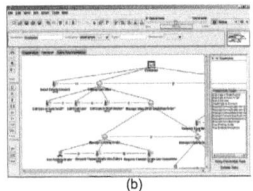

Figure 5.3: (a) Graphical CTT example (b) Graphical tool support for CTT task modeling.

Task Models and Markup Languages

To overcome quality problems due to modeling limitations, task models that describe the essential tasks users can perform while interacting with the system have gained much acceptance. Task models support the construction of UIs for different devices in a task oriented and interaction centered manner [FDM04]. To achieve more than device adaptation, the task sequence can be dynamically changed, for example, to shorten a process sequence. The *Concurrent Task Tree* (CTT) notation, introduced by Paterno [Pat99], is widely used to describe such task models in a hierarchical tree structure (cf. figure 5.3(a)) and offers graphical tool support, such as TERESA [MPS04], for defining these models (cf. figure 5.3(b)). The three central elements of a CTT model are *tasks, user interaction,* and *computation processes* without the need of user interaction. To indicate temporal dependencies between elements, nine temporal operations can be used. The most important operator is *hierarchy* that defines a hierarchy of subtasks (cf. figure 5.3(a)). Additionally, eight other temporal operations can be used, including choices between tasks, concurrency of tasks, or sequential enabling of tasks. A detailed description can be found in the corresponding text book on CTTs [Pat99]. In the context of wearable application environments, task models are deemed to be well suited because they support users in a task dependent manner. Thus, a task-centered specification of the user interface could ease its definition.

Another way to describe user interfaces in a platform independent way, is to use various special markup languages. For example, the User Interface Markup Language (UIML) [APB+99] addresses this issue. It supports a declarative description of a UI in a device independent manner. However, it does not support model-based approaches well, because it provides no notion of tasks. XIML [PE02] (eXtensible Interface Markup Language) also supports a device independent UI description. It provides a mechanism to completely describe the user interface, its attributes, and relations between elements of the interface without paying attention on how they will be implemented. Beside these mentioned markup languages there are many more tailored to specific aspects and applications. A survey on some more has been reported in [Nic06] including a brief summary of their strengths and weaknesses.

User Modeling

The current user context can strongly guide the adaptation process of an interface. To provide the user with an individual interface for a certain situation it is essential, to process all available knowledge about the user that encodes relevant user characteristics. To encode such information, user models are used. Murray [Mur87a, Mur87b] discussed many different meanings of user models. By introducing an "embedded user model" in [Mur87a] he referred to the type of model that is of interest for this thesis. That is a systems model that encodes "user characteristics for the purpose of tailoring the interaction or making the dialog between the user and the system adaptive" [Mur87a]. Thus, information from the user model is used to find appropriate modalities to ease interaction for a particular user. This requires the user model to be non-static, but updated dynamically with latest context information describing not only the user, but her behavior or current activity.

Research in user modeling has made significant progress over the last years and is still a vital area of research. As an in-depth discussion of latest technologies and approaches used is beyond the scope of this work, we recommend reading a survey on user modeling, its prospects and hazards, carried out by Kobsa [Kob93], as a starting point instead.

5.3   Enabling Tool Support Systems

Software tools that provide developers with some reusable or even out of the box solution for user interface development are quite common. There are many integrated development environments (IDEs) that support the entire development process of an application including its user interface. Here, often precast templates for recurring interaction sequences or even graphical user interface (GUI) builders are available to ease and accelerate their development. However, this is mainly true for software development of traditional desktop interfaces.

When moving from stationary to mobile application development, today's available tools are much more limited in terms of development support or a not yet developed [DA04]. Although a host of work has demonstrated that application development for mobile devices is far from trivial, interaction paradigms often fail because today's typically used devices fail in the dynamic mobile environment (cf. chapter 4).

For applications and user interfaces for wearable computers, where the potential of available sensors allow promising new developments, only very little work is known that tried to support the necessary development process. One of the most important works over the last years with regards to a basic underlying context acquisition and delivery infrastructure to implement context-aware applications is the so called *Context-Toolkit*. Dey et al. [DSA01] introduced the Context-Toolkit to provide developers with the general integration and use of context information within their applications. Central aim of the Context-Toolkit is an easy acquisition, interpreting, and use of context information gathered from the environment. The architecture of the toolkit was designed to fulfill requirements found through an extensive analysis of using context in applications [DA04]:

Separation of concerns One reason why context is not yet used in applications it that there is no common way of acquiring and handling context. An application can directly connect to sensors or indirectly using a kind of proxy server. The latter would be the preferred way because otherwise drivers to connect and acquire context are hard-wired into the application. Therefore, context should be handled in the same manner as user input is handled in an application, allowing a separation of application semantics from low-level input handling. Then, components are reusable as well.

Context interpretation Context information has to be interpreted on different levels to fulfill certain types of abstraction for an application, for example, reading an RFID tag and interpreting it using additional information like the user's name.

Transparent, distributed communication Unlike in desktop environments, where all devices are physically connected to the local computer, mobile environments are often highly distributed, i.e. running on different computers. Thus, communication between devices (sensors) should be transparent for both applications and sensors.

Constant availability of context acquisition When building traditional GUIs, interface components are directly instantiated, controlled, and used only by a single application. For context-aware applications, developers should not need to directly instantiate context providers other than those that can be used by more than one subscriber and should be maintained elsewhere to ease its use.

Context storage and history Linked to the previous requirement, this point stresses the importance of making context information persistent to be able to query past context data if needed for a certain kind of inference.

Resource discovery As mobile environments are not static and distributed, an easy way to use context sources (sensors) is needed that does not force developers to hard-wire a certain set of sensors to be used during implementation.

The Context-Toolkit is only one example of a middleware to facilitate context-aware application development. Meanwhile, there are similar systems like, for example, the Context Toolbox [BKLA06] or the context acquisition system described in [ST06].

5.4   Summary

The idea behind adaptive user interfaces is not only promising for stationary applications but also for applications running on wearable computers. However, even though reliable systems and tools exist to acquire context information from various sources, a reasonable application that makes use of them is the actual challenge. An inappropriate adaptation of interfaces will confuse users and rather leading to a decrease of usability than an increase. It is, therefore, essential to sufficiently understand how user interfaces for a certain computing paradigm have to be designed to work properly without any adaptation capabilities. Only then available context information will allow a reasonable approach to improve usability even further by automatically adapting the interface to its user and her environment. In the case of wearable computing, little knowledge on how their user interfaces should be designed has been established yet. Thus, fundamental research is still needed first. The remainder of the thesis will follow this approach of establishing fundamental findings first.

Part II

Design and Development of
Wearable User Interfaces

Chapter 6

An Approach for Developing Wearable User Interfaces

Proper interaction and usability design have become critical quality measures of software systems. Today, more attention is paid to a proper user interface design and its seamless integration into software development processes than years before. Since a productive integration of HCI knowledge into software development processes is not easy, a major challenge is to support ordinary software engineers, typically not familiar with latest HCI findings, with tools and methods to systematically build good user interfaces.

This chapter proposes a design and development process tailored to the special needs of wearable user interfaces, their developers, and researchers. It discusses how the proposed process can be integrated into existing software development processes. This includes the discussion of an envisioned evaluation method for wearable user interfaces as well as an envisioned software middleware for the actual implementation of these interfaces.

6.1 User Interface Design and Development

User-centered interface design and traditional software development use different approaches to accomplish their goals. Unlike user interface design, the traditional software development life cycle is characterized by independent parts that have to be completed before moving on to the next part in the cycle [SJWM05, p. 16]. The first published software process model that described the *classical life cycle* of software development is the "waterfall" model. It is shown in figure 6.1. Its name is derived from the cascade from one phase to another. A following phase should only start once the previous phase is completely finished. These sequential transitions are indicated with red arrows in figure 6.1.

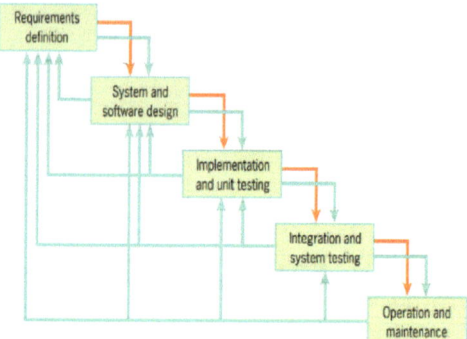

Figure 6.1: The classical software life cycle [Som04, p. 45].

Nowadays, software engineers accepted that a static top-down approach in software development, like the waterfall model, is too simplistic because of the many iterations and interactions needed between different phases (indicated in figure 6.1 with green arrows) [Som04]. For that reason, many modern software development processes now feature iterations and have become textbook knowledge such as Extreme Programming (XP).

The fundamental difference between the classical life cycle and user-centered interface design and development is the involvement of the user throughout the entire design life cycle [SJWM05, p. 16]. Additionally, interface design is highly iterative to continuously test and evaluate interfaces with respect to user requirements. Figure 6.2 illustrates a classical user interface design process. It basically consists of three major parts: *Design*, *prototyping*, and *user testing and evaluation*. Unlike the classical life cycle that leaves interface evaluation to the end of the process, the user-centered design process does not. This highlights the importance of evaluation during user interface design and development.

Although the user interface design process is iterative, the necessary knowledge to design and develop user interfaces is interleaved with no clear beginning or end. Designers obtain information from many sources. Some are drawn from specific and practical guidelines, middle-level principles, or high-level theories and models [SP05, p. 60]:

- *Practical guidelines:* Practical guidelines provide help for design problems and prevent from pitfalls, but may have only smaller applicability.

- *Middle-level principles:* Middle-level principles are wider applicable and help to analyze and compare design alternatives.

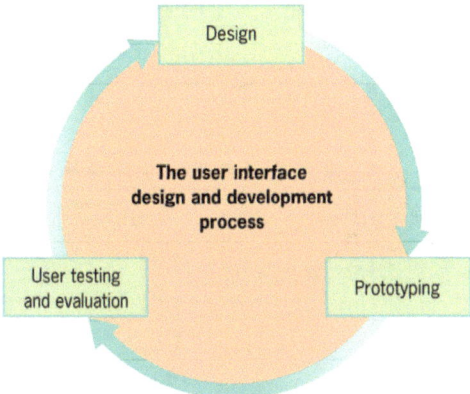

Figure 6.2: Iterative user interface design and evaluation process [Gre96].

- *High-level theories and models:* High-level theories and models provide more formalized or systematic approaches, for example, in predicting user behavior. However, even having the widest applicability their complexity requires detailed understanding to be used, which is often challenging for developers.

Standards, experiences, or information gained from past evaluations and experiments not yet available as guidelines or principles are other sources for design information. In particular, evaluation results on very specific aspects or application domains may never reach public awareness in terms of guidelines for developers, because they are often too tightly coupled to a specific application to allow broad applicability. Nevertheless, such results are very important for similar interface developments. For wearable computing applications, this issue may frequently occur due to the highly integrated and often task specific support wearable applications provide.

Wearable computing research considered user interfaces and their design only with minor emphasis over the past years [WNK06, CNPQ02, BNSS01, Cla00, SGBT00, BKM+97]. Instead, the research was focused on hardware, with an emphasis on wearable input and output devices and particularly the use of body-worn sensors to gather context (cf. chapter 4). As a consequence, there are only few available guidelines, principles, or methods on how to design, evaluate, and implement wearable user interfaces available today [Wit07a]. Because software developers usually have limited knowledge about HCI they have limited capabilities to design high quality and usable interfaces [OS06, Gre96]. Sometimes this leads to often cited "GUI Bloopers" that can easily fill entire books to illustrate what happens when existing HCI knowledge is ignored or applied in a wrong way by software

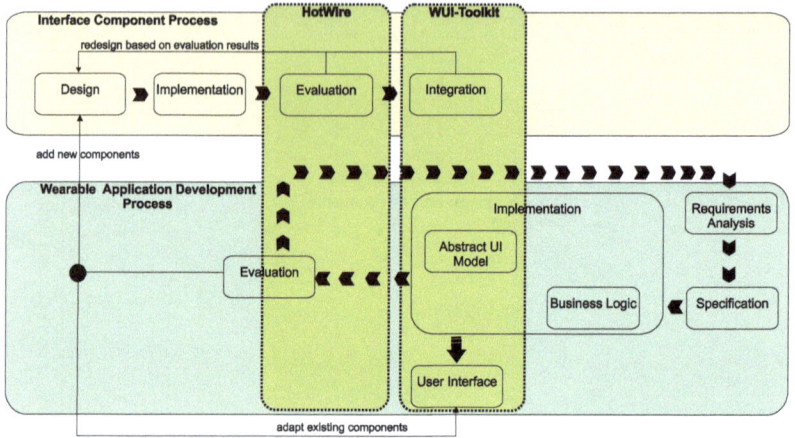

Figure 6.3: Overview of the wearable user interface development process.

developers (cf. [Joh00] for examples). This situation becomes even worse for mobile and wearable user interfaces, where we frequently see a re-use of the desktop paradigm which causes usability problems [KNW$^+$07]. A systematic exploration of evaluation methods, tools, and their application within a software development process is therefore needed for a successful deployment of wearable computing in the professional environment.

The remainder of this chapter will propose a structured user interface design and development approach to overcome the discussed problems for wearable applications and their user interfaces.

6.2 Wearable User Interface Development Process

The underlying assumption of the proposed development process, as discussed in the previous section, is that software developers are usually not sufficiently aware of the latest HCI knowledge, particularly not for wearable computers. This situation is most likely to continue in the foreseeable future, because wearable computing is still an emerging technology that has not become a business issue yet.

6.2.1 Overview

An overview of the proposed wearable user interface development process is shown in figure 6.3. It is a twofold approach where the focus in the first **interface component**

process is on design, implementation, and evaluation of basic user interface components and interaction concepts. Those components can be used in a later stage to assemble application specific user interfaces. The second **wearable application development process** focuses on the actual specification and development of a wearable computing application with emphasis on the user interface implementation. It builds on a sufficient number of tested interface components and interaction concepts provided through results of the *interface component process*. Due to its design, the *wearable application development process* seamlessly integrates itself into any iterative software development process.

Considerably more important than the detailed actions to be carried out in each process step are the envisioned tools and methods used during different phases in the process. Both sub-processes are supported by tools and methods tailored to support evaluation and implementation of wearable user interfaces. They are illustrated in figure 6.3 with vertically dashed boxes overlapping the two sub-processes:

- **HotWire**

  The *HotWire* is an apparatus envisioned to simulate physical primary tasks in a laboratory environment [WD06]. It is an evaluation method used to evaluate newly designed and developed interface components within the *interface component process*. The HotWire is an apparatus to abstract a real world primary task of an application domain, i.e. it allows simulating certain physical activities. The HotWire represents an evaluation method for wearable user interfaces that allows for the conducting of user experiments in a controlled laboratory environment to evaluate the usability of an interface component designed for a dual-task involvement of users.

  Besides individual or isolated interface component evaluations, the HotWire may also be partially used during the evaluation of an entire application in the *wearable application development process* once a controllable laboratory environment is better suited than the real application domain. A detailed discussion of the HotWire evaluation method and its usage will be given in chapter 7.

- **Wearable User Interface (WUI) Toolkit**

  The *WUI-Toolkit* is a concept proposed to provide facilitating tool support for the wearable user interface development with reusable components [WNK07, Wit05]. It is envisioned to be used as a framework by software developers in the *wearable application development process* similar to existing GUI libraries. Unlike GUI libraries, however, the idea is to implement a model-driven approach with semi-automatic interface generation capabilities rather than providing class libraries for the manual programming of actual interfaces. Software developers can take advantage of

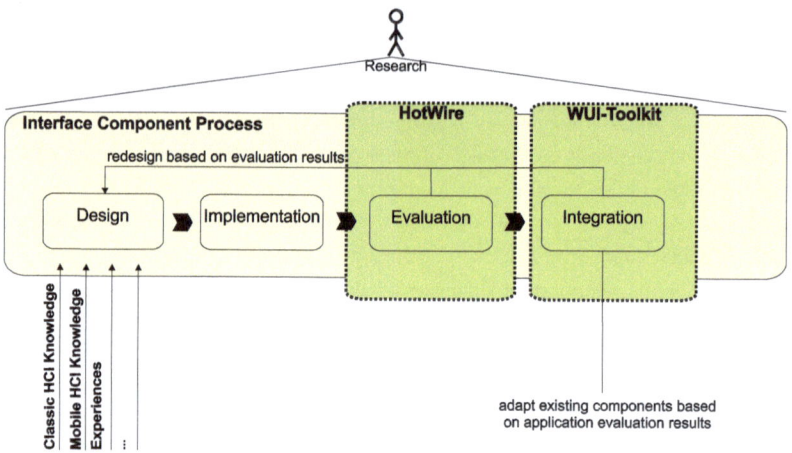

Figure 6.4: The user interface component development process.

the model-driven approach without taking care of the actual design and rendering process of a required user interface.

Once a number of interface components for the composition of wearable user interfaces are available, the *interface component process* can run in parallel to the *wearable application development process*. From that time on, it is a continuously ongoing process, where resulting interface components or new findings can be integrated into the WUI-Toolkit to make them reusable for forthcoming applications. A prototypical implementation of the envisioned WUI-Toolkit and its usage will be presented in chapter 11.

6.2.2   Interface Component Process

User interfaces are composed of different interface components that enable an interaction between the system and the user. GUI libraries are available for the classical direct manipulation of user interfaces [Shn83], that ease their development by providing reusable *standard* interface components like windows, buttons, scrollbars, and related interface layouts, including interaction paradigms. Their applicability in wearable user interfaces is limited though. This is because of the widely implemented WIMP (Windows Icons Menus Pointer) metaphor within those libraries, which is inappropriate for most wearable computing applications [KNW+07, Sta02a, Sta01b].

The interface component process, shown in figure 6.4, offers a systematic approach to develop and evaluate new user interface components for wearable computing applications. Also, it supports the adaptation of already existing components from the desktop and mobile computing area, instead of directly reusing those existing components to prevent from usability pitfalls.

Today's most important interaction paradigms and their corresponding interface components were initially invented or proposed by the HCI research community and only later on refined by the industry. Therefore, the interface component process primarily focuses on *research* as the initial driver of the process. HCI researchers are familiar with fundamental HCI principles and latest findings in wearable computing. Their basic research is needed prior to application development, because proper applications rely on proper and approved designs and interface artifacts.

Design and Implementation Phase

Although the control of most wearable user interfaces is different to desktop or mobile interfaces because of the different I/O devices used (cf. chapter 4), interface component design for wearable systems does not always need to be entirely started from scratch [Wit07a]. Inspirations can be taken from classical and mobile HCI research as long as they do not conflict with the fundamental properties of wearable computing (cf. section 2.1). Of course, interface component design can be influenced by many more sources such as own experiences or observations of specific problems with wearable computing technology (cf. figure 6.4). In particular, special purpose devices require special purpose interface components to be easily usable. The VuMan [BKM+97], for example, was the first wearable computer to have its characteristics of the provided interaction device directly taken from the user interface and its design.

Evaluation Phase

Once a new interface component was designed and implemented by a researcher, the most important issue is to evaluate its usability with real users. The objective of the evaluation phase is to verify, whether or not the new component is not only useful and usable in theory (heuristic evaluation), but also in practice (user-centered evaluation). As the interface component developed within this subprocess is required to be decoupled from any specific application, resulting interface components are deemed to be applicable in many different applications. In order to validate this applicability, the implementation phase is followed by the evaluation phase. Experiments conducted have to abstract from any specific usage scenario while simultaneously retaining the basic properties of wearable computing. To do this, the HotWire evaluation method is used to simulate a physical primary task from the real world. The wearable computer system that runs the new interface component, serves as the secondary computer task during evaluation. With this, a realistic evaluation of a new interface component in a dual-task situation, which is characteristic for many tasks of an application domain (e.g. maintenance), can be carried out. Once an experiment has been successfully conducted with a positive result, a tested component can be treated as 'preliminarily approved'. With this, it is ready for use in wearable applications in a following integration phase. If an interface component has not successfully passed the evaluation phase, a new iteration of the entire process has to be triggered. That begins with the redesign of the component based on the results of the previous evaluation.

Integration Phase

In the final integration phase the new component can be integrated in the WUI-Toolkit. This makes the component reusable and available for application developers. The WUI-Toolkit then serves as a kind of knowledge base that developers can access and use to model an interface similar to GUI libraries for desktop computing. Although direct access to an interface component is basically possible, the abstract model specifications defined by application developers later on result in a rendering that may use certain interface components when being appropriate. With the integration into the WUI-Toolkit, the interface component process is completed. It may be reinvoked on the same component once new evaluation results are available that identify usability problems or optimization potentials of that component. Such results can either be outcomes of the evaluation phase of the wearable application development process, or a side effect of related interface component evaluations.

6.2.3   Wearable Application Development Process

Every software application needs a user interface to communicate with its users. Because wearable user interfaces are different from today's deployed interfaces for desktop and mobile applications, an adaptation of software life cycles that reflects these differences must be beneficial. In particular, implementation and evaluation phases can be enhanced with special tools that ease and support the development and evaluation of wearable user interfaces. Suitable tools cannot rely on sophisticated knowledge of application developers and should be able to guide developers through the development process even though their knowledge about wearable computing is limited.

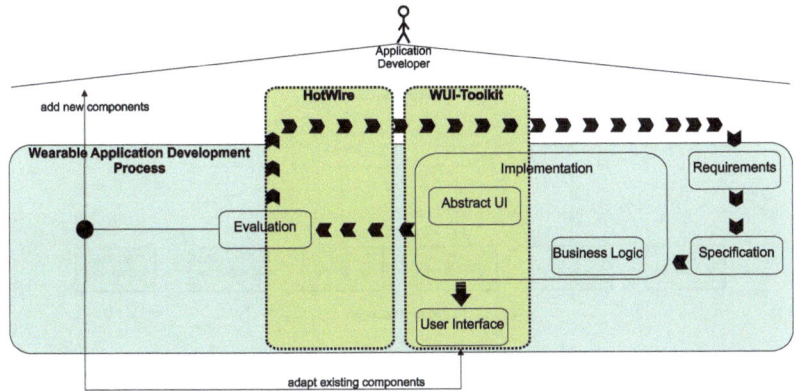

Figure 6.5: The process of developing a wearable application including its user interface.

The wearable application development process, shown in figure 6.5, enhances existing software development life cycles with special tools. The special software toolkit eases the implementation phase and empowers application developers to implement user interfaces while almost completely omitting interaction and design issues of wearable user interfaces.

Requirements Analysis and Specification Phase

In its requirements engineering and specification phases the wearable application development process is identical with the fundamental activities and techniques usually applied in other software development processes. Requirements engineering involves various activities needed to create and maintain system requirements that finally lead to a system requirements document [Som04, p. 122]. Activities to assemble such a document include requirements specification and validation or feasibility studies. Similar to the various activities in requirements engineering, there is a variety of different techniques to assess system requirements. In a user-centered approach, techniques such as interviews, observations, video documentations, or workshops are used to analyze tasks and help understand requirements (cf. section 4.5). Dykstra et. al [DEMA01] analyzed a range of techniques that are particularly useful for interaction design and related requirements and argued that the selection of a technique depends on the project structure, team skills, and the culture of the company doing the analysis. Independent of those company properties is the primary task of the user that always has to be carefully examined in the wearable application development process. It is the primary task of the user that may significantly

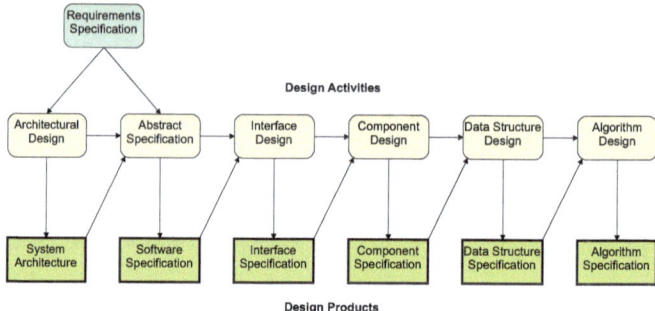

Figure 6.6: A general model of the software design process (adapted from [Som04, p. 75]).

impact the usability of the interface, once the wearable application is deployed as a secondary task. Therefore, neglecting this fact is fatal for wearable applications. This is what is inherently different in requirements engineering and the specification phase of wearable and desktop applications; a desktop application does not care about a secondary task because there usually is none.

Implementation Phase

The implementation phase in a software development process is dedicated to the conversion of system specifications that have been created from system requirements to an executable system [Som04, p. 56]. This always involves software design and programming activities. Because software design is a complex but crucial activity for an application, it is divided into different sub activities. Figure 6.6 illustrates the activities, their sequential order, and resulting products. In the depicted classical version, the process is meant to be the same for all parts of an application including the user interface. The wearable application development process, however, is different to the classical approach in the implementation phase.

For reoccurring standard problems in software design, comprehensive software design patterns are widely known and applied by software developers [GHJV95]. The Model-View-Controller (MVC) pattern, first introduced by Renskaug [Ree79] in 1979, is still frequently used. It basically separates the presentation (user interface) of an application from its business logic, i.e. from data structures and algorithms used to manipulate application data. This separation is implemented with clear interfaces that allow splitting the development of the application into two concurrent processes. While some application developers can work on the basic business logic to manipulate data objects in the right way, others can work on the implementation of the user interface.

The implementation phase of the wearable application development process adopts this approach and splits activities in two parts (cf. figure 6.5). Data structures are defined and manipulated in the *Business Logic* activity, the *Abstract UI* activity deals with modeling the envisioned wearable user interface. Instead of directly programming the user interface with available GUI libraries, the *Abstract UI* activity involves a model-driven specification to *describe* the envisioned interface. This means, the interface is described in an abstract manner rather than implemented with specific components. Developers are requested to provide an abstract model of the envisioned user interface based on application requirements. Hence, there is no need to consider design related issues of wearable user interfaces by developers in detail. Instead, the abstract specification features a simplistic interaction design through a definition of the basic input and output data needed to represent a business process. The interpretation and resulting rendering of the abstract model is then completely left to the WUI-Toolkit. The toolkit generates an interface representation based on the abstract model specification as well as additional context information.

Evaluation Phase

Because wearable interfaces often cannot make use of standard WIMP interfaces with ordinary mouse devices and keyboards, different methods for their evaluation are needed [WD06]. Software development processes in their evaluation phase have to be enhanced with new methods able to support the evaluation of deployed interfaces of wearable computing applications.

As figure 6.5 indicates, the evaluation phase of the wearable application development process may but does not necessarily have to make use of the HotWire evaluation method. If the HotWire is not applicable, evaluation of the application should make use of qualitative rather than quantitative evaluation methods such as interviews, workshops, or questionnaires to overcome evaluation challenges resulting from the tight coupling between the wearable system, its peripherals, and the user [LS01]. Thereof independent, the evaluation phase outcomes can have basically two consequences based on their scope:

1. **Generalizable Findings**

    Evaluation results that yielded new insights regarding design, usage, or usability of user interface components are handled in two different ways. Generic or generalizable findings that are new and not yet included in the WUI-Toolkit, cause the interface component process to be invoked. In this case, the process starts with an initial design of a new component representing the new findings. This is followed by the already known sequence of implementation, evaluation, and finally integration of the new component into the WUI-Toolkit.

If findings provide new insights into already existing user interface components, the interface component process is also invoked. However, the design phase will basically redesign and adapt existing components rather than defining new components. The purpose of this case is the *improvement* or *adaptation* of existing components and their reevaluation. Finally, an updated version of the component, that encodes latest findings, can be integrated as the new "state-of-the-art" component into the WUI-Toolkit.

2. **Application Specific Findings**
   Once evaluation results indicate usability problems or implementation errors, the entire life cycle has to be reiterated in order to solve discovered problems. Note that this has exactly the same impact that similar evaluation results would have in any other software development process independent of the particular application or the underlying computing paradigm.

6.3   Conclusion

The presented user interface development process can be seamlessly integrated into other software development life cycles. It enriches existing software processes with tools and methods to support the implementation and evaluation of wearable computing applications and particularly its user interfaces. The envisioned tools and methods can be used without significantly changing existing workflows [Wit07a]. Only few details of existing development phases within a certain software development process are affected or need to be slightly modified:

- *Requirements Analysis Phase*
  In the requirements analysis phase, the primary physical tasks end-users are requested to carry out, need to be thoroughly examined. It is the primary task of the user that significantly impacts on the usability of a newly developed application including its user interface once the wearable computing application is deployed and the user has to handle his secondary task as well. Therefore, the quality of the developed application will strongly depend on designing the application towards the characteristics of the primary task that need to be carried out.

- *Implementation Phase*

  In the implementation phase of a wearable user interface, developers are requested to implement an abstract model of the envisioned user interface instead of manually programming it in a classical way. This includes that specific design and interaction paradigms do not need to be considered. The model-based approach eases interface development in the sense that it offers developers with limited knowledge about HCI issues of wearable computers the possibility to model an interface that will later be automatically rendered by the WUI-Toolkit in an appropriate way.

- *Evaluation Phase*

  The evaluation phase is also affected by the proposed process. The HotWire evaluation method provides a new possibility to test wearable user interfaces for dual-task applications. Because dual-task applications are usually not in focus of classical evaluation methods for desktop or mobile applications, evaluation phases have to be adapted to allow applying the HotWire method.

The remainder of this thesis will elaborate on the application of the proposed development process. First, the HotWire evaluation method, as the central tool in the *interface component process*, will be introduced. This is followed by a number of interface component evaluations that use the HotWire to establish basic interaction and interface component knowledge proposed in the *interface component process*. Secondly, the *application development process* will be in focus with its central software tool that aids interface implementation. A prototypical implementation of the envisioned WUI-Toolkit including example applications will be presented. Here, presented applications were systematically built according to the *application development process* to demonstrate feasibility and usability of the proposed process.

Part III

Evaluation of Wearable User Interfaces

Chapter 7

The HotWire Apparatus

The last chapter discussed a general and systematic approach for the design, implementation, and evaluation of user interfaces for wearable computers. This chapter introduces the evaluation method already described in that development process.

When conducting user studies to evaluate a certain aspect of a wearable user interface, a major challenge is to simulate the real-world primary tasks that users have to perform while using a wearable computing application [WD06]. The presented evaluation method can be used to evaluate user interface components or applications in a laboratory environment, where the primary task is characterized by a mobile, physical, and manual activity.

7.1 Introduction

Unlike stationary applications, where environmental conditions remain rather stable over time and users typically perform only one task at a time with a computer, wearable applications are affected by changing conditions and multitasking. Conditions change due to the user's mobility, the environment, or task complexity of the primary task the user performs. For instance, in aircraft maintenance a wearable system may be used to guide the user through complex maintenance procedures. Because the actual maintenance procedure requires maintainers to work on physical objects with their hands, this can temporarily affect the workers mobility and cognitive or physical abilities [MW07]. In order to evaluate such applications and their user interfaces in a realistic but controlled environment, the application domain and its task characteristics have to be considered during evaluation. Physical tasks that are frequently found in wearable computing and that require users to work with their hands in their "personal space", i.e. within arm's reach, are called *manual tasks* [Cut97].

Different user studies [WK07, VPL⁺06, DWPS06, NDL⁺05, DNL⁺04] already demonstrated that by introducing realistic wearable computing tasks, many findings known from stationary and mobile computing can be confirmed. However, there are also new findings that point out that there are inherent differences in wearable computing due to its specific constraints mainly originated by mobility and the physical primary tasks performed. In connection with this, Witt and Drugge [WD06] formulated a set of basic and fundamental requirements to be fulfilled by an evaluation method for the laboratory environment to study interaction aspects in wearable computing in a realistic manner:

1. **Real physical task abstraction**
   Primary tasks in wearable computing are often manual tasks. The evaluation system has to realistically simulate such manual activities by abstracting their fundamental characteristics.

2. **Easy to learn**
   The system has to be easy to learn by users to reduce errors in the experiment data due to a misunderstanding of the experiment setup. The time to make the user proficient and fully trained should be short enough to add a sufficient practice period before the actual experiment, so that the user's performance will remain steady throughout the study.

3. **Adaptable to different simulations**
   The system has to be adaptable to provide the simulation of different primary tasks with different characteristics. That is, the simulator has to be capable of modeling, for example, different levels of task complexity, physical and attention demands as well as task lengths.

7.2   The HotWire Primary Task Simulator

The so-called *HotWire* apparatus is designed and developed according to the discussed requirements for a primary task simulator in the previous section. It offers a reproducible simulation of a real world manual task in a controlled laboratory environment. With this property it provides the foundation for a new method to evaluate wearable user interfaces under dual-task conditions.

The basic concept of the apparatus is inspired by a children's game originally intended to train motor skills as well as the ability to concentrate on a certain task over a longer period of time. In Germany this game is known as "Der heiße Draht" which translates to

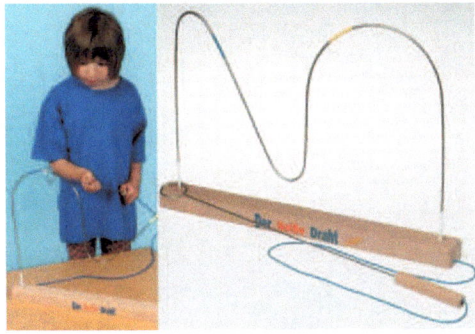

Figure 7.1: Commercial product of the HotWire game for children[1].

English as "the hot wire". It can be bought as a commercial product[1] (cf. figure 7.1). The toy version consists of a bent metallic wire, with both ends mounted onto a base plate, and a wooden hand-held tool with a metal ring. The idea of the game is that a person has to pass the ring of the hand-held tool from one end of the wire to the other end without touching the wire itself. If the wire is touched, an acoustic signal will be generated. Once such a signal occurs, the person has to restart from the beginning. To prevent children from fatigue by allowing them to rest while playing, small insulated colored segments are mounted on the metallic wire (cf. figure 7.1).

7.2.1   Construction of the HotWire Apparatus

The HotWire apparatus, developed for wearable user interface evaluations, is different to the commercial product developed to train children's motoric skills. To be applicable for user interface evaluations, it has a much more flexible design and a different technical setup compared to the commercial version. Most notably, the HotWire apparatus features a special metallic wire construction. The wire is made from different smaller wire segments. Each of those segments is connected to another segment with special windings. This offers high flexibility, because it allows varying the difficulty and characteristics of the manual primary task by replacing or changing the sequence or shape of connected segments. Hence, it makes the apparatus adaptable to different tasks. Unlike the original HotWire game, the metallic wire is only mounted on one side to the base plate. This allows for an easier and more flexible technical setup and also overcomes the drawback that the ring of a hand-held tool cannot be easily removed from the wire if both ends are attached to the

---

[1]Purchasable product found at http://www.sport-thieme.de (11/06/2006)

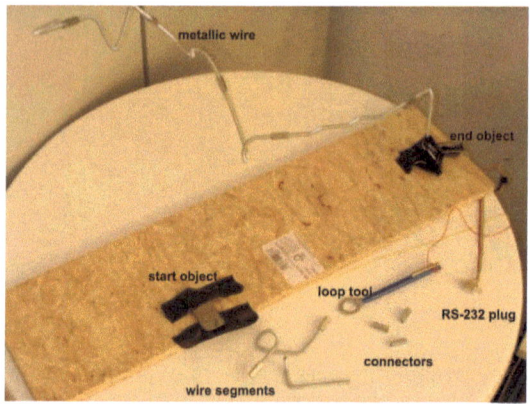

Figure 7.2: First prototype of the HotWire apparatus for simulating manual primary tasks in a laboratory environment.

base plate. In the original version, the tool always has to be passed back over the entire track to restart the game. This turns into a problem, once the length of the wire needs to be significantly long to model a certain primary task. The first prototype of the HotWire apparatus is shown in figure 7.2.

Performing the HotWire Task during an Experiment

To begin the HotWire task during an experiment, the user has to manually indicate that he is ready to start. By touching a special metallic object, attached to the base plate (*start object*), with the ring of the hand-held tool. Then, the user can immediately proceed to pass the ring of the hand-held tool as accurately as possible over the wire without touching it. To finally finish the HotWire task, the base plate features at its very end another metallic object that indicates the end of the task once being touched with the ring of the hand-held tool (*end object*). An overview of the used parts to build the HotWire apparatus as well as the location of start and end objects of the first prototype can be derived from figure 7.2.

Technical Setup of the Apparatus

The basic technical setup of the apparatus is straight forward. To gather quantitative data about the task performance of a user, the HotWire is connected to a computer. To automatically measure beginning, end, and errors made during the task, i.e. the number

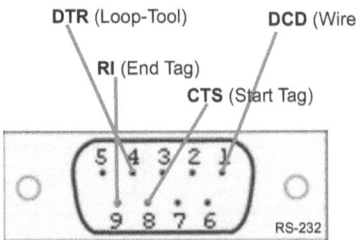

Figure 7.3: RS-232 connection schema for the HotWire apparatus.

of contacts between the metallic ring of the hand-held tool and the metallic wire, the
start and stop indicator objects, the tool, and the metallic wire itself were connected to a
RS-232 serial connector:

- For *errors*, the *data carrier detect* (DCD) pin is connected to the metallic wire.

- For the *beginning* of the task, the start object is connected to the *clear to send*
  (CTS) pin.

- For the *end* of the task, the *ring indicator* (RI) pin is connected to the stop object.

- The *data terminal ready* (DTR) pin is connected to the hand-held tool.

The connections are summarized in figure 7.3. The DCD, CTS, and RI are input
channels for the RS-232 interface. Only the hand-held tool is connected to the DTR
output channel. This is why each time the hand-held tool touches one of the other
components, the electrical circuit is closed and can be detected on the RS-232 interface.
Any software listening on the different state changes of the serial port connection is able
to detect these events. It is worth mentioning that there is no additional power source
needed to run the HotWire. The power provided by the serial RS-232 hardware interface
is sufficient. Although a serial RS-232 interface was chosen, other systems can be easily
used as well to connect the electronics of the HotWire to a computer. If computers do
not have a RS-232 interfaces, there are, for example, systems like the IO-Warrior[2] that
provide an USB interface and allow connecting multiple input and output channels.

---

[2]IO-Warrior - Generic USB I/O Controller, http://www.codemercs.com

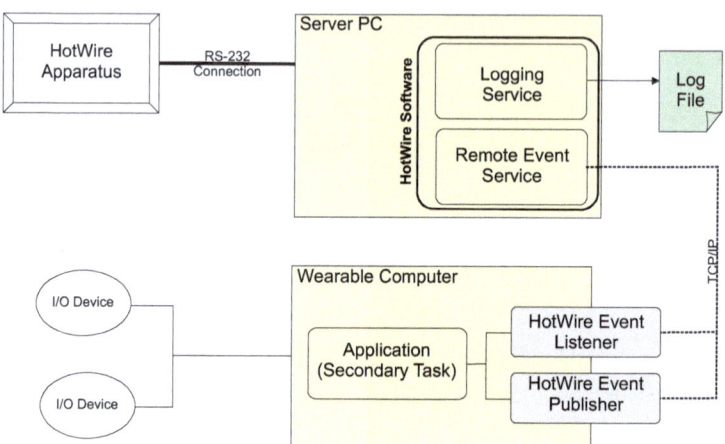

Figure 7.4: Example application of the HotWire apparatus including its software in a user study.

7.2.2   Monitoring Software

To easily integrate the HotWire apparatus in different user studies and experiment setups, special simulation software was developed that monitors the user's performance while performing the HotWire task.

Figure 7.4 shows an example of how the HotWire software can be integrated in an experiment setup. A stationary computer (*Server PC*) is connected to the HotWire apparatus and runs the HotWire software. The wearable application (*Secondary Task*), which is to be evaluated within the user study, runs on a separate wearable computer, but features a network connection. To communicate with the server, the wearable application uses special handlers provided by the HotWire software to publish and listen for events.

Provided Services

The HotWire software consists of two main services that implement basic logging and remote event dispatching functionalities:

1. **Logging Service**

   The *logging service* records all data (coming from the HotWire apparatus) important throughout a user study. For instance, the time needed by a subject to complete the HotWire task or the number of wire contacts being made:

- task completion time ($t_{\text{end}} - t_{\text{start}}$)
- overall errors ($\sum_{i=t_{\text{start}}}^{t_{\text{end}}} contact(i)$)
- error rate ($\frac{overall\ errors}{task\ completion\ time}$)

Besides logging HotWire events, the service also provides an API for logging custom events, for example, those coming from other software components, offering a mechanism to centralize all log messages of a user study. Because wearable computing applications are often composed of distributed entities, the logging service also handles logging information from remote devices by utilizing an *Event Publisher*. This publisher is part of the *Remote Event Service*. For easier post processing, all recorded data is written to one single log file per user at the end of a session.

2. **Remote Event Service**

   As already mentioned, wearable applications are often physically distributed. The *Remote Event Service* provides an extensible plug-in architecture for arbitrary remote event dispatching. Other software components can access HotWire logging event data at runtime by using *Event Subscribers*. For this, a publisher-subscriber design pattern was implemented. If software components are running on the same system, direct function calls are used for event delivery. If components are distributed but connected through a network infrastructure, the remote event service offers a plug-in for TCP/IP-based event dispatching.

7.3   Modeling Primary Tasks with the HotWire

Although the HotWire apparatus is designed to meet a wide range of different primary tasks that to some extent involve manual work, the HotWire needs to be reconfigured and adapted to realistically model a certain real world task. For example, to conduct a user study in the area of aircraft maintenance, the wire should be shaped in a way that subjects are forced to move as well as to adopt different postures while performing a HotWire task that was found to be characteristical for that domain [MW07]. The specific set of characteristical motions or postures that authentically model a manual task depend on the application domain.

There are many qualitative methods that can be used to analyze application domains regarding characteristical user tasks that could affect the usability of an application or its interface (cf. section 4.5). Usually, these are summarized under the topic of *task analysis*. Techniques to conduct a task analysis include interviews, observations, or work place studies [RW03]. As the detailed procedure to carry out a task analysis is beyond the scope of this thesis, we recommend reading related text books [PPRS06, BTT05, DL04].

7.3.1 Manual Task Characteristics

Manual tasks can be very different, ranging from rather simple tasks like moving heavy objects between different places, to very complex ones like the assembly of a wristwatch. All such tasks encompass special challenges and require certain abilities from the person performing the task. In industrial environments, manual tasks often demand a certain level of physical, perceptual, or cognitive ability that affect interaction with a wearable computer. With respect to a manual task that should be abstracted by the HotWire apparatus, the following properties have to be examined in detail *before* an adaptation of the apparatus to a particular activity:

- **Visual Attention**
  Visual attention is very important to accomplish a manual task. Almost every manual task requires some form of visual attention on the physical objects or tools needed to perform the task. Here, vision is needed by humans to close the hand-eye coordination feedback loop. The amount of visual attention required to perform a manual task varies dependent on operator characteristics, task characteristics, and the environment [Duk06]. Unlike our knowledge of physical demands required by a manual task, the effects of visual demands on performance of manual tasks are not well documented [LH99].

  Because visual attention is focused and cannot be easily divided onto different tasks, humans can only actively change their visual attention to a secondary task, which in turn produces mental load on them (cf. section 3.4). This is why proper interruption handling is very important for user interaction with a wearable computer. Even though the secondary computer task is primarily meant to be a supporting one, every instruction or assistance comes along with an interruption the user has to deal with. Chapters 8 and 9 will discuss interruption aspects with respect to gesture and speech interaction in wearable computing.

- **Physical Demands**
  Physical demands describe how physically demanding it is to carry out a task. Unlike visual attention, knowledge of ergonomics is quite extensive in regard of physical demands and in particular on what musculoskeletal disorders can be caused by physically demanding activities [BB97]. Tasks may force humans to bend down, crawl on the floor, lift and carry objects, or simply move over distances. All these

activities produce load on the human body and can impact task performance. With respect to a secondary computer task, those physical demands can be limiting factors for interaction and presentation.

Similar to visual demands, physical demands also influence a human's interruptibility, but may also impact the number of possible interaction styles during a particular task sequence. Often physical demands of manual tasks are accompanied by a temporary occupation or limitation of extremities or the mobility of the body in general. Holding a tool in a hand, or kneeling down in a narrow area can make it hard to use hands for both working on a manual task and interacting with a computer. For example, the use of gesture interaction in a narrow landing gear compartment of an aircraft may be inappropriate due to the limited freedom of movement of the technician. Chapters 9 and 10 examine the impact of body postures on interaction as well as the use of "hands-free" speech interaction in physically demanding scenarios.

- **Cognitive Demands**
  Although almost always needed, the cognitive demands of tasks are strongly coupled to the individual human performing a task, his experiences with it, and the problem solving strategy applied [EK05, p. 434]. Therefore, it is hard to determine cognitive demands of an activity. In general, tasks can be ranked as being more cognitively demanding than others. For example, a complex task requiring special expert knowledge to be successfully accomplished is likely to be more demanding cognitively than a comparatively easy task that requires almost none or every day knowledge to be accomplished. Because problem solving and expertise is a separate filed of cognitive research, details are omitted here. Instead, we refer to [EK05] as well as the NASA-TLX (Task Load Index) [HS88].The NASA-TLX is a subjective, post-hoc workload assessment questionnaire to determine a user's workload. It allows users to perform subjective workload assessments for their work with various human-machine systems. NASA-TLX is based on a multi-dimensional rating procedure that derives an overall workload score from a weighted average of ratings on six subscales. The subscales include, for example, mental demands, temporal demands, own performance, effort and frustration.

7.3.2   Modifiable Parameters

To model a primary manual task with the HotWire apparatus, there are different parameters available that can be modified. To realistically abstract a manual task or a number of task characteristics of a class of tasks, the wire track and the hand-held tool can be modified:

1. **Wire segments**

   - *Shape*
   - *Diameter*
   - *Number*

   By modifying the *shape*, *diameter*, or changing the *number* of wire segments used to build the wire track, a wide range of characteristics can be modeled. Because the wire track is the central element of the HotWire apparatus, it is considered to be the most important parameter to be varied. With different wire segments task complexity and task length can be modeled.

2. **Hand-held tool**

   - *Diameter*
   - *Weight*
   - *Number*

   Changing the *diameter* and *weight* of the hand-held tool allows modeling task complexity as well as visual and physical demands. Additionally, changing the *number* of hand-held tools to be used while performing the HotWire task, allows for the modeling of physical and cognitive demands such as an occupancy of both hands or their coordination during the task.

Before giving some specific modeling examples on how a certain real-world task can be modeled by tuning the different parameters of the HotWire in the following section, figure 7.5 summarizes the major areas a parameter change on the HotWire might affect.

7.3.3   Modeling Examples

Tasks that require visual attention and cognitive effort to be accomplished can, for example, be either modeled with wire segments that are intricately bent, i.e. where it is difficult to pass the ring over the wire without contact, or by changing the diameter of the ring of the hand-held tool. To model only visual attention demands, the track has to be modeled in such a way that makes it difficult to pass the ring over the wire, but not how this has to be done. The latter would additionally require users to think about a solution

| | HotWire Task | | Task Demands | | |
	Length	Complexity	Visual	Physical	Cognitive
Wire-Segments Shape		▬	▬	▬	▬
Diameter		▬	▬		
Number	▬				▬
Hand-held Tool Weight		▬		▬	
Diameter		▬	▬		
Number		▬	▬		▬

Figure 7.5: Overview of the different HotWire parameters and their associated effects on the characteristics of the HotWire task including the task demands they usually impose on a user carrying out the HotWire task.

on how to move or hold the hand-held tool to pass a section without an error, which raises cognitive demands. Also, changing the diameter of the ring, in connection with a fixed wire diameter, changes visual attention demands. A reduction or increase of the diameter of the ring, increases visual attention or decreases it, respectively. In combination with an intricately bent wire segment the diameter of the ring can also be used to raise cognitive demands.

Tasks that include physical demands related to mobility are modeled by forcing users to adopt different body postures to accomplish the HotWire task. These, however, can only be modeled by considering the overall shape of the wire track. The detailed forming of the wire strongly depends on the certain postures to be modeled. For example, to model a HotWire track that forces users to kneel down at a certain point, the wire has to be shaped in a way that it leaves the "standard level" towards a significantly lower level that can only be reached when users bend or kneel. Figure 7.6 shows a HotWire that was built to model physical demanding tasks with respect to different postures.

Another level of physical demands is imposed by the weight of the hand-held tool. Adjusting the weight of the hand-held tool to the same weight of tools used while performing the real-world task in the application domain, makes the HotWire task abstraction even more similar and realistic.

A very specific parameter to be varied is the number of hand-held tools. Unlike the number of wire segments that basically vary the length of a task, the number of hand-held tools is used to impose cognitive or coordinative demands of a task. Without changing the hardware setup, the use of two hand-held tools while performing the HotWire task shows the option to model tasks that can only be accomplished when permanently using

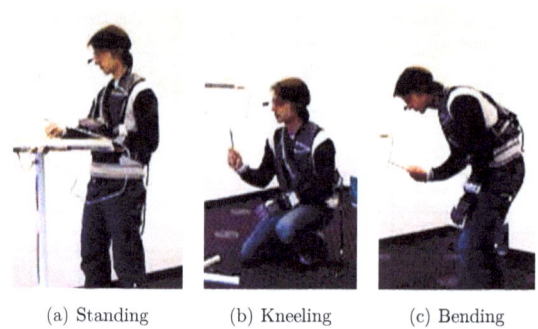

(a) Standing   (b) Kneeling   (c) Bending

Figure 7.6: Different body postures users were forced to take up by a HotWire apparatus.

both hands. As it is challenging for humans to do two different things simultaneously, coordination skills are needed to compensate for errors.

7.4   Apparatus Enhancements

Although the HotWire apparatus was successfully used in different studies (cf. chapters 8, 9, and 10), there are still enhancements possible to either ease or enhance data gathering during an experiment or to test the effect of properties of the apparatus when changing different parameters as described in section 7.3.2 to simulate certain situations.

Vision-based Tracking

The HotWire software (cf. section 7.2.2) allows for the monitoring and automatic logging of basic data relevant for post-hoc analysis of an experiment including the number of contacts made between the hand-held tool and the wire. In [DWPS06] it was shown that the pure contacts count is sometimes difficult to handle during analysis. Along with the location of a fault, i.e. where a contact happened on the wire track, analysis can be enhanced with respect to questions like: 'Did the contact occur in a difficult or easy section on the track?'.

To explore the general feasibility of determining the position where a contact occurred on the track, vision-based tracking was prototypically implemented. The prototype was built with a single web camera capturing the user performing the HotWire task. By tracking a user's hand that passes the hand-held tool over the wire track, the position of a contact can be determined. To track the hand-held tool, the ARToolkit [ART07] was

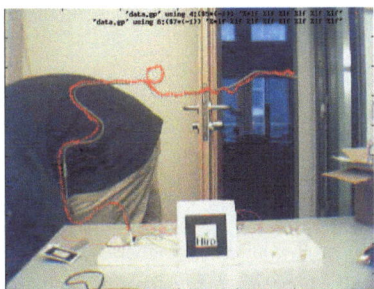

(a) Used ARToolkit marker.   (b) Overlay of tracking data plot with scene
                               photo.

Figure 7.7: Vision-based tracking of HotWire handheld tool.

used. The ARToolkit is a software package to facilitate the development of augmented reality applications. Its original use is to augment vision by adding virtual objects into the video stream so that they appear to be attached to real life markers (cf. e.g. [BCPK02]). This is done by locating a marker's position through observing its angle and size in the video stream.

The ARToolkit comes with some printable default markers that were used as markers to track the ring of the hand-held tool. The chosen markers are made of a large black frame surrounded by a white border and a special text symbol in the center (cf. figure 7.7(a)). In our prototype, the marker was approximately 8 x 8 cm in size. To get best tracking results, four of these markers were mounted around the grip of the hand-held tool to form a cube. To determine the position of the hand-held tool, another marker needed to be attached to the HotWire apparatus itself as reference. With this marker setup, the ARToolkit can calculate the 2D position from the camera's point-of-view (POV) as well as the 3D position of both markers. For visualizing calculated tracking information and contacts in the prototype application, we used an additional photo of the scene captured by the video camera and overlaid it with a plot of the recorded tracking data. Figure 7.7(b) depicts such an overlay.

Although the first proof of concept prototype showed the feasibility of the vision-based tracking approach, different improvements are needed to be fully applicable in a user study. Most important is the replacement of the used web camera by a high quality video camera. This will allow for the reduction of the marker size mounted on the hand-held tool. Also the use of spotlights for better scene illumination should improve the tracking system further. Obviously, a second video camera will increase tracking accuracy and can compensate tracking breaks but makes the entire setup much more complex and difficult to deploy.

7.5 Conclusion

This chapter introduced the HotWire primary task simulator as a new method for user interface evaluation of wearable computing applications. The HotWire simulator can be used in a controlled laboratory environment. The specific properties of wearable computing domains, where primary tasks are dominated by mainly manual work and secondary tasks by using a wearable computer are reflected in the design of the apparatus. The HotWire provides a physical primary task that is easy to learn and which can be configured for different levels of difficulty and task durations. It features a number of tunable parameters to model different manual tasks. For a realistic evaluation setup in the laboratory environment, visual, physical, and cognitive demands can be modeled.

Special logging software is available to monitor the user's performance while performing the HotWire task. Additionally, the software architecture provides interfaces to monitor secondary tasks that can be either situated on the same computer running the logging software or on a remote computer. The HotWire can be easily integrated in different user studies and experiment setups with the provided software.

It is worth to mention that although the HotWire allows realistic modeling of real world tasks, they remain an abstraction. The underlying essence of a set of real world tasks is extracted by removing any dependence on real world objects. Therefore, a certain task is not rebuilt for the laboratory experiment because this would only provide an evaluation for that particular task which makes any generalization of findings challenging.

The new evaluation method provided by the HotWire will be used in the following three chapters to examine interruption aspects in combination with different input techniques to guide the design of wearable user interfaces. The focus will be on dual-task situations with primary manual tasks often found in maintenance and assembly domains. The evaluations conducted particularly consider visual and physical demands of primary tasks as well as cognitive and workload demands mainly caused by a secondary computer task.

Chapter 8

Interruption Methods for Gesture Interaction

Since users of wearable computers are often involved in real world tasks of a critical nature, the management and handling of interruptions is one of the most crucial issues in wearable user interface design [DWPS06]. The appropriate management of interruptions is the foundation for an efficient interaction design and allows for optimizing task performance.

This chapter studies different ways to interrupt a user while performing a physical primary task. It investigates the correlations between physical and cognitive engagement, interruption type, and overall performance of users. The conducted user study was the first extensive study using the new HotWire evaluation method. It builds on related work described in [DNL+04] that also examined interruptions in wearable computing but with a virtual primary and stationary task. The HotWire study examines in particular the impact of interruptions in combination with data glove based gesture interaction.

8.1 Introduction

In a typical wearable computing application, a primary task involves real world physical actions, while the secondary task is often dedicated to interacting with the computer. As these two tasks often interfere, studying interruption aspects in wearable computing is of major interest in order to build wearable user interfaces that support users during work with minimized visual and cognitive load (cf. section 4.4).

Limitations of human attention have been widely studied over decades in psychological science. What we commonly understand as attention consists of several different but interrelated abilities [Lun01]. In wearable computing we are particularly interested in divided attention, i.e. the ability of humans to direct their attention to different simultaneously occurring tasks. It is already known that divided attention is affected by different factors such as task similarity, task difference, and practice (cf. section 3.4).

Although studying divided attention has already provided detailed findings, applying and validating them for wearable computing is still a challenging issue. Once approved, they can be used in wearable user interface design, for example, to adapt the interface to the wearer's environment and task. Furthermore, being able to measure such attention enables the specification of heuristics that can help to design the interface towards maximal performance and minimal investment in attention [Sta02a]. Here, however, a major problem is the simulation of typical real world primary tasks under laboratory conditions. Such a simulation is needed to analyze coherence between attention on a primary task and user performance in different interaction styles as isolated variables.

8.2   Hypotheses

The hypotheses to be verified with a user study are:

H1. The HotWire apparatus can be used to simulate a primary physical task in a controlled laboratory environment and retains basic properties of wearable computing such as mobility and adaptation of different postures by users.

H2. Imposing a physical primary HotWire task instead of a virtual and stationary one will impact interruption handling and causes the ranking of appropriate interruption methods to change compared to [DNL+04], where a stationary and virtual simulation was used.

H3. Novel glove-based gesture interaction with our *Scipio* data glove [WLKK06], despite being easy to use, impairs interruption handling in terms of task performance and error rate with negotiated methods where lengthier interaction is needed.

8.3   Experiment

The experiment addresses how different methods of interrupting the user of a wearable computer affect that person's task performance. The scenario involves the user performing a primary task in the real world, while interruptions originate from the wearable computer, requiring the user to handle them. By observing the user's performance in the primary task and in the interruption task, conclusions can be drawn on what methods for handling interruptions are appropriate to use. In order to measure the user's performance in both

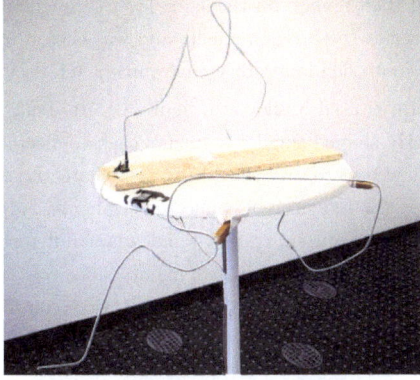

Figure 8.1: The HotWire apparatus used to simulate the primary task subjects had to perform.

task types, these must be represented in an experimental model. Following, each task and how both are combined in the experiment will be described.

8.3.1   Primary Task

The primary task needs to be one that represents the typical scenarios in which wearable computers are being used. For the purpose of this study, the task has to be easy to learn by novice users to reduce errors in the experiment caused by misunderstandings or lack of proficiency. The time to make the user proficient and fully trained should also be short enough to make a practice period just before the actual experiment sufficient, so that the

(a) Kneeling work   (b) Bending work position
position.

Figure 8.2: Different working positions observed during aircraft maintenance procedures. Copyright EADS CCR.

user's performance will then remain on the same level throughout the experiment. The HotWire apparatus satisfies those requirements and was chosen to simulate the primary task of this study in a controlled laboratory environment (cf. section 7.1).

The HotWire apparatus used is shown in figure 8.1. Its bent metallic wire was constructed out of differently shaped smaller segments each connected with windings to another segment. This allowed us to vary the difficulty or characteristics of the primary task by replacing or changing the sequence of connected segments. Additionally, the shape of the wire was designed to force users to move and adapt different characteristical body postures, for example, to be found in aircraft maintenance (cf. figure 8.2). To do this, HotWire modeling guidelines, discussed in section 7.3, were considered.

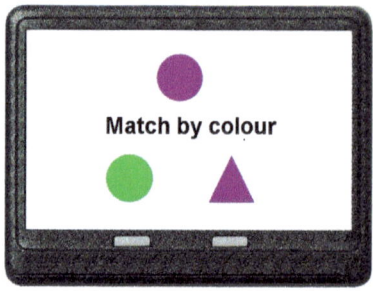

Figure 8.3: The matching task presented in the HMD to simulate the interruption task subjects had to perform in parallel to the primary task.

8.3.2   Interruption Task

The secondary task consists of matching tasks presented in the user's HMD and was adapted from [McF99]. An example of this is shown in figure 8.3. Three figures of random shape and color are shown. The user must match the figure on top with either the left or the right figure at the bottom of the display. A text instructs the user to match either by color or by shape, making the task always require some mental effort to answer correctly. There are 3 possible shapes (square, circle, and triangle) and 6 possible colors (red, yellow, cyan, green, blue, purple). These are used to generate a large number of combinations. New tasks are created at random and if the user is unable to handle them fast enough, they will be added to a queue of pending tasks.

8.3.3   Methods for Handling Interruptions

The methods tested for managing interruptions are based on the four approaches described in McFarlane's taxonomy (cf. section 4.4). During all of these methods the user performs the HotWire primary task while being subjected to interruption. The methods and assigned time frames for the experiment are as follows:

- **Immediate:** Matching tasks are created at random and presented to the user in the instant they are created.

- **Negotiated:** When a matching task is randomly created, the user is notified by either a visual or audio signal, and can then decide, when to present the task and handle it. For the visual case a short flash in the HMD is used for notification. Audio notifications are indicated with an abstract earcon.

- **Scheduled:** Matching tasks are created at random but presented to the user only at specific time intervals of 25 seconds. Typically this causes the matching tasks to queue up and cluster.

- **Mediated:** The presentation of matching tasks is withheld during times when the user appears to be in a difficult section of the HotWire. The algorithm used is simple; based on the time when a contact was last made with the wire, there is a time window of 5 seconds during which no matching task will be presented. The idea is that when a lot of errors are made, the user is likely to be in a difficult section of the HotWire, so no interruption should take place until the situation has improved.

In addition to these methods, there are also two base cases included serving as baseline. These are:

- **HotWire only:** The user performs only the HotWire primary task without any interruptions, allowing for a theoretically best case performance of this task.

- **Match only:** The user performs only the matching tasks for 90 seconds, approximately the same period of time it takes to complete a HotWire game. This allows for a theoretically best case performance.

Taken together, and having two variants (audio and visual notification) for the negotiated method, there are seven methods that will be tested in the study.

Figure 8.4: Experiment performed by a user.

8.4   User Study

A total of 21 subjects were selected from students and staff at the local university for participation—13 males and 8 females aged between 22–67 years (mean 30.8). All subjects were screened not to be color blind. The study uses a *within subjects design* with the interruption method as the single independent variable, meaning that all subjects will test every method. To avoid bias and learning effects, the subjects are divided into counterbalanced groups where the order of methods differs. As there are seven methods to test, a Latin Square of the same order was used to distribute the 21 participants evenly into 7 groups with 3 subjects each.

A single test session consisted of one practice round where the subject got to practice the HotWire and matching tasks, followed by one experimental round during which data was collected for analysis. The time to complete a HotWire task naturally varies depending on how fast the subject is, but on average, pilot studies indicated that it would take around 90–120 seconds for one single run over the wire. With 7 methods of interruption to test, one practice and one experimental round, plus time for questions and instructions, the total time required for a session is around 40–45 minutes.

8.4.1   Apparatus

The apparatus used in the study is depicted in figure 8.4, where the HotWire is shown together with a user holding the hand-held tool and wearing an HMD and a data glove. The HotWire is mounted around a table with a wire track of approximately 4 meters in length. To avoid vibrations because of its length, the wire was stabilized with electrically

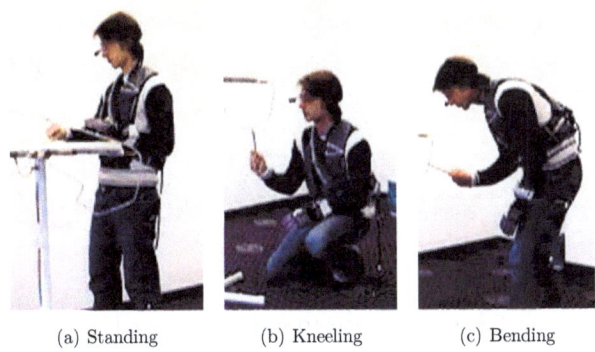

(a) Standing   (b) Kneeling   (c) Bending

Figure 8.5: Different body positions observed.

insulated screws in the table. An opening in the ring allowed the subject to move the ring past the screws while still staying on track. To follow the wire with the hand-held tool, the user needs to move around the table over the course of the experiment. The user may also need to kneel down or reach upwards to follow the wire, furthermore emphasizing the mobile manner in which wearable computers are used as well as body postures maintenance workers are often forced to adopt during work [MW07]. Figure 8.5 illustrates the variety of body positions observed during the study.

In the current setup, the user is not wearing a wearable computer per se, as the HMD and the hand-held tool are connected to a stationary computer running the experiment to prevent technical problems during the experiment. However, as the wires and cables for the HMD and hand-held tool are still coupled to the user to avoid tangling, this should not influence the outcome compared to a situation with a truly wearable computer, in particular, because the users had to wear a special textile vest during the experiment (cf. figure 8.6). The vest was designed to unobtrusively carry a wearable computer as well as all needed cables for an HMD without affecting the wearers' freedom in movement. To have an even more realistic situation an OQO micro computer was put in the vest to simulate the weight wearable computer equipment would have outside the laboratory environment.

8.4.2   Gesture Interaction

The matching tasks were presented in a non-transparent SV-6 monocular HMD from MicroOptical. The so-called *Scipio* data glove, presented by Witt et al. [WLKK06], is worn on the user's left hand serving as the interface to control the matching tasks. To

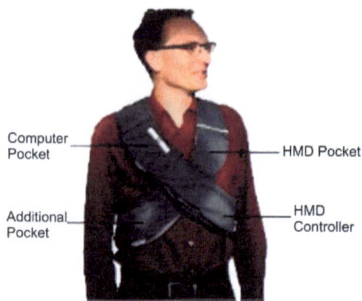

Figure 8.6: Textile vest to unobtrusively carry wearable equipment.

ensure maximum freedom of movement for the user, the data glove uses a Bluetooth interface for communication with the computer. The glove is shown in figure 8.7. By tapping index finger and thumb together, an event is triggered through a magnetic switch sensor based on the position of the user's hand at the time. Using a tilt sensor with earth gravity as reference, the glove can sense the hand being held with the thumb pointing left, right or upwards. When the hand is held in a neutral position with the thumb up, the first of any pending matching tasks in the queue is presented to the user in the HMD. When the hand is rotated to the left or to the right, the corresponding object is chosen in the matching task. For the negotiated methods, the user taps once to bring the new matching tasks up and subsequently rotates the hand to the left or right and taps to answer them. For the immediate and mediated methods, where matching tasks appear without notification, the user only needs to rotate left or right and tap.

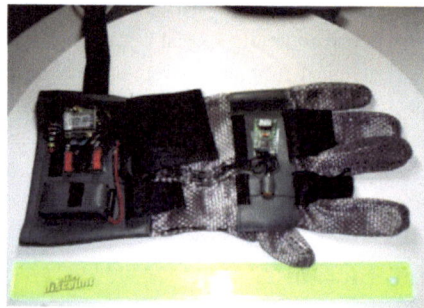

Figure 8.7: Scipio data glove used for gesture interaction throughout the experiment to answer matching tasks.

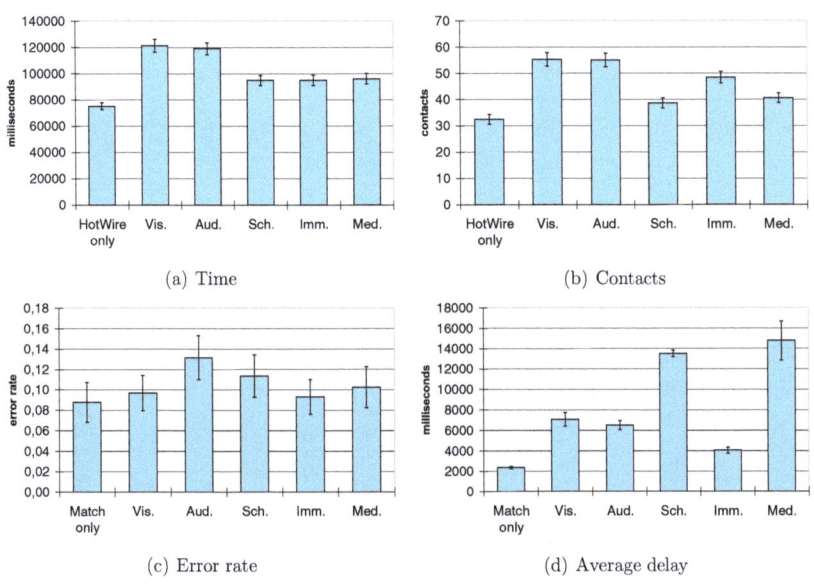

(a) Time

(b) Contacts

(c) Error rate

(d) Average delay

Figure 8.8: Averages of user performance.

Because of the novelty of the interface, feedback is required to let the user know, when an action has been performed. In general, any feedback will risk interference with the experiment and notifications used. In the current setup an abstract earcon (beep signal), generated by the on board speaker of the Scipio glove hardware, was used as feedback for the activation of a magnetic switch on the fingertips. To give selection feedback for the matching tasks an auditory icon sounding like a gun shot was used. The gun shot represents the metaphor of a shooting gallery. Both feedbacks were deemed to be least invasive for the task (cf. section 4.2.2 for properties of auditory icons and earcons).

8.5   Results

After all data had been collected in the user study, the data was analyzed to study which effect different methods had on user performance. For this analysis the following metrics were used:

- **Time:** The time required for the subject to complete the HotWire track from start to end.

- **Contacts:** The number of contacts the subject made between the ring and the wire.

- **Error rate:** The percentage of matching tasks the subject answered incorrectly.

- **Average delay:** The average time from when a matching task was created until the subject answered it, i.e. its average delay.

The graphs in figure 8.8 summarize the overall user performance by showing the averages of the metrics together with one standard error.

A repeated measures ANOVA was performed to see whether there existed any significant differences among the methods used. The results are shown in table 8.1. For all metrics except the error rate, strong significance ($p<0.001$) was found indicating that differences do exist.

Metric	P-value
Time	<0.001
Contacts	<0.001
Error rate	0.973
Average delay	<0.001

Table 8.1: Repeated measures ANOVA.

To investigate these differences in more detail, paired samples t-tests were performed comparing the two base cases (HotWire only and Match only) to each of the five interruption methods. The results are shown in table 8.2. To accommodate for multiple comparisons, a Bonferroni corrected alpha value of 0.003 (0.05/15) was used when testing for significance.

Metric	Vis.	Aud.	Sch.	Imm.	Med.
Time	<0.0001	<0.0001	<0.0001	0.0002	0.0003
Contacts	<0.0001	<0.0001	0.0022	<0.0001	0.0004
Error rate	0.7035	0.1108	0.0668	0.8973	0.4979
Average delay	0.0012	0.0001	<0.0001	0.0194	0.0046

Table 8.2: Base case comparison t-tests.

All of these differences are expected. The completion time will be longer when there are matching tasks to do at the same time and the error rate is likely to increase because of that reason, too. Also, the average delay is expected to be longer than for the base case since the user is involved with the HotWire, when matching tasks appear and both the scheduled and mediated methods will by definition cause matching tasks to queue up with increased delay as a result. It was unexpected that no significant differences in the matching tasks' error rate were found. Intuitively, we assumed that there should be more mistakes made when the subject is involved in a primary task. However, when looking at the data collected, most subjects answered the tasks as well in the interruption methods as they did in the base case of match only. Since there was nothing in the primary task that "forced" the subjects to make mistakes as, for example, imposing a short time limit on the tasks would certainly have done, the subjects mainly gave accurate rather than quick and erroneous answers. All in all, this comparison of methods with base cases shows that in general, adding interruptions and a dual-task scenario with a physical and mobile primary task will be more difficult for the subject to carry out successfully.

Time	Vis.	Aud.	Sch.	Imm.	Med.
Vis.	-	0.6859	**<0.0001**	**0.0001**	**<0.0001**
Aud.	0.6859	-	**0.0003**	**<0.0001**	**<0.0001**
Sch.	**<0.0001**	**0.0003**	-	0.9773	0.8157
Imm.	**0.0001**	**<0.0001**	0.9773	-	0.7988
Med.	**<0.0001**	**<0.0001**	0.8157	0.7988	-

Contacts	Vis.	Aud.	Sch.	Imm.	Med.
Vis.	-	0.9434	**0.0002**	0.1508	**0.0006**
Aud.	0.9434	-	**<0.0001**	**0.0240**	**0.0002**
Sch.	**0.0002**	**<0.0001**	-	**0.0038**	0.4217
Imm.	0.1508	**0.0240**	**0.0038**	-	**0.0031**
Med.	**0.0006**	**0.0002**	0.4217	**0.0031**	-

Error rate	Vis.	Aud.	Sch.	Imm.	Med.
Vis.	-	0.2744	0.4335	0.9041	0.8153
Aud.	0.2744	-	0.5258	0.3356	0.1039
Sch.	0.4335	0.5258	-	0.5852	0.6118
Imm.	0.9041	0.3356	0.5852	-	0.7668
Med.	0.8153	0.1039	0.6118	0.7668	-

Average delay	Vis.	Aud.	Sch.	Imm.	Med.
Vis.	-	0.5758	**0.0001**	**0.0470**	0.2180
Aud.	0.5758	-	**<0.0001**	**0.0170**	0.1411
Sch.	**0.0001**	**<0.0001**	-	**<0.0001**	0.3256
Imm.	**0.0470**	**0.0170**	**<0.0001**	-	**0.0061**
Med.	0.2180	0.1411	0.3256	**0.0061**	-

Table 8.3: Pairwise t-tests of methods.

Following, we compared the five interruption methods with each other using a paired samples t-test. The results are shown in table 8.3. It can be seen that a number of significant differences were found between the interruption methods. We will now analyze each of the metrics in turn to learn more about the characteristics of each method.

8.5.1 Time

With regards to the completion time, the interruption methods can be divided into two groups, one for the two negotiated methods (visual and audio), and one for the remaining three methods (scheduled, immediate and mediated). There are strong significant differences between the two groups, but not between the methods in the same group. The reason for the higher completion time of the negotiated methods is the extra effort required by the user to present matching tasks. Because the additional interaction required to bring the tasks up is likely to slow the user down, this result was expected (H3). An important finding was, however, that the overhead (24.8 seconds higher, an increase of 26%) was much higher than expected. Considering the relative ease—in theory—of holding the thumb upwards and tapping thumb and finger together to present the matching tasks, we expected a lower overhead. In practice the subjects found this method difficult when doing it simultaneously to the HotWire primary task. The data glove itself accurately recognizes the desired gestures when done right, but the problem is that the subjects experienced problems, because they lost their sense of direction when doing the physical task. This was something we noticed when watching videos of the subjects in retrospect. This finding would support that H3 may be right in that glove-based gesture interaction, even being very simple, impairs negotiated handling methods. Chapter 10 will investigate glove-based gesture interaction with respect to this finding in more detail.

Relating current results to findings in [DNL+04], where the primary task was less physical as the user sat in front of a computer and interacted using a keyboard, we see that even seemingly simple ways to interact can have a much higher impact, when used in wearable computing scenarios. This supports H2, stating that a physical primary task like the HotWire will impact interruption handling in a different (more realistic) way than a virtual task. Therefore, it can be argued that using a more physical primary task may increase the validity of user studies in wearable computing.

8.5.2 Contacts

Looking at the number of contacts between the ring and the wire, i.e. the number of physical errors the subjects made in this primary task, we can discern three groups for the methods. The two negotiated methods form one group, where the additional interaction required to present matching tasks also cause more contacts with the wire. The scheduled and mediated methods form a second group with the lowest number of HotWire contacts.

The immediate method lies in between and significant differences for this method were only found for the scheduled and mediated methods. It is of interest to know the causes of these differences: interference with the subject's motor sense because of the dual tasks, or some other underlying factor.

As can be seen, there is a correlation between the completion time and the error rate, which can be interpreted as indicating that the number of contacts made depends mainly on the time spent in the HotWire track and is not affected by the different interruption methods per se. To analyze this further, the rate r of contacts over time was examined.

$$r = \frac{contacts}{time}$$

When comparing the rates of all interruption methods, no significant differences were found. This can be expected because of the correlation of time and contacts made. However, since there are both easy and more difficult sections of the HotWire, such a naive way of computing the overall contact rate risks nullifying these changes in track difficulty. To examine the error rate in detail and take the HotWire track itself in account, assuming the user moved the ring with a constant average speed, we divided the track in 20 segments (cf. figure 8.9(a)) and compared the rate r_i per segment i between the methods[1]. However, no significant differences could be found here either. This suggests that our experiment was unable to uncover the impact of the interruption method as a whole, if such an effect exists, on the amount of contacts made in the HotWire.

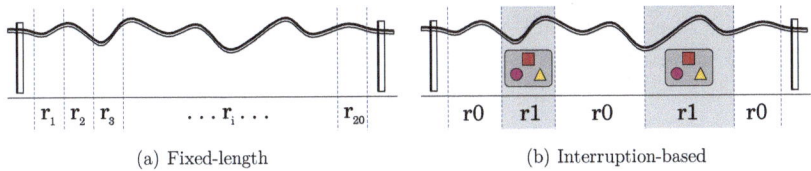

(a) Fixed-length   (b) Interruption-based

Figure 8.9: Segmenting the track for analysis.

Assuming that solely the appearance of matching tasks in the HMD cause more contacts to be made, we decided to test this hypothesis. The contact rates were divided in two categories, $r0$ indicated the rate of contacts over time when no matching task was present in the HMD, while $r1$ indicated the rate of contacts over time with a matching task visible (cf. figure 8.9(b)). The rates $r0$ and $r1$ then underwent a paired samples t-test for each of the interruption methods, to see whether the means of these two kinds of rates differed. According to the hypothesis, having a matching task present in the

---

[1]To get a more accurate segmentation, the ring's position on the track would need to be monitored over time, something our current apparatus does not yet support.

HMD should increase the contact rate $r1$ compared to the rate $r0$, when no matching task is present. Surprisingly, no significant difference was found. This can be taken as indication that either no difference exists, or more likely, that the number of contacts made by our HotWire apparatus is too random so that the underlying effects of having a matching task present got lost in this noise. As the initial version of the HotWire apparatus [WD06] could reveal these differences with stronger significance in pilot studies, it suggests the version used in this larger study simply became too difficult. Since the user now needed to walk around the track and change into different body positions, this would cause more random contacts being made than with a version where the user stands still, thereby causing so big variance in the data collected that small differences caused by the matching task or interruption method cannot be found.

To determine whether the methods influence the subject overall and make her more prone to make errors, we firstly compared the rate $r1$ between different methods, and then $r0$ in the same manner. For $r1$, when there was a matching task shown, the mediated interruption method had the lowest contact rate (0.38) while immediate had the highest rate (0.69), yet with p=0.04 this is not significant enough to state with certainty, when Bonferroni correction is applied. For $r0$, however, the mediated interruption method still had the lowest contact rate (0.33), while the two negotiated methods had the highest (both 0.48), and this difference was observed with significance p<0.003 confirming the hypothesis that the mediated method will help reduce this number. This finding shows that the algorithm we used for the mediated method can make the user perform the primary task slightly better in between interruptions, compared to letting her negotiate and decide for herself when to present the matching tasks.

8.5.3   Error Rate

The error rate for the matching tasks exhibited no significant differences regardless of method. One reason for this may be that a majority of the subjects answered all matching tasks correctly (the median was zero for all methods except negotiated). While four subjects had very high consistent error rates (20~70%) through all methods, including the base case, that contributed to a high variance. In other words, the matching task may be a bit too easy for most people, while some can find it very difficult to perform.

What is of interest is that when comparing these numbers with the error rate in an earlier study [DNL$^+$04], the rate is approximately twice as large when using the HotWire and data glove rather than the game and keyboard setup. Again this indicates H2 may be true. This would also indicate that users are more prone to make errors in the interruption task, once the primary task is made more wearable and mobile.

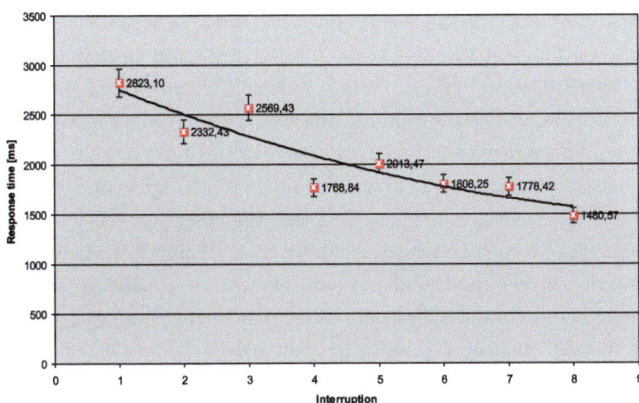

Figure 8.10: Average time needed by subjects to answer matching tasks in the order they occurred after the first 25 seconds of the scheduled interruption treatment.

Another difference found compared to [DNL$^+$04] is that the error rates for negotiated audio and visual have been exchanged so that audio, rather than visual, now exhibits worse performance. Although this cannot be said with statistical certainty in either case, it may indicate that differences do exist between subjects and their preference, and most likely also by the kind of primary task being done.

8.5.4 Average Delay

Naturally, the average delay is expected to be the highest for the scheduled method, since the matching tasks are by definition queued for expected 12.5 seconds on average. This was also found with strong statistical significance (p<0.0001) for all methods but mediated. With an overall average delay of 13.5 seconds on average for all answered matching tasks, and an by definition expected delay of 12.5 seconds, this means the user—in theory—only spent an average of approximately 1 second to respond to the queued matching tasks in the scheduled treatment. Comparing this to the immediate (4.1 sec) and negotiated (6.5 and 7.1 sec) methods, this is significantly (p≤0.0002) faster, probably because the need to mentally switch between primary and matching task is reduced because of the clustering.

When testing the scheduled interruption method, we observed that users were apparently able to increase their secondary task performance from the first queued matching task till the last. In order to examine this further, we computed the time needed to answer each matching task from the queue of pending tasks, i.e. the time from the visibility of a matching task until it was answered. To minimize errors in that metric, caused by fatigue, motivation loss, or general primary task performance of subjects, we only analyzed matching tasks answered within the first batch, presented after the first 25 seconds. Users answered an average of 7.10 queued matching tasks in the first batch. To answer them, they needed for each task an average of 1.47 seconds. By taking the order in which matching tasks occurred into account, we found that users were indeed able to reduce their response time to each matching task over time. Figure 8.10 shows this coherency by presenting the average time needed by subjects to answer matching tasks in the order they occurred. The trend line (black) indicates, that the response time decreases for the sequence of the eight matching tasks to be answered in the first batch. An explanation for this may be on the one hand the reduced need to mentally switch between primary and secondary task, as an effect of the task clustering. On the other hand, optimized usage of the data glove interaction is another explanation. In line with our observations, users were able to optimize their response time by maintaining the same rotational angle of their hands over a longer period of time. For instance, when subjects selected the left answer of a matching task, they frequently kept this hand position until the next queued matching task was presented. If the correct answer of the next task was again the left answer, subjects only needed to press the forefinger button without any additional hand rotation. With this strategy, users were able to speed up the answering process in case a sequence of tasks required the same answer in regard to their assigned position (left or right). Because the assignment of correct answers to either the left or right alternative was done at random, this alone does not entirely explain the reduction in response time. However, in a combination with the reduced need to mentally switch between primary and secondary task it may do.

The mediated interruption method exhibited such high variance in its data, about an order of magnitude larger than for the other methods, that no real significant differences could be shown. The reason for this high variance is that the mediated algorithm was based on a fixed time window, and for some users who made errors very frequently, this time window was simply too large so that the queued matching tasks showed up very seldom.

8.6 Evaluation of the HotWire Apparatus

Since the HotWire has been proposed as an apparatus for evaluating wearable user interfaces, it is important to determine how suitable it is compared to other laboratory setups. In [DNL+04] a computer game and keyboard was used in a non-mobile setting where the user sat still during the course of the study, and we will use this as reference setup for the comparison.

The interruption task was the same in both studies, with minor differences in task frequency and the head-mounted display used presentation. Moreover, the physical means to interact with the task were different. The metrics that are comparable across the studies—the error rate and the average delay—had a better significance in the former study. This could indicate that our current setup is less likely to uncover differences, if any exist, compared to the former non-mobile setup. Reasons may be that our study used a shorter time span for each method and that a novel interaction method was used, thereby increasing the variance of the data collected and diminishing the significance by which differences can be observed.

The primary task cannot easily be compared across studies. In the former study the number of errors was bounded and time was kept constant, whereas in our new study both errors and completion time are variable and unbounded. The former study thus had the errors as the only metric, whereas the HotWire offers both errors and time as metrics of performance. What can be seen is that in the former study no real significant differences could be found for the error metric between methods. With the HotWire, strong significant differences were observed in a majority of the tests for both the error and time metrics. This shows that differences do indeed exist between the interruption methods, and that these can more easily be uncovered by the HotWire apparatus, supporting our hypothesizes H1 and H2. Therefore, as the HotWire apparatus is more mobile, physical, and more realistically represents a wearable computing scenario, it can be argued that using this in favor of the stationary setup might be better for evaluating and studying wearable user interfaces. Particularly, because our mobile setup could uncover new problems with respect to subjects loosing orientation, when being forced to carry out secondary tasks while moving, bending, and walking that cannot be found with a stationary setup. Recently, an experiment carried out by Vadas et al. [VPL+06] also showed that a mobile primary task is more suited to identify problems in regard to the accomplishment of reading comprehensions on a mobile computer while walking. Vadas et al. found that experiment results significantly change when changing the primary task from a stationary to a mobile task.

Considering the fact that very few significant differences could be observed when looking in detail at the errors over time, as discussed in section 8.5.2, this basically indicates that there are more factors that need to be taken in account for research in wearable interaction. Ease of interaction, mobility, walking, changing body position, using both hands to handle the dual tasks—all of these factors cause errors being made in the primary task, while the effects of interruption and the modality used have less impact. Thus, it can be argued that the HotWire aids in focusing on the problems most relevant in wearable computing interaction, as details that are of less importance in the first stages are clearly not revealed until the important problems are dealt with (H1). In our study, we used a data glove that is conceptually simple to operate—the user can select left, right, or up—yet even this was shown to be too difficult when operated in a more realistic and mobile wearable computing scenario.

8.7 Conclusion

The recommendation for implementing efficient interruption handling in wearable computing scenarios with hand gestures is to examine the needs of the primary and secondary task and to choose the method which best adheres to these constraints, as there are specific advantages and drawbacks with each method. The HotWire study both confirms and complements the findings in [DNL+04] and [NDL+05] applied in a wearable computing scenario. It supports our hypothesis that imposing a physical primary task, like the HotWire, instead of a virtual one, will more realistically impact interruption handling and will therefore improve interaction research in wearable computing.

Overall, the scheduled, immediate, and mediated handling methods result in fewer errors than the negotiated methods and therefore are a better choice for safety critical primary tasks, where errors cannot be compensated. Scheduled and mediated methods cause a slower response to the matching tasks, whereas the immediate method allows for quicker response at the cost of more errors in the primary task. Hence, if a secondary computer task is to assist a primary task with additional information, our studies' recommendations are the scheduled and mediated methods, as these can suppress interruptions over a longer period of time and do not force users to pay attention to an interrupting task in the instance they are occurring.

The algorithm used in the mediated method was, despite its simplicity, able to reduce the error rate in the primary task in between the matching tasks compared to the negotiated method. Therefore, it is better in certain situations for interaction designers to utilize context-awareness by taking the primary task in account, rather than explicitly allowing the user to decide when matching tasks should be presented. If technically possible, a mediated method can be very flexible but is not as transparent for the user in its behavior as a scheduled method that also suppresses interruptions for a certain time. The studie's recommendation is therefore to use scheduled methods for primary tasks of a critical nature where the wearable system has no access to reliable context information. A mediated handling method should be considered where context-awareness can be achieved with high accuracy and an easy to implement algorithm.

The new metric of completion time indicated that a significant overhead is imposed on the primary task when subjects get to negotiate and decide, when to present the matching tasks, which results in a larger number of errors being made (H3). The cause of this were unforeseen difficulties in the interaction, even though a conceptually simple data glove was used to control the matching task. Study results therefore suggest that efforts should primarily be focused on improving the interaction style and ease of use of gesture interaction, while the actual methods used for interruption are of secondary importance. In general, the recommendation is that negotiated interruption methods should not be used in gesture interaction design, once primary tasks need to be accomplished in a short time and with high quality. The negotiation process will always impose a higher error probability, when using gesture input due to the second gesture needed and may overburden users, while in the midst of an attention demanding manual primary task.

The architectural implications of the different methods are relevant to consider in any case. Assuming the wearable computer is part of a more complex system where interruptions originate from elsewhere, the immediate and negotiated methods both require continuous network access so that the task to handle can be forwarded to the user immediately. On the other hand, the clustering of tasks that result from the scheduled and mediated methods may only require sporadic access, for example, at wireless hot-spots or certain areas in the working place with adequate network coverage. Therefore, scheduled and mediated interruption methods are preferred when no permanent network connection is available or energy constraints of the wearable computer prevent this.

The HotWire apparatus itself demonstrated that many findings from non-mobile interruption studies could be confirmed, while also pointing out that there are inherent differences in wearable computing due to mobility and the performing of physical primary tasks (H2). These differences cause some findings obtained with the HotWire evaluation method to stand out stronger than others. Additionally, as the apparatus more accurately resembles a realistic wearable computing scenario, study results recommend to use the HotWire to simulate the attention demanded by a primary manual tasks instead of using virtual and stationary tasks. The HotWire will help to guide research in wearable interaction design for dual-task environments, where the primary task is characterized by manual work than stationary or virtual tasks.

Without doubt, the interaction device used to handle interruptions impacts performance and errors being made. The data glove used in this study is a novel device that users were not familiar with, when taking part in the study. Therefore, the next chapter will report on results gathered from a second user study that repeated the interruption experiment by using "hands-free" speech interaction instead of gestures, to determine more thoroughly the impact of the interaction device on the best choice of an interruption method in dual-task situations. Chapter 10 will then come back to some important findings of this study to explore the properties of gesture interaction with data gloves in more detail. It will take up gathered observations throughout the study and will investigate the impact of different body postures on loosing orientation, as well as explore the question of whether visual feedback is able to prevent users from loosing their orientation and makes gesture input easier to use for novices.

Chapter 9

Interruption Methods for Speech Interaction

The last chapter examined the design of an interruption handling for wearable user interfaces operated with gestures using a data glove device. This chapter presents a second user study conducted to investigate the properties of speech interaction to coordinate interruptions. Compared to glove-based gesture interaction, speech interaction offers real hands-free operation without even sporadically occupying a user's hand during interaction. To relate findings and to make them comparable to previous findings for gesture interaction, the conducted experiment was closely related in its experiment setup to the previously presented experiment in chapter 8.

9.1 Introduction

Unlike interaction methods such as gestures, speech is probably the most natural way to interact with a computer. Nowadays, available speech recognition software has overcome many technical problems it once suffered from, and is ready to be used at least for simpler interaction in different applications [Wit07b]. A major advantage of speech interaction, compared to other interaction techniques, is its "hands-free" nature, i.e. users do not need their hands to control the interaction device. This feature is particularly important for wearable computing where a casual and easy use of the computer and its user interface is needed. While being involved in a primary physical task that typically requires substantial attention of the user, speech interaction is therefore a promising interaction technique for wearable user interfaces. Although being promising, speech input has to be used with care in interaction design, since it has to overcome several challenges such as background noise or social acceptance [Sta02c, SS00]. However, as humans naturally speak, learning efforts are deemed to be lower compared to other interaction techniques like gestures.

Little work on wearable audio interfaces and interruptibility has been carried out so far (cf. section 4.2.2). An early version was NomadicRadio [SS00], a wearable platform with an auditory interface for managing voice and text-based messages. The SWAN system [WL06] aided users in navigation and awareness of features in the environment through an audio interface. Because a systematic evaluation of the fundamental interruption methods introduced by McFarlane (cf. section 4.4) is essential for the proper integration of speech interaction techniques in wearable user interfaces, the remainder of this chapter will investigate this issue for wearable computing in dual-task environments.

9.2 Hypotheses

The hypotheses to be verified with a user study are:

H1. Speech interaction allows maintaining focus on a primary HotWire task easier than our glove-based gesture interaction does and results in better performance on the primary task.

H2. Audio notifications are better for speech interaction to indicate interruptions than visual notifications, when a primary manual task like the HotWire needs to be carried out at the same time.

H3. A negotiated method with audio notifications to handle interruptions is preferred by users, when being simultaneously involved in the HotWire task and lets users feel least interrupted.

9.3 Experiment

Similar to the experiment presented in chapter 8, the current experiment also addresses the question of how different interruption methods affect a person's performance when using a wearable computer. Again, the scenario involves the user performing a primary manual task in the real world, while interruptions originate from a wearable computer and have to be handled. Instead of using gestures, users are requested to handle interruptions by using speaker independent speech input. The objective of the study is to observe the user's performance in the primary and secondary task to draw conclusions on the most appropriate interruption methods to be used for handling interruptions with a speech input

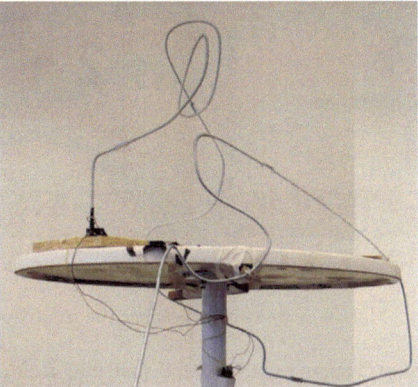

Figure 9.1: The HotWire apparatus used in the speech interaction experiment.

enabled wearable user interface. Additionally, results for speech input can be compared to those obtained for gesture interaction in chapter 8.

9.3.1 Primary Task

To let study outcomes relate more easily with previous work [NDL+05, DNL+04] and especially chapter 8, we decided to rebuild the HotWire primary task setup that was already used in chapter 8 to simulate the primary manual task in a controlled laboratory environment.

The rebuild of the HotWire apparatus for this experiment is shown in figure 9.1. It consists of a metallic wire that was bent in the same shape and mounted in the same way to a base plate like it was done in chapter 8. The resulting wire length of 4 meters is also identical. In contrast to the original hand-held tool of the previous experiment, which was found to have a too small ring diameter (cf. section 8.5.2), the hand-held tool for this experiment had a slightly larger diameter of 2.6 cm (an increase of 4 mm). Because the apparatus was mounted on a similar table of an identical height (1.20 meters), the difficulty and characteristicals of the primary task are almost identical.

9.3.2 Secondary Task

Unlike the primary task, the secondary computer task was slightly modified compared to the one of chapter 8, to include latest findings obtained throughout preceding experiments and pilot studies.

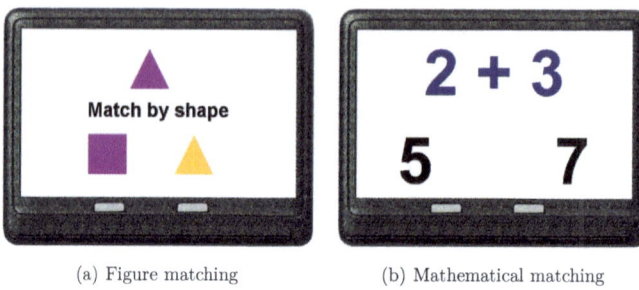

(a) Figure matching   (b) Mathematical matching

Figure 9.2: Matching tasks representing the interruption task.

The study presented in chapter 8 used a simple matching task. An example of which is shown in figure 9.2(a). The matching task was presented for the user in a head-mounted display. There, three figures of random shape and color were shown, and the user had to match the figure on top with either the left or the right figure at the bottom of the display. A text instructs the user to match either by color or by shape, and as there are 3 possible shapes and 6 colors, the task always require some mental effort to answer correctly.

To increase the cognitive workload of the user to more levels than just shape and color matching, a second matching task was added in form of a mathematical exercise (cf. figure 9.2(b)). The mathematical task presents an expression of type

$$X < operator > Y, < operator >:= +|-|*|/$$

Below an expression one correct answer is given and one erroneous answer assigned randomly to left and right. In the current experiment, the expressions and answers were limited to integers only ranging from 1 to 9, for the sake of simplicity and ensuring mainly correct responses while still requiring enough mental effort of the subjects tested.

All matching tasks are again created at random. Unlike the previously used matching tasks in chapter 8, matching tasks of this experiment may time out. That is, if the user is unable to handle a visible matching task within a 5 sec. time frame, the task automatically disappears (times out) and is treated as a wrong answer, as suggested in [DWPS06]. If tasks are created so frequently, that the user cannot answer them soon enough, they will be added to a queue of pending tasks.

9.3.3   Methods for Handling Interruptions

The methods tested to manage the interruptions in the experiment are basically the same as those tested in chapter 8, except for the mediated treatment that now implements a reduced time window. In parallel to all methods, the user again performs the HotWire task, while being subjected to interruption. For the sake of completeness, all methods used were defined as follows:

- **Immediate:** Matching tasks are created at random and presented to the user in the instant they are created.

- **Negotiated:** When a matching task is randomly created, the user is notified by either a visual or audio signal and can then decide, when to present the task and handle it. For the visual case the same short flash already used in chapter 8, was presented in the head-mounted display as notification. Audio notifications are indicated by the same abstract earcon already used in previous study.

- **Scheduled:** Matching tasks are created at random but presented to the user only at specific time intervals of 25 seconds. Typically this causes the matching tasks to queue up and cluster.

- **Mediated:** The presentation of matching tasks is withheld during times when the user appears to be in a difficult section of the HotWire. The algorithm used was as follows. Based on the time when a contact was last made with the wire there is a time window of 3 seconds during which no matching task will be presented. The idea is that when a lot of errors are made, the user is likely to be in a difficult section so that no interruption should take place until the situation has improved.

In addition to these methods, there are again the two base cases (HotWire only and Match only) that serve as baseline.

9.4 User Study

A total of 21 subjects were selected from students and staff at the local university for participation—13 males and 8 females aged between 21–55 years (mean 29.05). The study uses a *within subjects design* with the interruption method as the single independent variable, meaning that all subjects will test every method. All subjects were screened not to be color blind. To avoid bias and learning effects, the subjects are divided into counterbalanced groups where the order of methods differs.

A single test session consisted of one practice round where the subject gets to practice the primary and secondary task. This is followed by one experimental round during which data is collected for analysis. The time to complete the primary task naturally varies depending on how fast the subject is, but pilot studies indicated that on average it

Figure 9.3: Experiment performed by a user.

would take around 60–100 seconds for one single run over the wire. With 7 interruption methods to test, one practice and one experimental round, plus time for questions and instructions, the total time required for a session is around 40 minutes.

Technical Setup

The technical setup of the study is depicted in figure 9.3, where the HotWire is shown together with a user holding the hand-held tool and wearing an HMD as well as an audio headset (including earphones and microphone) for speech input.

In the current setup the user is not wearing a wearable computer as the used monocular HMD from MicroOptical, the audio headset, and the hand-held tool are connected to a stationary computer running the experiment. The wires and cables for the devices are still coupled to the user to avoid tangling though, but should not influence the outcome compared to a situation where a truly wearable computer is used.

To model a realistic situation we again used the special textile vest the users had to wear during the experiment, which was successfully used in the previous user study. It was designed to comfortably carry a wearable computer, as well as all needed cables for an HMD and the audio headset without affecting the wearers mobility. Moreover, we put an OQO computer in the vest to simulate the weight a wearable computer would have outside the laboratory environment.

The audio headset served as the interface to control the matching tasks through spoken commands. All tasks can be answered in an identical way. By simply saying "left" or "right", the left or right answer of a presented matching task is selected. To provide the user with feedback on her selection made, an auditory icon (gun shot), that was deemed

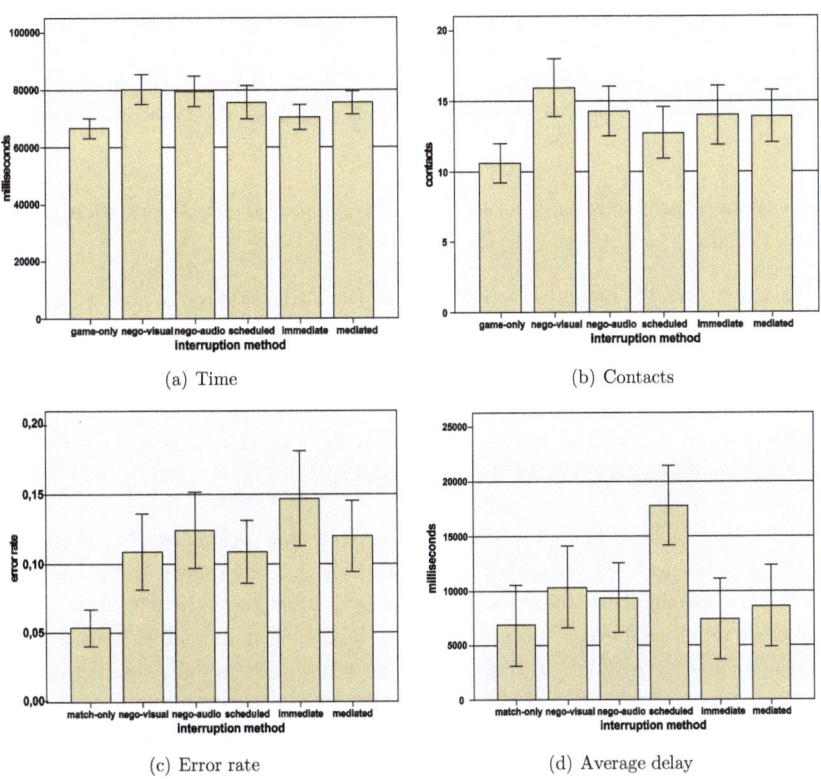

(a) Time   (b) Contacts

(c) Error rate   (d) Average delay

Figure 9.4: Averages of user performance.

not to interfere with audio notifications of the negotiated method (earcon), was used. Because in the case of the negotiated interruption methods new matching tasks are only announced but not automatically presented to the user, a third spoken command was needed to bring a pending matching task in front. To do this, users had to say the command "show me". Hence, for the negotiated methods, the user has to say "show me" and only then select either left or right to answer the matching task with the corresponding "left" or "right" command. To compensate recognition errors due to a users accent or different pronunciations that often occur when having not only native speakers [WK07], speech recognizer parameters like detection thresholds and used grammars were optimized.

9.5 Results

After all data had been collected in the user study it was analyzed to examine the effect different methods had on user performance. For this analysis, the following metrics were considered:

- **Time:** The time required for the subject to complete the HotWire track from start to end.

- **Contacts:** The number of contacts the subject made between the ring and the wire.

- **Error rate:** The percentage of matching tasks the subject answered wrongly or that timed out.

- **Average delay:** The average time from when a matching task was created until the subject answered it, i.e. its average delay.

The four graphs in figure 9.4 visualize the overall user performance in each method by showing the achieved averages of metrics together with one standard error. An informal visual examination of the graphs already suggests that there are differences between the interruption methods. To get statistical certainty, our data analysis started with a repeated measures ANOVA to see whether there were significant differences between the methods tested. Table 9.1 shows the results. For all metrics, except error rate, significance was found, indicating that differences do exist. Average delay showed even strong significance ($p<0.001$).

Metric	df	F	P-value*
Time	125	5.840	**0.001**
Contacts	125	4.330	**0.003**
Error rate	125	2.171	0.083
Average delay	125	147.827	**<0.001**

* with Greenhouse-Geisser *df* adjustment applied.

Table 9.1: Repeated measures ANOVA.

To explore these differences in more detail, paired samples t-tests ($\alpha=0.05$) were performed comparing the two base cases (HotWire only and Match only) with each of the five interruption methods. To accommodate for multiple comparisons, a Bonferroni corrected alpha value was used for testing. Table 9.2 shows the results.

Already the base case comparison showed interesting results. Although we intuitively assumed that task complexity increases when being involved in a dual-task situation, which should actually cause errors and the completion time to increase, our data did not generally support this. Neither the scheduled nor the immediate treatment showed significant difference in completion time. All others did as expected. This indicates that either our data could not uncover all differences or that some methods are more appropriate than others when using speech input. Further examination is needed.

Metric	Nego-Vis.	Nego-Aud.	Sch.	Imm.	Med.
Time	**0.025**	**0.011**	0.539	1.000	**0.004**
Contacts	**0.023**	0.835	0.472	0.997	1.000
Error rate	0.822	0.463	0.522	0.102	0.199
Average delay	**<0.001**	**0.002**	**<0.001**	**<0.001**	**0.001**

Table 9.2: Base case comparison t-tests.

With regard to contacts being made on the HotWire, surprisingly a significant difference was found only for the negotiated visual method. One reason could be that the small increase in the ring diameter already resulted in a significant decrease of the HotWire's difficulty. On the other hand, the "hands-free" property of speech interaction that allowed subjects to hold the hand-held tool more accurately, for example, with both hands or to use the second hand to stabilize their body is another reasonable explanation, which is supported by our observations (cf. figures 9.10(b) and 9.10(c)).

Although results on error rate are similar to those reported in chapter 8 (all being non-significant), it was unexpected for this study. Since there was a time out integrated in each matching task that "forced" subjects to make more mistakes due to time pressure, subjects were expected to give, at least in some treatments, more rather fast and thus erroneous answers. This was at least what our pilot studies indicated.

In line with our expectations were the strongly significant ($p < 0.001$) differences found for the average delay metric. Since the user is involved in the HotWire task when matching tasks appear, and both the scheduled and mediated methods will by definition cause matching tasks to queue up, this causes the delay to increase.

Altogether, the initial comparison showed that adding interruptions to a dual-task scenario will make it more difficult to successfully carry out the tasks even when using speech input. Some interruption methods do better than others, though. This suggests that not necessarily those methods that were found best for gesture interaction in chapter 8 are also the best choice when applying speech interaction.

Time	Nego-Vis.	Nego-Aud.	Sch.	Imm.	Med.
Nego-Vis.	-	0.808	0.252	0.005	0.142
Nego-Aud.	0.808	-	0.144	0.002	0.105
Sch.	0.252	0.144	-	0.137	0.974
Imm.	0.005	0.002	0.137	-	0.009
Med.	0.142	0.105	0.974	0.009	-

Contacts	Nego-Vis.	Nego-Aud.	Sch.	Imm.	Med.
Nego-Vis.	-	0.056	0.031	0.066	0.093
Nego-Aud.	0.056	-	0.235	0.804	0.699
Sch.	0.031	0.235	-	0.319	0.349
Imm.	0.066	0.804	0.319	-	0.918
Med.	0.093	0.699	0.349	0.918	-

Error rate	Nego-Vis.	Nego-Aud.	Sch.	Imm.	Med.
Nego-Vis.	-	0.553	0.993	0.194	0.701
Nego-Aud.	0.553	-	0.658	0.546	0.893
Sch.	0.993	0.659	-	0.306	0.596
Imm.	0.194	0.546	0.306	-	0.389
Med.	0.701	0.893	0.596	0.389	-

Average delay	Nego-Vis.	Nego-Aud.	Sch.	Imm.	Med.
Nego-Vis.	-	0.101	<0.001	<0.001	<0.001
Nego-Aud.	0.101	-	<0.001	0.001	0.191
Sch.	<0.001	<0.001	-	<0.001	<0.001
Imm.	<0.001	0.001	<0.001	-	<0.001
Med.	<0.001	0.191	<0.001	<0.001	-

Table 9.3: Pairwise t-tests of methods.

Following, the five interruption methods were examined in more detail. The results of the Bonferroni corrected paired samples t-tests are shown in table 9.3. A number of differences were found that will be analyzed next.

9.5.1   Time

Regarding completion time, the tested methods can be divided into three groups with decreasing time needed for the HotWire task. One group is formed by the negotiated methods, one by the scheduled and mediated methods, and one by the remaining immediate method (cf. figure 9.4(a)). Although a clear difference of approx. 5 sec. exists between each group, only the negotiated audio and the immediate methods exhibited a significant difference. However, as negotiated visual was on average even 1 sec. slower than the negotiated audio method but with a smaller standard error, it is more likely that both negotiated methods in reality significantly differ from the immediate method, although our collected data could not uncover this difference.

In general, the reason for the higher completion time of the negotiated methods is because of the extra effort required by the user to present matching tasks. As the additional interaction requires subjects to bring up the tasks with the "show me" command, which slows down the user, this result was expected. Important was, however, that the overhead (6.6 seconds higher, an increase of 6%) was much lower than we expected. Although the speech recognizer needed around 700ms to recognize a command after it was said, which is much slower than what, for example, gesture recognition typically needs, the overhead is still clearly smaller than the overhead discovered in chapter 8 for gesture interaction. There, an overhead of 24.8 sec. increased completion time by about 26% for a similar experiment. This indicates that with speech input the extra effort (time) needed to bring up a matching task in negotiated methods is very small or almost negligible.

Relating these findings to previous work, where the primary task was less physical as the user sat in front of a computer and interacted using a keyboard [DNL+04], or more realistically using the HotWire together with gesture input (cf. chapter 8), we see that speech interaction has a certain advantage in wearable computing environments, where completion time is important. Users involved in a complex primary task with substantial visual attention demands and even one handed manual work to be carried out, may perform faster with speech than gestures. For our HotWire experiments this was found with certainty and indicates that H1 may be true.

9.5.2 Contacts

Unlike time, the number of contacts subjects made with the HotWire does not allow to derive any clear grouping of methods. Pairwise t-tests could not uncover any significant differences between the methods, if any exist. This suggests that H2 may be wrong with respect to errors made on the primary task, because negotiated methods did not show significant differences. However, negotiated visual gave on average the highest number of contacts (14.95) which would support H2. The scheduled method gave the lowest number (12.76). Our hypothesis was that the number of contacts should be less compared to chapter 8 (avg. 54 contacts). Although we used a 4 mm larger diameter for the ring of the hand-held tool to make the HotWire less challenging, and to avoid noise on the metric caused by too many and random contacts being made, approximately 74% less contacts on average compared to chapter 8 were unexpected. To find reasons for this, we continued with examining the rate r of contacts over time between methods.

$$r = \frac{contacts}{time}$$

This simple comparison was neither able to uncover significant differences nor could we gain other insight from it, probably because of the correlation between time and contacts made.

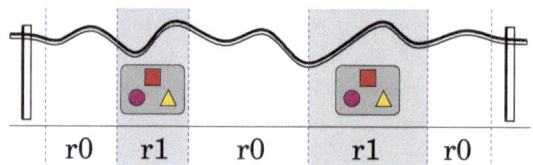

Figure 9.5: Interruption-based segmentation.

Because the pure contact metric can apparently not be used to examine its properties in detail, we considered related but more detailed metrics. Therefore, we want to further investigate, if there are any smaller underlying effects on contacts, when subjects are requested to answer matching tasks that cannot be uncovered with a plain contacts analysis.

The presence of matching tasks in the HMD should cause more contacts being made due to the transition from a single-task to a dual-task situation subjects have to undergo. To accomplish this second task, the visual attention has to be taken from the first task to answer the second task. To test this hypothesis we used the approach from chapter 8. The contact rates were divided in two categories; $r0$ indicated the rate of contacts over time, when no matching task was present in the HMD, while $r1$ indicated the rate of contacts over time with a matching task visible (cf. figure 9.5). The rates $r0$ and $r1$ then underwent a paired samples t-test for each of the interruption methods to see how the presence of matchings affected the number of contacts. As hypothesized, rates of $r1$ were always higher. More precisely, $r1$ of negotiated visual was significantly ($p < 0.003$) higher. For the mediated treatment, the difference was even strongly significantly ($p < 0.001$) higher. The latter significants was expected. The mediated algorithm required no contacts over a period of 3 sec. before it presented matching task, which causes $r1$ to rapidly increase, when contacts are being made during that time. More important, however, was the significance found for the negotiated visual treatment, which indicates a disadvantage of visual notifications, when being involved in an attention demanding primary task (H2). In turn, the negotiated audio method exhibited the lowest impact on contacts, when matching tasks were present. While nothing can be said with certainty, this would still support the fact that humans can more easily perceive sound sources located around them and do not necessary need focused attention like vision does [Bre03]. In our experiment, subjects did not need to divide their visual attention to bring up the matching tasks, which results in no significant difference in the number of contacts being made in $r0$ and $r1$.

To determine, whether the methods influenced the subject overall and make her more prone to make errors, we compared firstly the rate $r1$ between different methods and then $r0$ in the same manner. For $r1$, when there was a matching task shown, both negotiated audio and scheduled had the lowest contact rates (0.20), while the immediate method had the highest rate (0.25), yet neither were these differences significant, nor can the range of the absolute numbers (0.05) be considered as different at all. For $r0$, as expected due to its nature, the mediated method had the lowest rate (0.11), while the immediate method has the highest rate (0.21). Although the absolute range was still very small again, Bonferroni corrected paired samples t-tests showed significant differences between mediated vs. the negotiated visual method ($p = 0.003$), and the immediate vs. the mediated method ($p = 0.004$), respectively.

All in all, a clear ranking of methods only based on plain contact metric is difficult. In terms of the impact an interruption method has on the primary task, negotiated audio, scheduled, and immediate methods were lowest. The remaining two methods both showed significant impact. Next we will examine the matching tasks themselves.

9.5.3 Error Rate

Similar to results in chapter 8, the error rate for the matching tasks exhibited no significant differences, regardless of method. This was unexpected, because our current changes in the matching task (adding mathematical matching tasks and time limits) were designed to make matchings more challenging, i.e. causing more wrong answers. Indeed, subjects on average gave 12% wrong answers over all treatments, which is about 10% higher compared to chapter 8. Still, this was not enough to show significant differences between the methods, if they exist.

However, because we introduced a time limit to answer a matching task, this information can be used to estimate the amount of stress or mental load an interruption method puts on subjects. If matching tasks exceed their time limit, this means that the subject was probably not able to handle the task in time because of too much stress in the primary task. In turn, this stress will then supposedly cause an insufficient amount of attention and cognitive resources spent on the secondary task. Therefore, we compared the time out rate r_t among the methods, i.e. the number of timed out matchings divided by the number of all matching tasks presented during a treatment.

$$r_t = \frac{timed\ out\ matching\ tasks}{all\ matching\ tasks\ presented}$$

Although the differences between the methods were not significant, figure 9.6 shows, as expected, that most matching tasks exceeded their time limit in the immediate method.

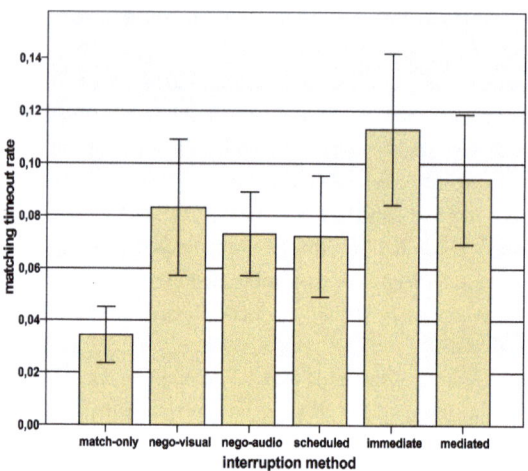

Figure 9.6: Matching task timeout rate.

This is probably, because tasks appeared completely at random and thus may have caused most stress. However, this cannot be stated with statistical certainty.

Only in the immediate method more than 10% of matching tasks exceeded their time limit. Although not being best, the mediated treatment showed that even very simple context-awareness could lower the stress level in our setup, which leaves more space for an accurate interaction. As already indicated when examining the other metrics above, the negotiated audio method tended to produce least stress. It is interesting to note that compared to our earlier study in chapter 8, where no time limit was given, the immediate method's error rate is now the worst rather than the best.

Finally, our observations uncovered something completely different but very important. Almost all of the 8 female subjects confused left and right selections very frequently. Females often said the opposite command of what they apparently intended to say. Consequently, they often had to repeat the command a second time to say the corrected command. This sometimes increased matching errors. Only one male subject showed similar problems during the course of the study. An in-depth analysis of this observation will require additional research.

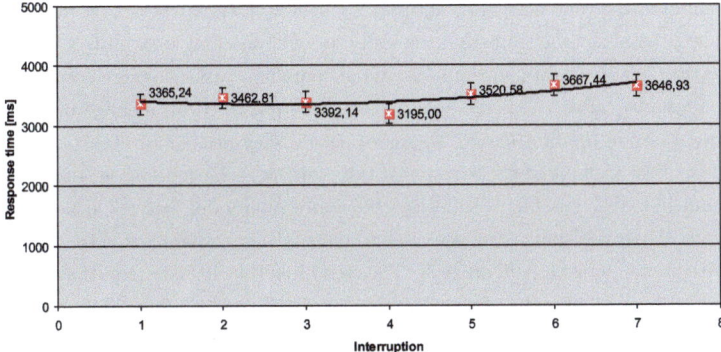

Figure 9.7: Average time needed by subjects to answer matching tasks in the order they occurred after the first 25 seconds of the scheduled interruption treatment.

9.5.4   Average Delay

Naturally, the average delay is expected to be the highest for the scheduled method, since the matching tasks are by definition queued and presented only in fixed time intervals. This was also found with strong significance ($p<0.001$) for all methods (cf. table 9.3). All other results showed significant differences between the methods except between the two negotiated methods and negotiated audio vs. the mediated method. Hence, the negotiated and mediate methods are likely to form a group with similar average delays, rather than one method being favorable over another.

The immediate method provided on average fastest response (7.44 sec.), followed by the mediated (8.62 sec.), negotiated audio (9.36 sec.), and negotiated visual method (10.35 sec.). With an overall average delay of 17.8 seconds for all answered matching tasks, the scheduled method exhibited the longest average delay, but with an expected delay of 12.5 seconds on average due to the queuing, this means the user—in theory—only spent on average approximately 5.2 seconds to respond to queued matching tasks, which is the fastest response of all methods. A possible explanation is that the need to mentally switch between primary and secondary task is reduced because of the clustering.

Unlike our observations in chapter 8, we could not observe in this experiment that users were able to increase their secondary task performance from the first queued matching task till the last with speech input in the scheduled treatment. To examine this further, we used the same approach already applied in our previous experiment for gesture interaction and computed the time needed by subjects to answer each matching task from the queue of pending tasks, i.e. the time from the visibility of a matching task until it was answered (cf. section 8.5.4). Again, we only analyzed matching tasks answered within the first batch, presented after the first 25 seconds. Users answered an average of 6.71 queued matching tasks in the first batch. To answer them, they needed for each task an average of 3.02 seconds. Compared to the response time subjects achieved with gesture interaction, this number is twice as high. Different to gesture interaction, we could not find in our quantitative analysis that users were able to reduce their response time to each matching task with speech input (cf. figure 9.7). The trend line (black) indicates, that the response time is not decreased for the sequence of matching tasks to be answered in the first batch. An explanation for this may be that the speech recognition process is a bottleneck, and that this bottleneck cannot be compensated by a reduced need to mentally switch between primary and secondary task, or other interaction strategies applied by subjects to improve their performance.

During our observation throughout the study we noticed that in the negotiated methods many subjects almost instantaneously used the "show me" command to bring up announced tasks and did not use the possibility to choose the "best" moment. They rather just choose a moment. With respect to average delay, this means that the obtained times are close to a best case scenario, which is apparently still sufficient to outperform some other methods in regards to time, contacts, and error rate.

Compared to our results in chapter 8, the observed average delays are all about 1 to 4 seconds longer. Probably, this is because of the approximately 700 ms needed by the speech recognizer to recognize commands and the implementation of the mathematical matching tasks. Mathematical tasks seemed to be more difficult for subjects to answer than figure matchings. The latter was confirmed by observations and subject comments during the experiment (a kind of think-aloud). Subjects apparently felt ashamed when having answered mathematical matchings wrongly and frequently excused themselves orally. For figure matchings we could not find similar behaviors.

In line with the interruption study reported in [DNL+04], the current data confirms the advantage of the audio notifications in the negotiated methods compared to visual ones. This indicates that although the HotWire more realistically abstracted a wearable computing environment, speech input is probably more suitable to compensate the typical challenges users have to deal with in dual-task environments with a manual primary task, than gesture input is able to. With speech input, users could maintain focus on the primary task easier due to hands-freeness and the non-existing interference with a manual task (cf. section 9.6.2). That is, speech input and audio notifications need the auditory stimulus of the user, while manual work needs her visual stimulus.

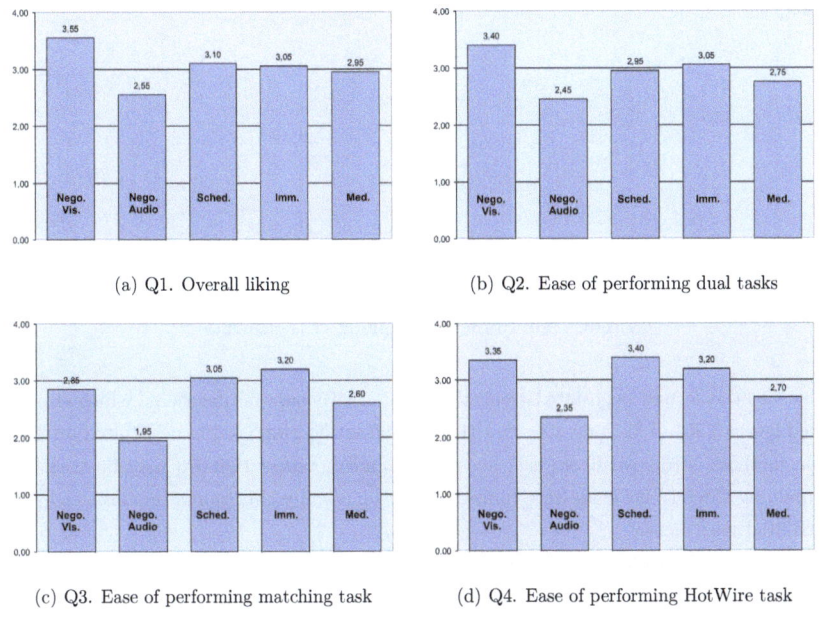

(a) Q1. Overall liking   (b) Q2. Ease of performing dual tasks

(c) Q3. Ease of performing matching task   (d) Q4. Ease of performing HotWire task

Figure 9.8: Subjective ranking of treatments.

9.6   Qualitative Results

Besides an analysis of quantitative data gathered throughout the experiment, qualitative
data available through questionnaires and observations may provide insights on how users,
apart from pure performance measures, liked the different interruption methods we tested.

9.6.1   Questionnaires

To determine the personal opinions of subjects on the different interruption methods
tested, post-experimental inquiry data of questionnaires was examined further (cf. appendix A.1). First, four questions of the inquiry were analyzed where subjects were asked
to rank the five experimental treatments on a Likart scale from 1 to 5 in ascending order
with the best first (1) and the worst last (5). The average rankings are shown in figure
9.8.

The first question concerned a subjects overall liking of a certain interruption method
(figure 9.8(a)). The negotiated audio treatment was liked most by subjects (2.55) as op-

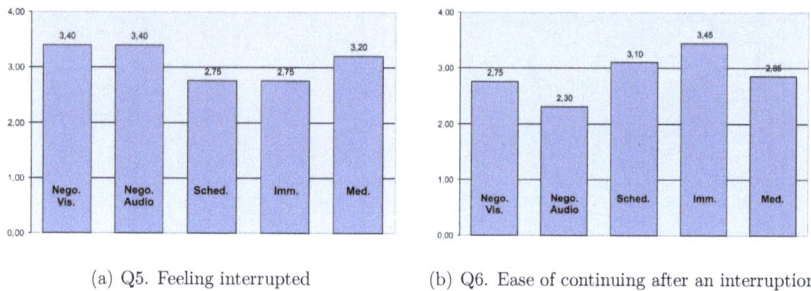

(a) Q5. Feeling interrupted   (b) Q6. Ease of continuing after an interruption

Figure 9.9: Subjective ranking of treatments.

posite to the second negotiated treatment, that used visual notifications, which subjects liked least (3.55). This indicates that the type of notification used in negotiated interruption methods strongly affects user acceptance and moreover that H3 may be true. The remaining three treatments were ranked almost identically with minor advantages for the mediated treatment.

The second question concerned the ease to perform the primary HotWire task and the secondary matching tasks (figure 9.8(b)). Again, subjects ranked the negotiated audio treatment best (2.45), and the negotiated visual treatment worst (3.40). The mediated treatment was, however, close to the negotiated audio treatment with a ranking of 2.75.

The third and fourth question asked how easy it was to perform the matching task and the HotWire task, respectively (figures 9.8(b) and 9.8(c)). Even though the negotiated audio treatment was preferred again in both cases, scheduled and immediate treatments were ranked worst. Although subjects apparently changed there opinion about the best interruption method, when being asked to think only of one task at a time, these changes are likely to be small. To state this with certainty more detailed analysis with more data is necessary. What can be derived from the four questions instead, is that negotiated audio treatment outperformed all other treatments in terms of preferred interruption methods by subjects, which strongly supports H3. Because the mediated method came second, this also indicates that the use of additional context information can provide benefits in interruption handling, even though subjects do not always prefer those methods to others.

To see whether or not the methods subjects liked most are also the methods that cause least feeling of being interrupted and make the continuation after an interruption as easy as possible, the answers of two further questions were analyzed. The average rankings of these questions are shown in figure 9.9. Note that for Q5 (figure 9.9(a)), methods were ranked in descending order with 5 being the rank for the least feeling of being interrupted.

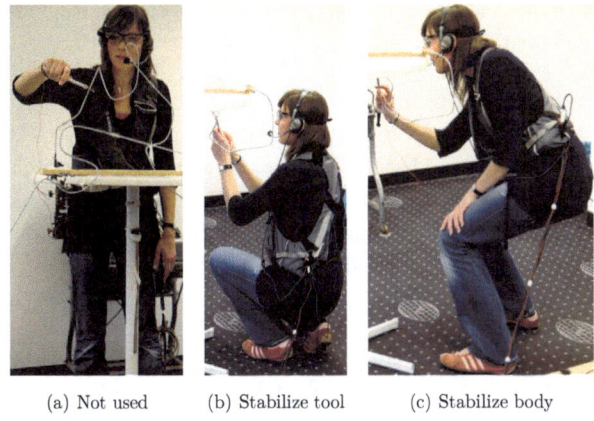

| (a) Not used | (b) Stabilize tool | (c) Stabilize body |

Figure 9.10: Different hand usages observed.

Subjects not only liked the negotiated audio method most, they also felt least interrupted (3.40). However, with the second negotiated method subjects also felt only low interruption. This indicates that negotiated methods will be preferred by subjects once an application offers speech interaction. If this, however, remains, once users experience the weaknesses of speech interaction, needs a long time evaluation in the field.

In line with the feeling of being interrupted, figure 9.9(b) indicates that negotiated methods allowed easiest continuation after an interruption. Again, the negotiated audio method was the preferred negotiated method and exhibited the best rank (2.30). Subjects had the most problems continuing after the interruption with the immediate method, compared to all other methods (3.45).

9.6.2   User Behavior Observations

Figure 9.10 illustrates a number of behaviors observed during the study regarding the use of the second free hand as well as the variety of body postures adopted by subjects. What can be directly derived from the three figures is that users were much more relaxed and unconstrained in terms of mobility compared to our experiment with gesture input (cf. chapter 8). The hand not holding the hand-held tool was used by subjects in more or less three different ways:

- **Not used**

  As indicated by figure 9.10(a), in situations, where the primary task was not that challenging, for example, because it temporarily did not impose too much visual attention or physical demands, users tended to hold the free hand in a comfortable and relaxed position.

- **Stabilize hand-held tool**
  When users encountered a challenging section in the primary task, they usually decided to use the second hand to improve the accuracy of their primary hand that holds the hand-held tool by holding the hand-held tool with both hands. Often, this behavior was found when users judged physical demands of a situation to stand out less than visual attention demands. Figure 9.10(b) illustrates such a situation.

- **Stabilize own body**
  Similar to use the free hand to stabilize the hand-held tool, observations indicated that users also used their free hand to stabilize their own body. This always happened in physically demanding sections of the HotWire task. For example, as shown in figure 9.10(c), when users were forced to adopt a body posture that made the primary task much more difficult to carry out without errors. Noticeable, transitions between stabilizing the hand-held tool and the user's body were observed more frequently than transitions to no usage of the free hand.

Summarizing these observations, they indicate that a second free hand is used during a primary task to automatically adapt and improve a user's subjective performance in a certain situation and especially in challenging situations. Although subjects participating in the gesture interaction study (cf. chapter 8) also had, at least temporarily, the same possibilities to use the hand wearing the data glove, when not needed for interaction, no similar behavior could be observed.

9.7   Conclusion

The presented user study showed that the particular interaction device used to control a wearable user interface impacts the selection of the best interruption method. Methods that were found superior for gesture interaction in dual-task situations (cf. chapter 8) are different to those when using speech interaction. Speech interaction was found well suited for complex primary tasks especially, when task performance is important. It easily allowed for maintaining visual focus on the primary task and did not significantly interfere with manual activities. Speech interaction in therefore recommended, when the primary task is characterized by manual work that requires a significant amount of visual attention and/or physical demands to be carried out successfully.

Although each tested interruption method exhibited strengths and weaknesses, the study found that overall the negotiated audio method exhibited most advantages in respect to both performance results and user preference (H2 + H3). The extra effort needed to bring up matching tasks was very small in both negotiated methods and increased completion time only about 6%, compared to the HotWire only task. With audio notifications, subjects kept focus on the primary task easily. The negotiated audio method also exhibited the lowest impact on the primary task's error rate, probably because hearing and speaking both use the same (auditory) stimulus as opposite to the visual negotiation method. User feedback in questionnaires strongly suggested this as well. The study's recommendation for interaction designers is therefore to use speech input instead of gestures, when offering users the interaction possibility to negotiate interruptions. Although there is always an overhead for the negotiation process, the overhead is significantly smaller for speech input than gesture input.

Subjects were fastest with the immediate method, even though it was not the most favored method. The completion time did not significantly increase compared to a single-task situation with only the primary task. While the negotiated audio method tended to produce least stress, the immediate method produced most stress, which resulted in the highest error rate on matchings with more than 10% timed out tasks. Similar to study outcomes for gesture interaction, the immediate method, in principle, results in fastest response to interruptions with speech input. Since user acceptance was low, the immediate handling method is only recommendable for few situations, where task performance is highly required and user acceptance and satisfaction are only secondary.

Unlike the findings in chapter 8 for gesture interaction, this study could not always identify an advantage of the mediated method. It might be that the algorithm applied was not sufficient to clearly show benefits for the easy to use speech interaction. Despite of this, users liked the mediated method although they did not think it would be always better than other methods. The scheduled method was found to give lowest response time. If many tasks queue up, it offers the opportunity of the fastest response to each task even with slow speech recognizers. User acceptance was, however, fairly low. In fact, only the negotiated visual method was liked less than the scheduled treatment. Although the study recommends the scheduled method for non time critical interruptions that can be answered in regular intervals, user acceptance for this method was fairly low and should consequently be avoided in interaction design for speech input.

Overall, the study suggests, similar to related work [NDL+05, DNL+04] and findings in chapter 8, that humans may compensate more of the challenges they have to deal with, with speech input, when being interrupted in a dual-task situation than with gesture input. This applies even when hands-freeness is not required by the primary task. Observations in the study showed that the hands-free nature of speech interaction gives users the freedom to use their hands to optimize task performance and/or accuracy, by stabilizing their bodies or working with two hands. Additionally, speech input makes performing tasks much more convenient for users, which is important in maintenance and assembly domains where tasks can be quit compelling, difficult to carry out, and computer acceptance is fairly low. Occasionally, environmental constraints such as noise, may prevent using speech interaction. In such cases, context information could be, however, used to implement automatic adaptation of interaction modes, for example, changing temporarily from speech to gesture input, based on the noise level.

Chapter 10

Visual Feedback and Frames of Reference for Gesture Interaction

A proper handling of interruptions can optimize user performance as discussed in the last two chapters. However, user performance is also influenced by the interaction method, which in turn can be affected or constrained by a person's mobility and physically involvement while performing a task.

This chapter presents a final empirical study to investigate two other important aspects in gesture interaction design for wearable user interfaces: The effect of visual feedback and different body postures on gesture interaction techniques in wearable computing. In chapter 8, users adapting different body postures while interacting were found to apparently lose orientation, which impaired their performance. A similar experiment conducted for interruption handling using speech input did, however, not reveal such findings. The objective of the experiment presented in this chapter is therefore to examine in more detail, whether visual feedback and a different gesture recognition algorithm can be used to optimize interruption handling using hand gestures.

10.1 Introduction

If highly mobile control of wearable user interfaces is needed, gestures are deemed to be a suitable interaction method, since they can be performed blindly based on kinesthetic feedback, while at the same time being to some extent hands-free. However, there are a number of problems associated with using gestures that have been discovered mainly in 3D and virtual reality user interface research, but not yet validated or adapted for wearable user interfaces, where gesture interaction is also used.

As shown in chapter 8, a device used to implement gesture interaction is a data glove equipped with sensors that recognize hand postures or gestures. A problem of data gloves and similar input devices that utilize accelerometers with earth's gravity as their fixed frame of reference in wearable applications is that users may risk losing their orientation when in the midst of performing a physical task in the real world. For example, an airplane technician crawling inside a narrow and sloping section of the plane can easily lose track of what direction is up and down in relation to a world-centered frame of reference, and thereby make user input less accurate and more erroneous. This problem was already briefly discussed in chapter 8, where some non-standard body postures appeared to cause problems in using hand gestures to select between two virtual objects shown in a head-mounted display (cf. section 8.5.1). Presumably, the problems occurred because the users had an incorrect sense of their hands' orientation in relation to the real world, i.e. they failed to transfer movements from their body-relative frame of reference to the static world frame used by the input device.

The remainder of this chapter explores interaction using hand gestures with optional feedback in regard to the described problem. The research question concerns how to make gesture-based interaction with a wearable computer more accurate in challenging environments, where the user is forced to perform highly mobile and physical tasks at the same time as operating the computer.

10.2 Hypotheses

The hypotheses to be verified with a user study are:

H1. Providing continuous visual feedback will be detrimental to the user's overall performance, and omitting such feedback will yield better performance in a typical wearable computing scenario.

H2. More accurate control can be achieved if hand gesture recognition uses a body-centric frame of reference for interpreting data, rather than a world-centric frame of reference.

10.3 User Feedback

As humans naturally support verbal communication with gestures, they have been researched in HCI for a long time. Pirhonen et al. [PBH02] demonstrated that gestures are convenient for mobile communication as most people can perform them while being on the move. Compared to common stylus-based interaction techniques for mobile computing that require visual feedback and thus inhibit our movement, gestures do not. A very common result of usability studies on interaction controlled by visual feedback is therefore that feedback interrupts users in their movement while interacting with the computer. But what happens if the display that shows the feedback is even perceivable without moving the head as in the case of head-mounted displays?

Brewster et al. [Bre03] evaluated two novel interfaces using sound and gestures for wearable computers. They demonstrated that non-visual interfaces using audio feedback can be an effective alternative to visual-centric interfaces, suggesting that feedback improves interaction.

Clawson et al. [CLSC05], however, showed in a user study that mobile text entry with mini-QWERY keyboards is more sensitive to the absence of visual feedback with respect to typing speed than, for example, when the Twiddler one-handed chording keyboard is used. These examples demonstrate that in wearable computing feedback does not always improve or impair interaction, but seems to depend on both the type of feedback and the interaction device used. In line with this, Marentakis et al. [MB06] also support this assumption in their work. They found that providing audio feedback for mobile interaction with a non-visual audio display decreased task performance rather than it increased it, while other metrics observed throughout the usability study yield opposite results.

The effect of providing visual feedback for gesture interfaces is, however, likely to provide proper user guidance. It is sometimes considered a necessity for user satisfaction, because users do not sufficiently feel how they performed a gesture in space and may want to receive guidance in case the interaction failed. Kallio et al. [KKMP06] evaluated the use of visualizing entire hand motions of performed gestures as feedback for interaction. They argued that such visualization can be useful for gesture feedback, but discovered also that users can get confused when obscure visualizations resulting from erroneous gesture recognition were presented. In contrast, it is known that users' internal sensation of body postures and performed motions allows them to feel how they control an input device without the need of looking at it or using visual feedback. This has been found an important factor, when users are involved in multiple tasks and therefore have to divide their attention [WNK06, BH99, FB97, MFPBS97].

In conclusion, this suggests that it is not yet entirely clear, what impact feedback provided for a certain interaction technique will have or how it interferes with other characteristics of the computing paradigm. For instance, one of the unique characteristics of wearable computing is its high degree of mobility involving different body postures of users being involved, for example, in a primary manual maintenance task. Thus, we are interested in our experiment not only in the impact visual feedback might have on hand

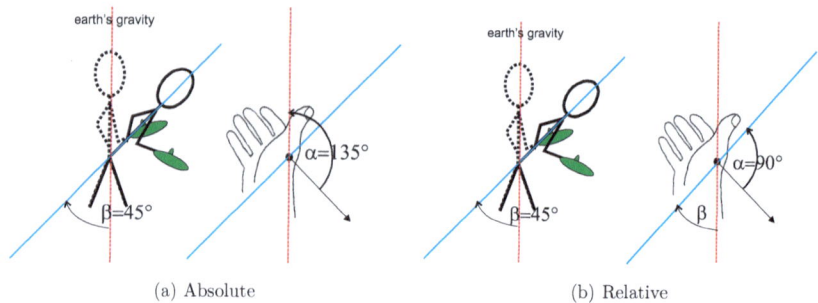

(a) Absolute   (b) Relative

Figure 10.1: Two alternative frames of reference.

gesture interaction for wearable computing, but also if different body postures interfere with them or have an impact on the interaction technique itself.

10.4   Different Frames of Reference and Gestures

What is common to almost all gesture devices (e.g. [WNK06, TP02]) and their used gesture recognition is that sensor data is interpreted in a static manner. Sensor data is usually interpreted in a static world-centered frame of reference that neglects the highly mobile property commonly present in wearable computing environments, i.e. an operation where the user is highly mobile and involved in a dual-task situation with a primary physical task in the real world and a secondary computer task. That these properties can make a difference compared to stationary computer use has also been argued in [WD06].

Utilizing different frames of reference in user interaction has been recently demonstrated for cameras automatically detecting their orientation using tilt sensors and automatically correcting photo orientation as well as interactively switching the display between landscape/portrait formats [HPHS05]. Here, the user can change the orientation of the camera device but still maintain her body-centric frame of reference. By automatically transforming the camera's output to the user's body-centric frame of reference, interpretation of the camera display is much easier and convenient for the user. Although not closely related to our work, up to now different frames of reference have been mostly studied for virtual reality and 3D user interface design. For example, Hinkley et al. [HPGK94] presented design issues for 3D user interfaces using different frames of reference and argued that "users may have trouble moving in a fixed, absolute coordinate frame". To overcome this, Hinkley et al. proposed interaction techniques to be based upon motions *relative* to the user's own body, rather than *absolute* to a static world-centric frame of reference.

Following Hinkley et al.'s definition, figure 10.1 depicts these two alternatives of using different frames of reference for hand gesture recognition. Figure 10.1(a) depicts the commonly used *absolute* approach for gesture interaction where (angular) calculations are done by calculating the differences of the current sensor data to the fixed world-centric frame of reference defined by earth's gravity. Opposite to this approach, figure 10.1(b) shows the *relative* approach where sensor data is interpreted in respect to a body-centric frame of reference that is defined by the user herself. As indicated in both figures, calculations result in different values of angle α. In the absolute method the user has to manually compensate the angular difference β in respect to her own body posture, which adds additional cognitive load that might effect interaction accuracy. Applying the relative method instead compensates all body-movements of the user automatically in a way that all interaction is relative to her body posture. For example, an absolute "thumb up" position is only reached once the thumb is turned back $-45°$, i.e., pointing toward the ceiling. For the relative method "thumb up" is reached, when the thumb is in line with the user's pitch, i.e. in the given case no adjustment is needed, because body and hand are tilted in the same angle. Note that while the user maintains an upright posture, the absolute and relative methods are equal.

10.5   Experiment

The experiment attempts to establish whether body-relative gesture recognition (henceforth denoted as the *relative method*) will offer the user better control, when using a data glove for interaction, compared to the current recognition (henceforth denoted as the *absolute method*), where the user needs to maintain a sense of the hand's orientation in relation to the real world and earth's gravity. In connection with exploring the differences between the relative and absolute method, the experiment also evaluates the impact of providing visual feedback while performing the interaction gestures. To test this, a user is set to perform a physical task in the real world, while simultaneously being forced to interact with a virtual task in the wearable computer. By comparing the user's performance of both tasks when using relative as opposed to absolute recognition, some conclusions can be drawn about the feasibility and accuracy of the two recognition models. Furthermore, additional conclusions can be drawn on how visual feedback interferes with the user's task performance, i.e. whether or not the presence of visual feedback in the relative or absolute gesture recognition could increase task performance. This section proceeds with presenting the physical and virtual task as well as the apparatus used to implement a user study.

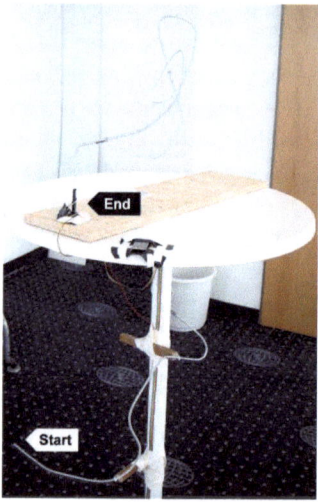

Figure 10.2: HotWire apparatus representing physical task.

10.5.1   Physical Task

The physical task needs to represent a typical situation encountered in different wearable computing scenarios. Examples of such tasks include mechanical assembly of vehicles, routine inspection and audit of machine components, and preparation of medical equipment in healthcare. Often, such a task requires the close proximity of the user, typically occupies one or both of the user's hands, and requires a major part of the user's attention. Furthermore, the tasks tend to be mobile in that the user needs to move around as well as transport parts or components from one place to another. To represent this kind of task, the HotWire evaluation method was chosen.

As the experiment is about the impact of body- versus world-relative positioning, the wire track is shaped in such a way that it will enforce users to bend and stretch, and in general get into body postures that would make them more prone to lose orientation. Furthermore, the sections of the track are varied in terms of difficulty, exposing the user to easier as well as trickier sections that require a higher degree of concentration on the physical task. Figure 10.2 shows the complete HotWire apparatus used in this experiment.

(a) Figure matching   (b) Mathematical matching

Figure 10.3: Matching tasks representing the virtual task.

10.5.2 Virtual Task

The virtual task consists of different matching tasks presented in the user's HMD. Similar to chapter 9, there are two types of matching tasks. The first is the color and shape figure matching task already used in chapter 8. The second is the mathematical task already used in chapter 9. Figure 10.3 shows the two types of matching tasks. By using the approach of chapter 8 users can answer matching tasks by rotating the hand wearing the data glove left or right. Once a matching task is answered users receive an acoustic feedback in form of an auditory icon (gun shot).

The matching tasks are considered abstract enough not to interfere cognitively with the physical task of the HotWire. It could be argued that the virtual task should be modeled as being more related to the physical task, for example, providing guidance on how to best proceed over a difficult section of the wire. However, it was deemed more suitable to keep the task as simple and easy to comprehend as possible, in order to focus the study on pure performance metrics for the interaction method used, and avoid any bias caused by the users' interpretation and handling of such guidance. Naturally, the findings from the experiment in terms of interaction style can then be directly applied to more specific virtual tasks in different application domains.

10.5.3 Sampling of Body Postures

The virtual task runs concurrently to the user performing the physical task so that matching tasks will be presented for the user at random time intervals. Each matching task will thereby interrupt the user and call for the user's attention in handling it. As this will occur at random points on the track, a wide variety of body postures will be sampled at the time the matching task is presented and handled. Because the user's performance in both the physical and virtual task is monitored, this sampling makes it possible to determine how well the virtual task can be handled in various situations, using various input methods. In turn, this enables us to draw conclusions about the usability of using either the relative or absolute input method, as their relative strengths and weaknesses will influence the user's performance of both tasks.

To increase the validity of the experiment, it is desirable to prevent the user from letting a queue of unanswered matching tasks build up. If a queue is allowed to build up, which allows the user to answer them all in one batch one after the other, this could allow the user to attempt to "cheat" by using various strategies. For example, by only answering the matching tasks when having reached the very end of the track, or waiting until a stable body posture has been achieved as a result of an easy section of the track, the user could improve some aspects of her performance (e.g. correctness in responding) while impairing other (e.g. time to respond). Therefore, to force the user to handle the matching tasks as soon as possible and provide correct answers, a time limit was imposed causing the matching task to disappear and be counted as an error unless it is handled soon enough.

Another reason not to let queues of matching tasks build up is that this can otherwise cause a bias in the experiment. Because the focus of the study is on the interaction aspect, having a long queue of tasks will allow the user to get accustomed to using the data glove for the first few tasks, and then being able to provide a more accurate, faster response on the remaining tasks in the queue. While the queuing of virtual tasks may well be the case in different scenarios applicable to wearable computing, we wish to avoid it in this specific case and instead consider only the case where the virtual tasks appear separately. This will also help make the results easier to generalize; a good performance with a single instance of the task is likely to improve further if tasks are queued and clustered, whereas the opposite is not necessarily true.

In the experiment, a time limit of 5 seconds was used for the matching tasks, as our initially conducted pilot study had shown this to be an adequate length of time for handling the task. To avoid queues building up, all matching tasks were interspersed with 1 second plus a random period of time of up to 5 seconds. Combined, this means a new matching task will appear on average every 8.5 seconds while performing the physical task.

10.5.4   The Data Glove

The data glove used for gesture interaction in the experiment is based on the SCIPIO [WLKK06] multi purpose sensor board that features an acceleration sensor, possibilities to connect different electrical switches, and a wireless communication using Bluetooth. A

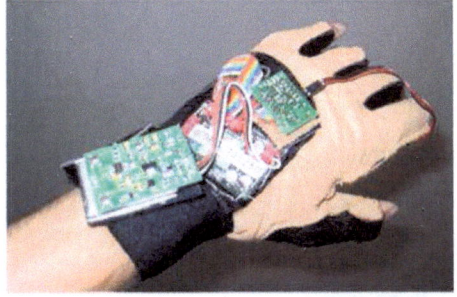

(a) Sensor board and battery pack mounted on the back of the leather glove.

(b) "Click" feedback buttons.

Figure 10.4: Prototype of the data glove used in the experiment for gesture interaction.

pair of leather fitness gloves was chosen as the basis for the data glove prototypes. The sensor board including a battery pack was mounted on the back of the hand of each glove. A trigger button, providing some tactile and acoustic "click" feedback, generated by the mechanics of the buttons when being pressed, was positioned on the forefinger to be easily accessible. The accelerometer gathered motion data for the gesture algorithm while the trigger was used to actually issue a gesture. Figure 10.4 depicts the data glove.

To let interaction gestures correspond to the way matching tasks are presented, two gestures for selecting either the left or right object were chosen: By rotating the glove to either left or right and exceeding a predefined threshold angle (45°), a gesture is activated. Once activated a gesture is finally issued to select an object by pressing the forefinger button. Note, this is the same approach taken already in chapter 8.

The two different gesture recognition algorithms tested in the experiment only differ in angular calculations. To determine whether a rotation angle is above the threshold the rotation angle is measured with respect to a "thumb up" position. In the *absolute* case "thumb up" is related to the static frame of reference that is defined by earth's gravity. In the *relative* case, however, "thumb up" is measured with respect to the users body-centric frame of reference. That is, once the user tilts her head/body to one side the body-centered frame of reference detaches from earth's gravity reference so that the "thumb up" position is reached once the thumb is in line with the current tilting angle of the users' body (cf. figure 10.1(b)).

To measure the required body-centric frame of reference, users have to wear a special headset, based on the SCIPIO [WLKK06] hardware, with an acceleration sensor centered above the user's head during the experiment. The tilting angle of the user during motion

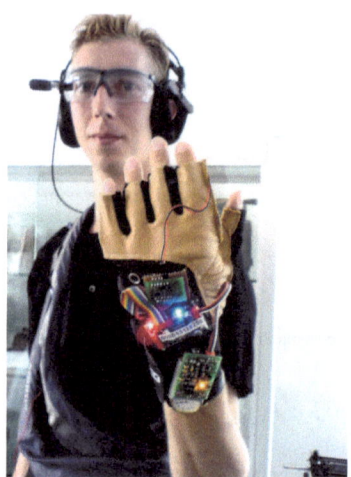

Figure 10.5: User wearing the headset for body posture measurements, the data glove for gesture interaction, an HMD for graphical output perception, and a vest to unobtrusively carry the wearable hardware.

with respect to earth's gravity was measured with this headset. A user wearing the headset as well as the data glove is shown in figure 10.5.

10.5.5   Visual Feedback

To provide the user with real-time information on the gestures for selecting either the left or right object in the virtual task, visual feedback could be provided in the head-mounted display, where the matching tasks are shown. The feedback consists of a continuously updated widget in which the data glove's current tilting angle is visible, together with the frame of reference marking the neutral position where neither left nor right is selected. For the absolute method the frame of reference is the earth's gravity vector, i.e. straight down regardless of how the user moves around (cf. figure 10.6(a)).

For the relative method, the frame of reference follows the tilting angle of the user's head (cf. figure 10.6(b)). The widget also shows two "activation areas" marked in red and green, that move along with the frame of reference. When the rotating angle (the orange line) of the user's hand reaches one of these areas, a colored square, corresponding to the color of the activation area, is shown in the center to let the user know an input event (left or right) can be triggered by pressing the button positioned on the forefinger.

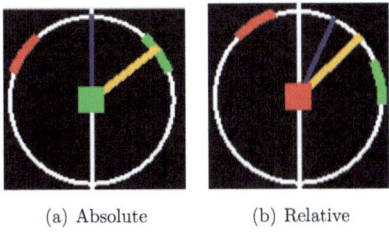

(a) Absolute   (b) Relative

Figure 10.6: Visual feedback with reference angle fixed to earth's gravity (left) or following the user's head (right).

Overall, the visual feedback provided guides the user how to move to make a left or right selection. The feedback was deliberately not integrated into the actual matching task, for example, through highlighting the left or right object, in order to serve as a "worst case" kind of feedback. It may be more complex than needed for the given situation but it is also more general and thus easier applicable in other scenarios. By testing the absolute and relative methods with and without this feedback, knowledge can be gained on what impact such feedback will have.

10.6 User Study

A total of 22 subjects were selected for participation from students and staff at the local university—14 males and 8 females aged between 23–43 years (mean 27.95). All subjects were screened not to be color blind. The study uses a *within subjects design* with the gesture recognition method and the inclusion or exclusion of visual feedback as the two independent variables. Eight treatments were used, one base case with only the physical HotWire task performed, three base cases with only the matching task performed (figure matching, mathematical matching, and both combined at random), plus four experimental treatments consisting of the absolute and relative methods with and without feedback.

Between each treatment the user had a chance to rest to reduce fatigue and prepare for the next treatment described verbally by one of the test leaders. To avoid bias and learning effects, the subjects were divided into counterbalanced groups where the order of the treatments differed.

A single test session consists of one practice round where the subject gets to practice running the physical and virtual tasks, followed by one experimental round during which data is collected for analysis. In the practice round, each treatment is performed once so that the user can learn the different combinations of absolute and relative methods with and without feedback. Although merely five runs over the HotWire are done in the practice round, this has shown to be enough for the subject to become sufficiently proficient to perform evenly for the remainder of the experiment.

In the experimental round, each of the eight treatments is performed twice to yield more data for statistical purposes. In practice, this is equal to providing a twice as long track. The time to complete the physical task naturally varies depending on how fast the subject is, but previously conducted pilot studies indicated an average of about 40–60 seconds for one single run over the wire. With one practice and one experimental round, eight treatments performed in each round, plus time for questions and instructions, the total time required for a complete session is around 45 minutes.

Running the Experiment

The experiment was conducted in an isolated room at the local university, with only the subject and two test leaders present to carry out the experiment. Upon arrival, each subject was asked to fill in a form with basic demographical questions such as age, gender, estimated proficiency with computers, and estimated ability to perform motor-driven tasks in general (cf. appendix A.1). The apparatus used in the experiment was then introduced to the subject, with the absolute and relative orientation recognition methods explained in terms of how they were operated.

For the absolute method, the subject was instructed that the earth's gravity was used as the frame of reference for gestures performed. For the relative method, the subject was instructed that the user's head was used as reference instead. This was followed by the initial practice round where the subject put on the wearable computer and the data glove, in order to learn how to operate them and to become familiar with performing the physical and virtual task. After this, the experimental round started during which data was collected for further analysis on the visual feedback's and orientation method's impact on user interaction. Having completed this, the subject was asked to fill in another form with questions regarding the experiment just performed. This form included questions about the user preference of the different orientation methods and the visual feedback provided, in order to collect qualitative data about the treatments performed.

10.7 Results

After the user study the collected data was analyzed to examine the impact of visual feedback and how the different orientation methods affected user performance. The following metrics were used in the analysis:

- **Time:** The time required for the subject to complete the HotWire track from start to end.

- **Contacts:** The number of contacts the subject made between the ring and the wire.

- **Error rate:** The percentage of matching tasks the subject answered wrongly.

- **Average delay:** The average time from when a matching task was created until the subject answered it.

The first two metrics, time and contacts, refer to the subject's performance in the physical task. The last two metrics, error rate and average delay, describe how the virtual tasks were performed. The lower the value of a metric is, the better the subject's performance is in that respect. The graphs in figure 10.7 summarize the overall user performance by showing the averages of the metrics together with one standard error.

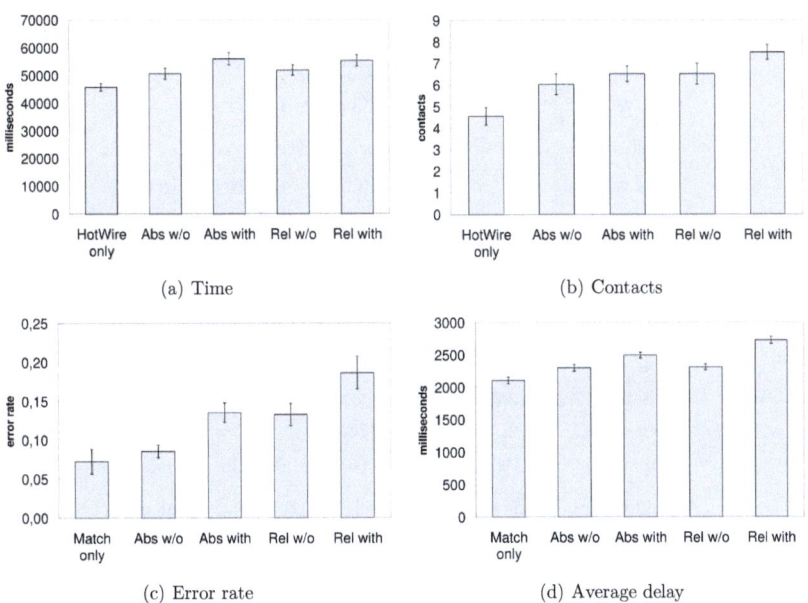

(a) Time

(b) Contacts

(c) Error rate

(d) Average delay

Figure 10.7: Averages of user performance.

A Two-factor repeated measures ANOVA was performed over the four experimental treatments where the absolute and relative methods, with and without feedback, were tested. Significant differences (F(1,84)=10.444, p<0.002) were found for the average delay metric in the performance of the virtual task. For the remaining three metrics, this initial analysis did not reveal any significant differences. This is however partially because interaction effects between the physical and virtual task will show up most clearly in the average delay metric, while the other metrics can be obscured and require a more in-depth analysis to reveal the differences.

Therefore, to further investigate the data in more detail, paired samples t-tests were performed comparing each of the four treatments with each other. The results of the metrics, where significant differences were found are shown in table 10.1. A Bonferroni corrected alpha value of 0.05/6=0.008 was used to accommodate for multiple comparisons. In the forthcoming sections the metrics and differences will be examined in further detail.

Time	Abs w/o	Abs with	Rel w/o	Rel with
Abs w/o	-	0.0061	0.1888	0.0013
Abs with	0.0061	-	0.0433	0.3669
Rel w/o	0.1888	0.0433	-	0.0371
Rel with	0.0013	0.3669	0.0371	-

Contacts	Abs w/o	Abs with	Rel w/o	Rel with
Abs w/o	-	0.1839	0.2116	0.0093
Abs with	0.1839	-	0.5000	0.0349
Rel w/o	0.2116	0.5000	-	0.0492
Rel with	0.0093	0.0349	0.0492	-

Error rate	Abs w/o	Abs with	Rel w/o	Rel with
Abs w/o	-	0.0718	0.1351	0.0323
Abs with	0.0718	-	0.4740	0.1165
Rel w/o	0.1351	0.4740	-	0.1112
Rel with	0.0323	0.1165	0.1112	-

Average delay	Abs w/o	Abs with	Rel w/o	Rel with
Abs w/o	-	0.0626	0.4414	0.0002
Abs with	0.0626	-	0.0552	0.0078
Rel w/o	0.4414	0.0552	-	0.0021
Rel with	0.0002	0.0078	0.0021	-

Table 10.1: Pairwise t-tests of treatments.

10.7.1   Completion Time of the Physical Task

Related work has found that users tend to stop or slow down their motions when interacting with a device in mobile settings (cf. section 4.2). Hence, the completion time will increase once the virtual task is introduced alongside the physical task, and this can also be seen in figure 10.7(a) showing the times for the base case of the physical task and the experimental treatments. Since matching tasks appear with the same frequency regardless of treatment, the overall slow down effect will be the same for all treatments.

Thus, the individual differences in completion time among the four treatments lies either in the method or feedback used. Interpreting the results of the t-tests, we can see that the completion time of the physical task is negatively affected by the use of visual feedback, while nothing can be stated with certainty whether the absolute or relative method is preferable.

For the absolute method, feedback caused significantly (t=-2.75, p<0.008) longer times than absolute without feedback. This was also seen (t=-3.4, p<0.008) when comparing the latter with the relative method using feedback. All other factors being equal, this shows that the inclusion of visual feedback for the absolute method degraded user performance of the physical task, thereby supporting hypothesis H1 stating this to be the case in wearable computing.

The reason that this visual feedback degrades the user's performance of the physical task probably is that it constitutes a closed feedback loop, which requires the user's continuous attention to be interpreted properly. Because the subject moves her hand, the widget is updated in real time and the user's attention is caught in the virtual domain, thereby reducing the performance of the task located in the physical domain.

The qualitative data from the post-experimental form reports that users could ignore the feedback, but apparently did not. It should be stressed that no user considered the feedback widget to be complex or difficult to interpret. On the contrary several users stated they fully understood and were able to use the information within it.

Therefore, the negative impact of visual feedback was not because of a bad implementation of the widget, but rather that it deprived them of the ability to focus their attention on the physical task. From a design perspective, the feedback was also meant only to serve as guidance for the users when needed, and not something they would use all the time to perform the gestures. This indicates that visual feedback, even in a form that is not required for the task at hand, can cause problems when implemented to assist gesture interaction.

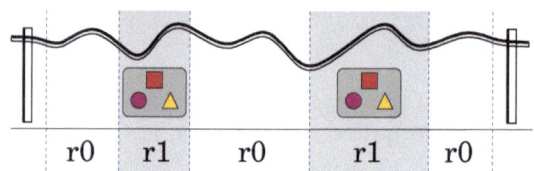

Figure 10.8: Contacts rates with and without matching task present.

10.7.2 Contacts in the Physical Task

In the initial t-tests performed, no significant differences were found for the number of HotWire contacts in the physical task, and therefore this metric needs to be examined in more detail. First, it was verified that the contact rate will be significantly higher compared to the base case when a virtual task is introduced, and as expected this was indeed the case because of the added interaction. The follow-up investigation then tried to establish whether the presence of a matching task in the HMD would affect the rate of contacts made over time. The contact rates were divided into two categories; $r0$ indicated the contact rate when no matching task was present, while $r1$ indicated the rate with a matching task visible (cf. figure 10.8). The rates $r0$ and $r1$ then underwent a Two-factor ANOVA and paired samples t-tests for the four treatments, but neither analysis revealed any significant findings.

10.7.3 Average Delay in the Virtual Task

By analyzing the average delay of the matching exercises in the virtual task, we found that relative with feedback exhibited the very worst performance (cf. figure 10.7(d)), and that the remaining three treatments were all significantly better. The fact that relative without feedback was significantly better (t=-3.22, p<0.003) than the same with feedback again indicates that visual feedback is detrimental, supporting hypothesis H1. With feedback included, the absolute method was significantly better (t=-2.63, p<0.008) than the relative method, providing one indication to disprove hypothesis H2 which stated that the relative method would be better.

Comparing the base case of match only (mixed mathematical and figure matching) with the four treatments, an ANOVA showed a significant (F(4,105)=5.98, p<0.0003) difference between the average delay metric in the different treatments. Following t-tests revealed strong significant differences between the base case and the absolute (t=-3.28, p<0.002) and relative (t=-4.43, p<0.001) methods in the case where visual feedback was present. Since the base case does not involve the physical task, this factor alone can contribute to a higher average delay overall, but does not explain the relative differences between the treatments themselves. These differences are thus caused either by the orientation method used or by the visual feedback. Because the two treatments where feedback is present exhibit a worse performance than the other two treatments without feedback, this suggests that the differences in average delay between the treatments can be attributed to the inclusion of visual feedback. Again, this indicates that visual feedback is detrimental to performance and causes a significantly higher time to handle matching tasks.

10.7.4   Error Rate in the Virtual Task

Comparing the error rate on matching tasks between the four treatments shows that errors are consistently slightly higher for the relative method compared to the absolute method, regardless of whether feedback is used or not (cf. figure 10.7(c)). An initial t-test between the treatments, however, showed that these differences in the error rate are not significant. To reveal, if this is caused by any underlying effect, a comparison of the four treatments to the base case of match only with mixed mathematical and figure matching was performed. Here, three factors can affect user performance, the burden of simultaneously performing the physical task, the inclusion of visual feedback, and the orientation method.

An ANOVA performed over these five treatments found no significant differences, indicating that error rate cannot be used to accept or reject H2, because either no difference between the methods exist, or it simply was not found yet.

10.7.5   Effort of Hand Gestures

The four metrics discussed so far are important for the performance and accomplishment of a certain task, although they only yield information about the user performance once an action has been made—not what events occurred or what interaction was made before that action was performed.

One aspect that a well designed user interface should help the user with, is to optimize user performance by avoiding needless or redundant interaction steps. For a user interface controlled via gestures, this means minimizing the movement of the user's hands to perform an action. Ideally, the user would rotate the hand to left or right and push the trigger to issue the event and perform the desired action.

If the user would for some reason rotate the hand back and forth a lot, this would generate unwanted interaction steps that serve no purpose (unless there is feedback and a matching task to handle, in which case the user may do it simply for the purpose of testing or thinking). Thus, it is of interest to analyze how the user's hand moved during the treatments, to test whether hypothesis H2 holds in its assumption that the hand will follow the user's body posture to a higher degree in the relative method than in the absolute method.

The assumption is that the number of rotating gestures, henceforth called *activations*, will be reduced in the relative method as the user's hand is coordinated with the body's frame of reference compared to the absolute method. Two t-tests were performed, comparing the absolute and relative methods first with feedback and then without feedback, for the case where no matching task was present, showed strong significant (t=-2.79/-4.03, p<0.01) differences between the number of activations made. The relative method, however, exhibited a higher number of activations than the absolute method. This was contrary to our assumption. If the user's hand would follow the body in the relative method the opposite situation would have occurred. Because the user's movement patterns are the same regardless of whether relative or absolute is used, the absolute method would exhibit a higher number of movements as the head motion alone causes activations. Note that for the relative method, the angular difference between the hand and head's frame of reference is used, and an activation can thus be caused either by rotating the hand or tilting the head.

Since relative exhibited a higher number of movements than absolute, it means that the user's head moves. Since the natural head motions when the user moves along the track can be assumed to be similar regardless of method tested, this implies that the user's hand is held still and kept in the world relative domain, rather than following the user's natural body movements, which would disprove H2.

To determine whether the presence of the visual feedback widget causes more activations being made, the data was further analyzed comparing the presence and absence of feedback, but this revealed no significant differences indicating either that our study could not show any differences, or alternatively explained as that the presence of feedback does not influence the natural behavior of the user.

10.7.6 Accuracy of Hand Gestures

Delving further into the interaction patterns of hand movements, it is of interest to know how many activations (rotating the user's hand above the threshold) are needed to handle a matching task. Ideally, exactly one activation is needed—rotating to the correct side directly when the task appears. To analyze this, we only consider the periods of time during which a matching task was presented in the HMD, and count the number of all activations needed from the appearance of the task until it was responded to.

In this case, it is the number of activations divided by the total number of matching tasks that is the relevant metric to compare subjects. Note, we do not divide by time, as that would give a performance related metric that can greatly vary between subjects, and which is not of interest when studying user behavior of the data glove as a concept. The case where no interaction occurred and the matching task timed out was ignored. Only tasks actually answered (correctly or not) were counted.

Performing pairwise t-tests between the four experimental treatments did however not reveal any differences, because users appeared to have answered each matching task in a similar manner regardless of treatment. In particular, the relative method was not worse in terms of accuracy when disregarding the response time, meaning that it is not necessarily less accurate compared to the absolute method.

10.7.7 Qualitative Data

In order to determine the subjects' personal opinions on the orientation methods and feedback used, the qualitative data from the post-experimental inquiry was analyzed further (cf. appendix A.1). Four questions were asked where the subjects ranked the four experimental treatments from 1 to 4, relative and absolute with and without feedback, in ascending order with the best first (1) and the worst last (4). The average rankings are shown in figure 10.9.

The first question concerned their overall liking of the treatments; absolute without feedback gained the best score (2.0), and relative with feedback the worst (3.05). Absolute with feedback was ranked better by subjects (2.25) than relative with feedback (3.05), indicating that the subjects did not like the relative method. The use of feedback further reduced a treatment's ranking, although the difference was in neither case significant.

The second question concerned the ease by which the treatments let subjects perform the two tasks. Here, the absence of feedback gained a better score for both absolute and relative, with the absolute method also being the preferred one (1.65).

The third and fourth question concerned the ease of performing the matching task and the physical task, respectively. For the matching task, subjects indicated that they considered the absolute method with feedback to be the preferred one (1.5), while the relative method had the worst score regardless of whether feedback was included (2.35 and 3.0). Without feedback, absolute was always ranked better than relative.

For the physical task, subjects again indicated a dislike of the use of feedback, and considered the absolute method to be the easiest one to use (1.95).

Users always ranked in roughly the same order, with absolute first and relative last in all questions, indicating that they did not like the relative method. These findings

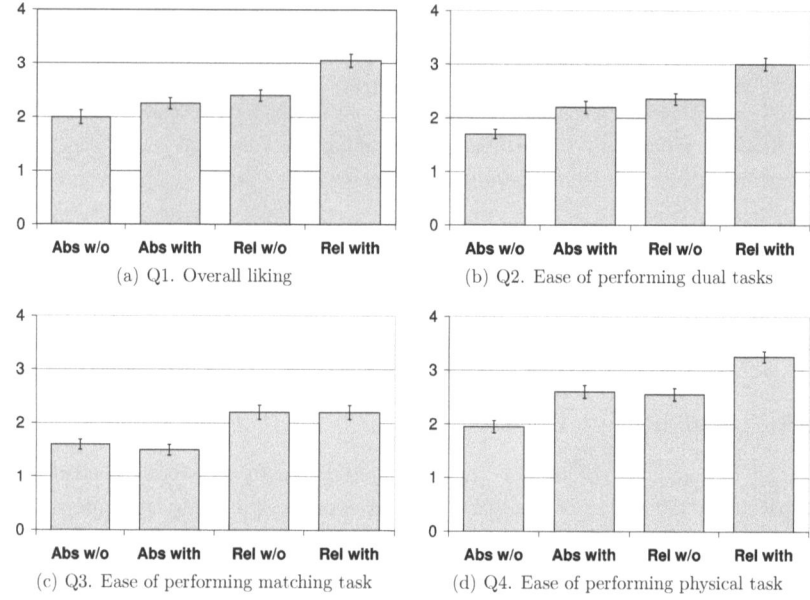

Figure 10.9: Qualitative ranking of treatments.

indicate that hypothesis H2 may be wrong. Differences were found between the absolute and relative methods, and absolute was consistently ranked as being better than relative in terms of overall liking and ease of use. Furthermore, hypothesis H1 is supported in that feedback will be detrimental to the user, and that this is the case not only for user performance but also for the user's liking and ease of using the orientation methods.

10.8 Discussion

With regards to the two hypotheses listed in the introduction, we will now discuss the results and conclude our findings.

10.8.1 The Problem of Immersive Feedback

A number of statistically significant differences were found when comparing treatments with and without feedback, indicating that the presence of the visual feedback widget reduced user performance in respect to many metrics. The most obvious metrics affected were those related to performance, i.e., the completion time of the HotWire physical task, and the average delay of a matching task until it was handled. Although the visual feedback widget was not integrated into the matching tasks, but rather shown below on the same HMD, the user could attempt to ignore it. Despite this, the presence of the feedback widget still proved to be detrimental to the user's performance of the physical task. According to the qualitative data from the forms, many users indicated that in general they did not like the use of visual feedback and that they could and did ignore the feedback because it was not needed. The latter is contradicted by the quantitative data which clearly shows that the feedback still had a negative impact on their performance, whether they were aware of it or not. Of interest is also that users considered feedback to have a more negative impact on the physical rather than the virtual task, making the former harder to perform even though the feedback has no relation to it. The probable cause for this difference in opinion is that when focusing on the physical task, the visual feedback would still be present and disrupt the user's attention.

The feedback in its current installation, where it is continuously updated, yet where every frame can be understood separately, constitutes a closed feedback loop that requires the user's constant attention. Therefore, we argue that providing this kind of closed-loop visual feedback in wearable computing scenarios can cause problems with the physical task. Continuous visual feedback for gestures should not be used if the primary task is attention demanding. This opinion has been known anecdotally in the wearable computing community [Sta02a]. The current study validates this and also points out that merely the presence of visual feedback can be detrimental, even in cases where the feedback is not necessary to successfully carry out the virtual task. The users were not able to ignore the visual feedback when performing the primary task, even though they reportedly tried to and considered themselves to manage it successfully.

Alternative methods such as tactile or audio based feedback may be preferable, as these neither require the user's visual attention nor stimulate her visual system to the same degree (cf. chapter 9). Because audio feedback also exhibits problems (cf. section 4.2.2), this highlights once again that feedback in mobile settings is still a problematic issue to implement correctly and has to be handled with great care during interface design.

10.8.2 The Novelty of Interaction Techniques

No evidence has been found that our implementation of the relative body-centric orientation method has any advantage over the absolute method that uses a commonly known world-centric frame of reference. One of the reasons for this finding is that users behave and move in a manner contrary to what would be considered natural. They were holding

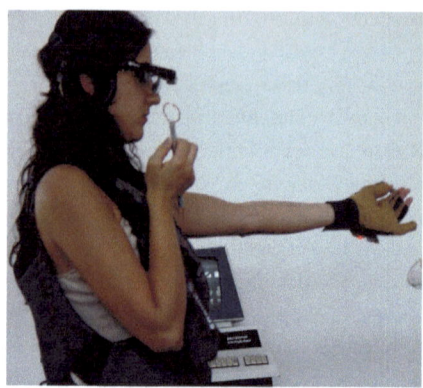 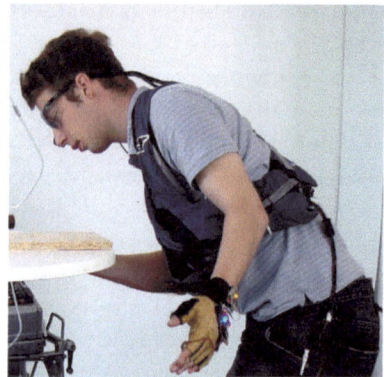

(a) Interaction without a primary task.   (b) Interaction with dual-task involvement.

Figure 10.10: Observed, unexpected and unrelaxed user behavior during gesture interaction.

the hand wearing the data glove in a rigid and static manner not following the movement of their body. This resulted in their head and hand moving independently of each other to a higher degree than it was the case for the absolute method.

One of the reasons for this is that the fixation of the user's hand in the real world's frame of reference was not the natural behavior we expected when hypothesis H2 was formulated, stating that a relative method will do better for a more accurate interaction than an absolute method. Post-experimental video and photo analysis of a number of subjects confirm this finding. The vast majority of users held the hand wearing the data glove unnaturally still, with their hand and/or arm straight out roughly aligned to the horizontal plane, in an unrelaxed and "robot-like" manner. Figure 10.10 depicts some of the unexpected user behaviors observed during interaction. This behavior will indeed cause a much higher number of activations to occur with the relative method used, as the user's head moves with the track, while the hand is held and maintained in a static position. This may be because of the novelty of the device, which made users use it in a manner they considered appropriate yet still unnatural. For the absolute method, this behavior makes for an ideal performance as the user's hand is always kept aligned with the real world, even though this would neither be a natural movement pattern for long term use nor can it be considered comfortable for the user.

This finding is supported by the analysis of the objective data collected, as well as through video and photos captured during the subjects' performance of the experiment. In the qualitative data, subjects consistently ranked absolute as being better than relative in terms of overall liking and ease of use. On the question whether the data glove was difficult or easy to use, the users did however find it easy or very easy to use on average, indicating that they did not consider their "unnatural" way of interacting with it to cause any problems.

Despite this, they still indicated a strong dislike for the relative method, probably because they did not use the interaction device as it was designed to be used and therefore found it more troublesome to use. Because they could not see the actual difference between the algorithms being used, their unfamiliarity with the relative method was what caused this negative feeling towards it. For interaction design this means that interaction methods not being transparent for the user in regard to its underlying working approach might have a disadvantage compared to very simple but comprehensible algorithms because users may have prejudices.

Besides all knowledge about natural body movement, users may behave entirely differently than anticipated, when a new and unfamiliar kind of interaction technique is presented to them. This is also the probable cause to why our user study failed to reveal the differences between using an absolute and relative frame of reference. However, a long term study where users can accommodate better to the novel interaction technique might be more suitable.

10.9   Conclusion

This chapter presented the results of a final empirical HotWire study investigating the effect of visual feedback and body postures on gesture interaction techniques in a dual-task setup. Visual feedback in a head-mounted display was found to impair user performance. The reason was that the presence of visual feedback caused the user's attention to be caught in a closed feedback loop.

Even though continuous feedback was not a prerequisite for successfully carrying out the gesture interaction, users were unable to ignore it and did not remain focused on the primary task. The recommendation of this study is to use visual feedback with care and to avoid continuous and closed feedback loops in this kind of setting. Instead, alternative means for feedback should be investigated further, for example, tactile feedback.

Furthermore, employing an alternative gesture recognition method using a body-centric frame of reference instead of a conventional world-centric one to improve usability, was shown to have a negative impact both on the performance and subjective perception of users. The primary reason for this was not technical in nature, but rather that users behaved both unpredictable and unnatural when using a novel interaction device which they may not have had experience with beforehand.

Results suggest that short term user studies may not accurately reflect long term natural usage of gesture interaction. For interaction designers this means to consider that users may require a long time before a natural usage pattern is developed. It is important to note that in short term user studies a user's opinion on ease of use and general liking is difficult to assess. Users apparently tend to adapt themselves more to a new technology than they consider that the new technology has been designed to be easily usable for them without requiring their unnatural adaptation.

Part IV

Development of Wearable User Interface

Chapter 11

The Wearable User Interface Toolkit

Chapter 6 proposed a process-driven approach to develop wearable user interfaces. An evaluation method and a special software tool where identified as the central elements to facilitate the evaluation and implementation of a wearable computing application. The last four chapters took up the proposed evaluation method and evaluated interface components as well as examining interaction issues. This chapter introduces a prototypical implementation of the envisioned software tool for wearable user interface development. It can take our findings and make them available for reuse in many different wearable computing applications. The software architecture of the toolkit is presented along with its central technical aspects, and we will look at how the toolkit can be used by developers in the application development process.

11.1 Basic Requirements

The ability to ease user interface development for wearable computing applications during an application development process is obviously the overall requirement of the WUI-Toolkit. Following, the most important requirements of the toolkit are discussed. A more detailed discussion of the requirements of a WUI-Toolkit is given in [Wit05].

- **Device independent interface specifications**
  Usually, wearable systems have no fixed or default I/O device configuration like desktop computers, where the presence of display, keyboard, and mouse can always be assumed. Instead, wearable applications can make use of, for example, gesture devices or chording keyboards and an HMD instead of an audio headset (cf. sections 4.2 and 4.3). Therefore, a user interface for a wearable computing system should be preferably specified rather independently of any specific I/O devices or modalities than dependent on a specific I/O configuration.

- **Support for context-aware interfaces**

  One advantage of wearable computing is the use of sensors to detect environmental conditions or user activities and the ability to react accordingly. Research already showed how sensors are successfully applied to recognize a wide range of contexts. Moreover, there are software packages available that allow constructing context-aware applications (cf. section 5.3). Once the user interface of an application is, however, specified in a device-independent way, context-related adaptation of the interface has to happen within the device-specific part of the toolkit, based on available context information. Context detection itself is therefore not part of the toolkit, but a connector to use other context detection software available.

- **Support for automatic interface adaptation**

  Context awareness of user interfaces is often achieved by attaching available context information to the application in a "hard-wired" manner. Unfortunately, in wearable computing, there are a lot of dynamic contexts or environmental conditions that can adversely affect the usability of a user interface. Some of these factors can be adjusted automatically. For example, by permanently changing color contrast according to changing environmental illumination (cf. section 3.2.3). A WUI-Toolkit should feature some global knowledge repository about general properties that may affect perception of interfaces. Simple examples include font size or colors. By using this knowledge, the toolkit should be able to automatically reconfigure or adapt interfaces.

Obviously, special interface components including appropriate interaction concepts are needed by the toolkit during rendering. They are made available by the corresponding *interface component process*, presented in chapter 6 through evaluations as those discussed in the previous three chapters.

11.2 Intended Use of the Toolkit

The basic idea of the toolkit is to support the user interface development process of wearable applications, by facilitating the design and implementation of the actual user interface needed. While doing so, it addresses two user groups in a slightly different way.

1. *Researchers* can use the toolkit to rapidly develop interface prototypes needed during user studies (cf. e.g. [WK07]). It provides the opportunity to immediately concentrate on the design, implementation, and testing of new interface components, instead of dealing with underlying software infrastructures each time, including I/O

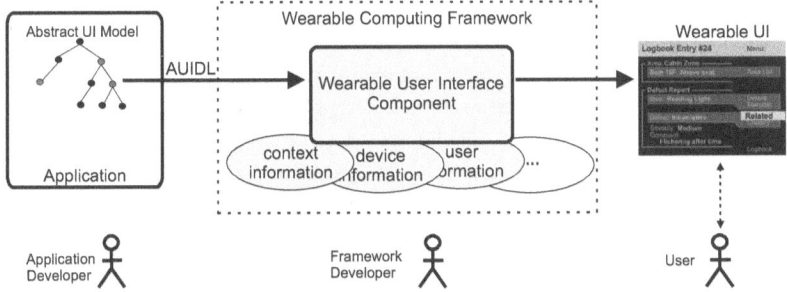

Figure 11.1: Actors using the WUI-Toolkit.

device management, event queuing, access to low-level context sources, or rendering. The toolkit provides a plug-in infrastructure to add new interface components for rapid prototyping of test applications.

2. Besides a research oriented use of the toolkit, *application developers* are the major group of users. Here, the toolkit provides the underlying infrastructure for user interface development, but additionally offers a mechanism to build envisioned interfaces, while paying minimal attention to wearable HCI knowledge. For this, the toolkit offers a model-driven approach that allows the specification of interfaces with a limited number of high level expressions. These expressions do not require developers to consider rendering or interaction aspects. Instead, an envisioned interface is specified on an abstract level by defining needed inputs from the user, and provided output to the user.

Development Process

Independent of the particular interests, the toolkit's intended usage is organized in a process chain. Figure 11.1 shows the *separation of concerns* approach taken by the toolkit. To generate a user interface, the toolkit requires an abstract model specification of the envisioned interface that models its capabilities. To accomplish this, application developers do not pay attention to specific interaction devices or graphical representations of interface components. To generate a user interface that reflects the properties of the abstract model, the model is evaluated *at runtime*. Hence, the generation of user interfaces is not static but dynamic. Because the evaluation of the abstract model is done at runtime, the system state, including additional information such as available I/O capabilities, can be taken into account. Although this offers a wide range of possibilities in reconfiguring the system according to the actual context of use, it comes at the price of taking full control of the final user interface away from the application developer. Moreover, it leaves the burden to ensure flexibility and runtime configuration to *framework developers*. This is inherently different to classical user interface development, were developers usually have to implement an interface with special interface artifacts of an interface library.

Framework developers and researchers participating in the *interface component process* work closely together to ensure an appropriate representation of a given abstract model. The challenge is to map parts of the abstract model to a set of available interface components. Because this requires framework developers to understand HCI and wearable computing challenges, the toolkit itself can be seen as a kind of knowledge repository. It encodes knowledge about how user interfaces should be designed for wearable computers, when certain capabilities are needed.

To let a *user* control a generated user interface of the toolkit, two basic steps are needed:

1. Specification of an abstract model of the user interface that is independent of any specific I/O device, interaction style, or modality to be used.

2. Configuration of the toolkit's underlying software core infrastructure for device management, etc. This step is not mandatory. It is only required, if the default configuration does not meet the specific requirements of an application.

The remainder of this chapter will elaborate more on the specification of the abstract model and the rendering process of the prototypical implementation.

11.3 Overview of the Software Architecture

The overall design of the WUI-Toolkit follows an event-driven approach and makes frequent use of the observer design pattern (sometimes also called publisher/subscriber design pattern) [GHJV95]. Figure 11.2 shows the basic components of the architecture, their interfaces to other systems, and the possible separation of components into different runtime environments. Only shaded components in figure 11.2 belong to the actual core components of the WUI-Toolkit.

The envisioned user interface for a wearable computing application is specified by the application developer through the *Abstract UI API*. While doing so, an abstract model of the interface is formed that holds its properties and capabilities. The abstract model can be serialized into another representation, the so-called *Abstract User Interface Description Language* (AUIDL), for remote communication and internal management purposes.

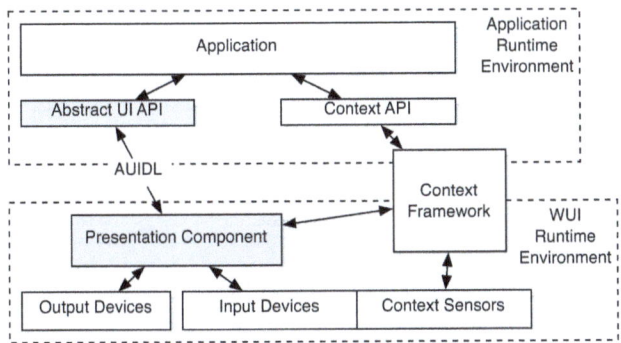

Figure 11.2: Basic software architecture of the WUI-Toolkit including interfaces to other systems.

The *Presentation Component* receives information about the envisioned user interface to be rendered in form of AUIDL. Its purpose is to mediate between the application and the user through a generated user interface. By interpreting the abstract user interface model and mapping abstract entities to suitable interface components, the presentation component delivers the actual user interface to the user. Additionally, it receives input from the user. If user input is received by the presentation component through input devices relevant for the application, for example, the execution of a database query that changes the application's model, user input is forwarded to notify the application.

If there are multiple options during the mapping of abstract entities to specific interface components, the presentation component has to decide which components and devices to use. For example, a text string can be rendered as written text on a display device, or as speech output on an audio output device. To decide this, rules and constraints are used that are encoded as expert knowledge into the presentation component. The user's context may also be considered during the decision process. For instance, light conditions of the environment are used to determine colors and font sizes for text rendering on display devices.

While the presentation component is running, the context of the user may change. To receive notification when such changes occur, an interface to a *context framework* is needed that informs, whenever sufficiently large context changes happen. Then, the decision process may be restarted, which might change the configuration of already instantiated interface components, but may also switch I/O from one device to another.

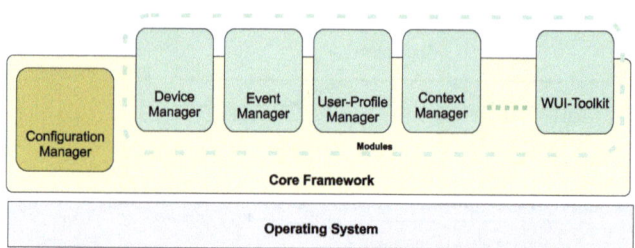

Figure 11.3: Services provided by the Core Framework.

For low-level aspects such as communication with I/O devices, event queuing, or configuration management of the toolkit, a *Core Framework* is used that provides a low-level abstraction layer.

11.4 Core Framework

Nowadays, desktop and mobile user interface development is usually done by utilizing special GUI libraries that provide standardized solutions for common problems and reoccurring procedures. In most situations, developers do not have to deal with low-level software aspects such as device driver management or event dispatching. This is all done by the libraries used for interface implementation. When it comes to interface development for wearable systems, though, the provided low-level services of these libraries are often not sufficient [Wit07a]. This is because provided functionalities have been selected and designed for desktop or mobile systems. For example, standard libraries for WIMP interface design have only a notion of a single focus and do not allow the user to simultaneously interact with two mouse devices per se. For desktop systems, where only a mouse and a keyboard are the default input devices, this is sufficient. In wearable computing it can, however, limit interaction design to direct manipulation interfaces.

The core framework of the WUI-Toolkit, therefore, provides a set of services that were developed independently of any interaction style to provide a flexible use of I/O devices and event dispatching services. Figure 11.3 shows the five most important service modules available in the core framework. Note, the WUI-Toolkit itself is also implemented as a module, but the configuration management is not.

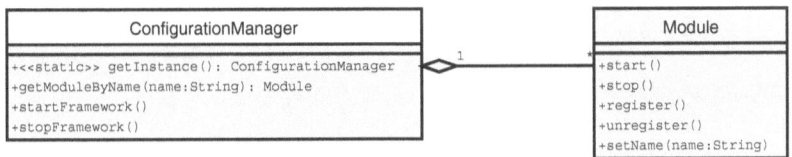

ConfigurationManager
+<<static>> getInstance(): ConfigurationManager
+getModuleByName(name:String): Module
+startFramework()
+stopFramework()

Module
+start()
+stop()
+register()
+unregister()
+setName(name:String)

Figure 11.4: UML diagram of the ConfigurationManager and its associated Modules.

11.4.1 Configuration and Bootstrap Process

Because the WUI-Toolkit was implemented as a module of the core framework, the initial bootstrap process and configuration of core modules is coordinated within the core framework. In particular, the ConfigurationManager is responsible for managing this process. Unlike all other managers in the core framework, the ConfigurationManager is not designed as a module (cf. figure 11.3) but as a broker, being able to coordinate the proper instantiation of modules with all their dependencies. To solve this classical form of configuration management, *Inversion of Control* is frequently used and specifically *Dependency Injection* [Fow03]. With the so-called "Hollywood Principle" ("don't call us, we call you"), framework code invokes application code and coordinates the overall workflow of a system, rather then having application code invoking particular framework code [JHA+05]. The *Spring Framework* [Spr06] is a lightweight framework that offers a variety of services to facilitate framework development needed by the WUI-Toolkit. It is based on dependency injection and offers an XML-based specification of framework configurations. The Spring framework's configuration functionality is used by the ConfigurationManager to provide a standardized mechanism for the specification of a particular system configuration based on XML. This offers an easy reconfiguration of the system without the need of recompiling source code in case of configuration changes, which may frequently occur in the wearable computing case.

```
public static void main(String args[] ) {
...
   // start the core framework
   ConfigurationManager cm = ConfigurationManager.getInstance();

   cm.startFramework();

   // get the toolkit instance (loaded module) from the core framework
   WUIToolkit wui_toolkit = (WUIToolkit) cm.getModuleByName(
                            "WUIToolkit" );

   if ( wui_toolkit != null ) {

      // do something with the toolkit ...

   }
}
```

Listing 11.1: Core framework startup with accessing the WUI-Toolkit module.

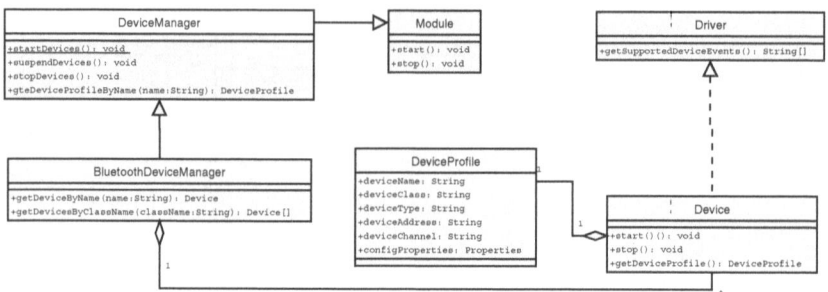

Figure 11.5: UML diagram of the DeviceManager and its associated Modules.

As indicated in figure 11.4, the ConfigurationManager instantiates and manages different Modules. The number of modules to be loaded as well as existing dependencies between modules are specified in a central XML configuration file (cf. appendix B.3). To parse the XML file and to instantiate corresponding module objects the Spring framework is used. Once the core framework has been successfully started using the startFramework method, all modules are available for service. Listing 11.1 shows code that starts the core framework and accesses the instance of the WUI-Toolkit.

11.4.2   Management of I/O Devices

The I/O device management service controls all I/O devices accessible by the wearable computer system, i.e. devices that are connected to the wearable computer. Although sensors are input devices as well, the DeviceManager considers interaction devices only. Devices that can be treated as a sensor's subsystem are typically managed by a context system, which needs to directly communicate with the devices to acquire latest sensor values [ST06].

The core framework currently features a single instance for devices management, the BluetoothDeviceManager, that provides access to Bluetooth devices through the JSR82 Java Bluetooth API[1]. Additionally, the device manager can handle devices that are typically managed by the operating system, for example, devices such as a graphics card or the keyboard (cf. figure 11.5). A number of device drivers, important for basic interaction, are available so far:

---

[1]http://jcp.org/aboutJava/communityprocess/review/jsr082/index.html

- **Gesture Input**

  Interaction using hand gestures is available via a data glove device. The available driver supports data gloves that are based on the SCIPIO [WLKK06] hardware and feature a 3D acceleration sensor, or a tilt sensor. The SCIPIO hardware itself offers a multichannel reusable sensor board that can be accessed via Bluetooth. The implemented gesture interaction used in chapters 8 and 10 was using this driver.

- **Speech Input**

  Drivers for voice based interaction are currently available for two different speech recognition engines that both can run on a mobile system with limited computing power. Speech interaction drivers for the Multitel[2] and Vocon[3] systems are available. The latter was used in chapter 9. The Multitel driver was used for an application that will be presented in section 12.3.

- **Text Input**

  Applications often rely on some kind of text input. A driver that abstracts all operating system managed keyboard devices is available. To do this, the driver accesses the event queue of the OS as well as needed native device drivers. It was used in [NSK+06] to implement text input with a wireless half-size QWERTY keyboard and will be discussed in section 12.1.

- **Pointing**

  Although pointer based interaction is inappropriate for most wearable computing applications, a device driver is available that implements it. However, it's purpose is for testing in the implementation phase only. With a pointer, application developers can easily test the basic functionalities of there visual applications by using the pointing device (mouse) attached by default to the desktop system they are typically developing applications on.

Similar to the ConfigurationManager, the BluetoothDeviceManager also utilizes the Spring configuration mechanism to load the systems I/O device configuration specified in a dedicated XML file (cf. appendix B.3). Although the central device configuration file describes a static configuration of I/O devices for a wearable computer system, it rather specifies a set of *possible* I/O devices that can be used by an application, instead of *requiring* specified devices to be present and accessible all the time. For instance, an I/O device configuration may contain a speech input device and a gesture input device. This does not automatically imply that either one or the other can be used by the application,

---

[2]http://www.multitel.be

[3]http://www.nuance.com/vocon

```
<bean id="device15" class="org.tzi.device.DeviceProfile"/>
    <property name="deviceName" value="Wireless Data-Glove"/>
    <property name="driverClass" value="org.tzi.device.service.DataGloveDriver"/>
    <property name="deviceType" value="Bluetooth"/>
    <property name="deviceAddress" value="000B531337DD"/>
    <property name="deviceChannel" value="1"/>
    <property name="configurationProperties">
        <props>
                <!-- no additional properties needed for this device -->
        </props>
    </property>
</bean>
```

Figure 11.6: Device profile of a data glove input device specified in XML.

neither does it specify that both can be used as substitutes for the others. The decision
which device to use in an application is context dependent. The decision is made by the
presentation component that is responsible for generating an appropriated interface based
on the abstract model and available context information.

Device Profiles

Figure 11.5 also illustrates that I/O devices managed by the BluetoothDeviceManager
have a DeviceProfile containing a Meta description of the actual device. The profile is a
set of identical properties for all devices such as a device name, a driver location, or a
device address. Because device configurations can become quite complex for some devices,
device profiles provide the option to store arbitrary additional properties (cf. figure 11.6
or appendix B.3).

The Driver interfaces, implemented by each Device, require the specification of a number of supported events, the device is able to provide (getSupportedDeviceEvents). Supported event types in conjunction with an event hierarchy are used by the toolkit to
determine, which set of I/O devices to use for a wearable user interface. Each device
profile is part of a global XML configuration file accessed by the device manager. An
example for a data glove device connected over Bluetooth is given in figure 11.6.

11.4.3 Event Queuing and Event Dispatching

The software architecture of the WUI-Toolkit including all subcomponents is highly event-
driven. The DeviceEventManager implements a central event queuing and dispatching infrastructure for low-level device events. It is similar to the event queue of an operating
system where all device events are posted and can be consumed by interested entities. Although Java in principle already features an API to access an underlying operating system
event queue, the provided interface is designed for applications using direct manipulation

interfaces built with AWT, Swing, or similar libraries. To overcome this limitation for the
scope of wearable user interfaces with arbitrary interaction paradigms, the existing Java
event infrastructure was extended. The DeviceEventManager provides an infrastructure
that is able to handle DeviceEvents that do not inherit from AWTEvent of the Java API.

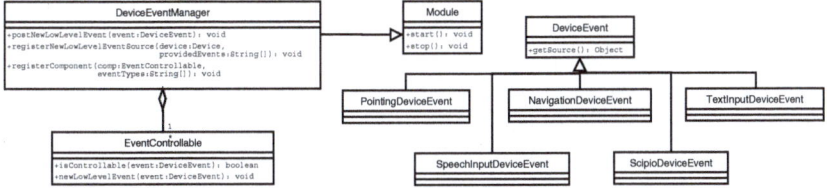

Figure 11.7: UML diagram of the DeviceEventManger including DeviceEvent hierarchy.

The DeviceEventManager is a module of the core framework. It uses an observer design
pattern to notify listeners about newly posted device events. Figure 11.7 shows the overall
design of the DeviceEventManager and its associated components. Listeners that want to
be notified on new events have to implement the EventControllable interface. Additionally,
a component that wants to be notified on device events has to initially register itself with
the DeviceEventManager with registerComponent. While doing this, a list of device events
can be declared to indicate classes of device events the component is interested in. Unlike
standard GUI programming, the declaration of the event class does not directly target a
certain device, but will notify the component on all available events of that class. The
current implementation of the core framework is aware of four device event classes that
directly correspond to the available device drivers discussed above.

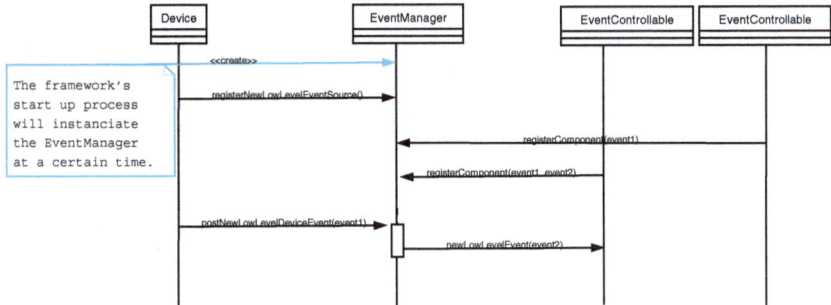

Figure 11.8: Exemplary sequence of event source registration, event posting, and event
forwarding.

Figure 11.8 illustrates the general life cycle sequence of the DeviceEventManger including an example of how events are dispatched by Devices and received by system components that implement the EventControllable interface. The EventManager is instantiated during the framework's startup sequence coordinated by the ConfigurationManager. Once the framework is initialized, Devices register themselves as event sources for a set of DeviceEvents they provide. In parallel, EventControllable objects can register themselves as listeners for a set of DeviceEvents as well. A mapping between event listeners and event providers is established once a corresponding pair of an event publisher and subscriber for a certain event class is present in the wearable system. This implies that mappings are also released at runtime, if devices disappear from the wearable system infrastructure and unregister themselves. With its flexible and abstract design it also provides the option to implement multi-modal interaction like the combination of gestures and spoken commands to operate an interface (cf. section 12.3).

11.4.4   Additional Service Modules

Besides the above mentioned three core modules that all provide very low-level services, figure 11.3 depicted five modules in total. Because their complexity is comparatively simple to the other modules, a detailed discussion including their design is omitted here. A short overview is given instead:

The *User Profile Manager* offers basic services for handling different user profiles by an application. Applications can store and retrieve arbitrary user properties of interest during the entire lifetime of an application. Each user profile is implemented as a container and has a textual XML representation that warrants easy editing and modification (cf. appendix B.3.3). User profiles can be used, for example, during the rendering process of an interface to determine the users visual acuity in order to adjust screen fonts accordingly (cf. section 11.7).

The *Context Manager* serves as an interface to access third party context recognition systems and wraps their functionalities. The current implementation provides interfaces to the context system developed in the wearIT@work project [ST06]. It is accessed, for example, by application developers to enrich the abstract model of the user interface with dynamic context information (cf. section 11.5.3) or directly during the rendering or adaptation phase by the toolkit (cf. section 11.7).

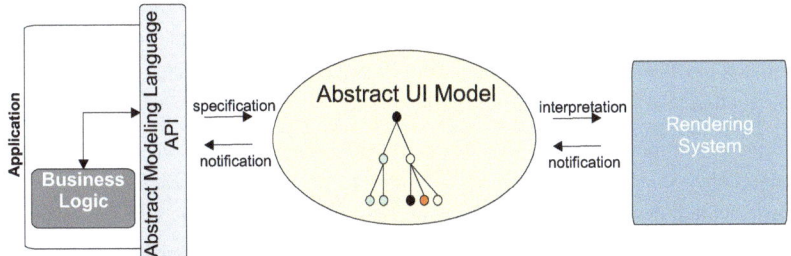

Figure 11.9: Communication flow between an application and rendering system through the AbstractUIModel.

11.5 Abstract User Interface Description Layer

Unlike common interface development libraries that describe the semantically and, in particular, the syntactical structure of a user interface, the abstract user interface description layer provides an abstract but semantic specification of an interface without making specific rendering assumptions or specifications.

The central element of the description layer is the AbstractUIModel that holds a model of the user interface specified with the abstract modeling language API. Similar to other abstract user interface specification approaches, like Concurrent Task Trees (CTTs) [Pat99], the abstract model is encoded in a hierarchical tree structure. Here, the root element of the tree specifies the first "screen" of the interface (cf. section 5.2.2).

The AbstactUIModel provides an application interface to access and interpret its semantical structure including a communication channel. Figure 11.9 illustrates the role of the AbstractUIModel in the communication between an application and a rendering system. The WUI-Toolkit module, as an instance of a rendering system, obviously interprets the model for rendering purposes and may post notifications to trigger data manipulations of the application. With the abstract modeling language API, application developers create an AbstractUIModel of the user interface and use communication channels to connect the application's business logic with the abstract model.

11.5.1 Abstract Modeling Language

The AbstractUIModel is independent of any particular I/O device or interaction style and contains only elements that are needed to interpret semantic relations within an envisioned interface. For instance, there is actually no way to declare that a certain set of interface components always has to be presented to the user on a single screen. Instead, it is possible to model a set of elements semantically belonging together. The actual implementation, however, is left to the rendering system, i.e. the WUI-Toolkit module. Consequently, the number of elements available to represent or describe information to be presented, is more reduced than in common interface libraries.

To ease the specification of the AbstractUIModel, the abstract modeling language API supports the declaration of an envisioned interface in a dialog or task based style. This is, even though developers actually have no control of the rendering, the API is designed so that developers can think in hierarchies of steps in sequential order, where each step represents a single "screen" presented to the user [WNK07]. This is similar to programming practice of standard GUIs, where different "screens" will usually be encapsulated in separate classes that are recursively linked together to a tree structure with its root in a main window class.

The current implementation of the abstract user interface modeling language supports a total of seven elements, five basic elements to specify static I/O dialogs and two further elements offering asynchronous communication for context-aware behaviors. Since the data of an application is usually not static and known a priori, the actual instantiation of elements in the AbstractUIModel is done on demand, i.e. the AbstractUIModel itself is responsible for the instantiation process. This allows for implementing performance optimizations sometimes crucial in wearable computing, such as caching of objects. Another aspect that drove the design decision was the requirement to support distributed wearable computing applications, where the actual rendering and the application may run on different systems [Wit05].

Following, the available elements to specify an interface are introduced. A specification of the language with Backus-Naur formalism (BNF) is given in appendix B.2.1.

Information

An Information represents an atomic piece of information presented to the user. In most cases it contains text data, but may also contain multimedia content such as an image, a sound, a video, or a combination of alternate contents. With the latter mechanism, the toolkit can offer different representations of the same piece of information appropriate in a particular situation. To annotate information items further, special properties can be set to indicate, for example, the priority or importance an information item has in a certain context. The rendering system can then select an appropriate rendering accordingly.

Group

A Group is derived from an Information. It is used to structure semantically related information. With its abstract design, it can group arbitrary abstract elements, in particular other Groups. For example, each dialog presented to the user might be on the top level a group indicating that a set of elements belong to each other.

Selection List

A SelectionList is a specialization of a Group. It can be composed of a set of Information elements and a set of Triggers which apply a function to an item in the list.

Explicit Trigger

An ExplicitTrigger represents an action of the user. To activate the trigger, explicit interaction with the user interface is requested from the user. An example would be an action that involves a change in the applications data. For instance, a "save changes" action would be specified using an ExplicitTrigger.

Explicit Text Input

In contrast to an ExplicitTrigger that offers Boolean results, an ExplicitTextInput can be used to gather text input from the user. The use of an ExplicitTextInput is restricted to real text input entered by the user. The actual input device that gathers the input can be any device that provides a transformation of input to a text representation. Devices such as speech recognizers, keyboards, or sign language recognizers are all examples for suitable devices.

11.5.2 Dynamic Changes and Asynchronous Communication

All elements introduced so far can be used to specify a range of standard interfaces [WNK07]. However, neither of those can handle complex processing or a significant computation load that would not delay feedback, nor can they notify the user or the rendering system about events occurred asynchronously in the background of a running business logic. Both aspects are crucial though. The first calls for a concept similar to threads that allows the application to continue without freezing. Since application and rendering system communicate only through the AbstractUIModel and may be hosted on different systems, simple threads are not possible.

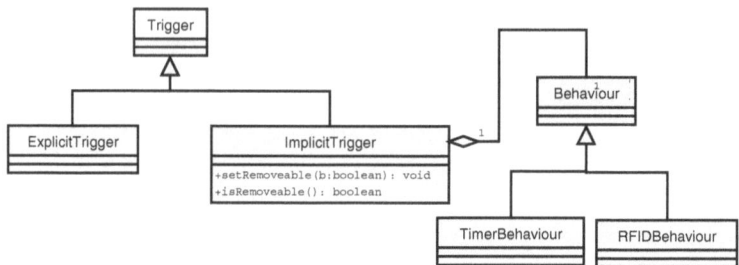

Figure 11.10: UML showing the design of the ImplicitTrigger.

Process

The abstract Process element is designed for this purpose. It provides a structure to encapsulate complex and time consuming code execution sequences. If a Process is used, its contained code will be executed, once activated, in a separate thread on the system running the application. Entities interpreting or querying the AbstractUIModel will be informed about the progress of a running process. With this, the rendering system can provide needed user feedback if operations executed last for a longer period. Additionally, knowing ahead of rendering of a potentially time consuming and computationally intensive step can be used by the toolkit to change rendering outcomes.

Implicit Trigger

In wearable computing, the availability of context information is one of the major advantages. Implicit interaction, is what may change the user interface, but is not explicitly triggered by the user (cf. section 4.3.1). To make use of it, asynchronous communication is essential. Context systems usually acquire and infer sensor information continuously. Thus, context changes are likely to occur asynchronously to the execution of a program that makes use of them and call for a notification mechanism similar to a publisher/subscriber design pattern.

An ImplicitTrigger element is available to handle implicit interaction in the abstract model. It can be activated either indirectly by the user or independently of the user, based on its specific behavior. The behavior of a trigger, i.e. what has to happen to activate the trigger, is encapsulated in a Behavior object (cf. figure 11.10). To implement context-awareness of an envisioned user interface, custom behaviors can be designed. For instance, similar to the behavior of the wearable application reported in [MKS+07], a recognized user activity during an assembly task may activate an ImplicitTrigger that causes the user interface to automatically proceed to the next assembly step. Here, a user is not requested to explicitly interact with the application in order to reach the next assembly step.

There are some "default" behaviors available including a TimerBehavior that can be configured to activate a trigger once a given time period has elapsed or an RFIDBehavior that allows activating a trigger once a corresponding RFID tag was scanned (cf. listing 11.2).

Because there are situations in which context-awareness is wanted to be ubiquitous over the entire life cycle of the running application and other situations in which this is not wanted at all, each ImplicitTrigger features the possibility to define an *operating range*. To set this range the setRemoveable method is used (cf. figure 11.10). By setting it to *local*, the trigger and its behavior will only be active once its surrounding elements are active, i.e. currently rendered on a device. Otherwise the operating range is set to *global*, which makes the behavior active also when the ImplicitTrigger is not rendered. To offer, for instance, the possibility for users to always use an RFID reader to execute specific actions, the RFIDBehavior can be used with setting the operating range of a corresponding trigger to *global*. Due to the hierarchical structure of the AbstractUIModel, the operating range of the global case can vary. For a tree hierarchy of height n and a trigger located at height $m, m \geq n$, the operating range is $m - n$. That is, it is active from level m downward in that branch. Accordingly, a behavior active throughout the entire application has to be placed in the root $(m = 0)$ of the model.

```
package org.tzi.abstractui;

import java.io.Serializable;

import org.tzi.abstractui.core.InformationImpl;
import org.tzi.device.event.*;
import org.tzi.vui.configuration.WUIConfigurationManager;
import org.tzi.vui.rendering.controller.Behaviour;

/**
 * Represents a scanned RFID tag. When a certain tag was
 * scanned the correspondig ImplicitTrigger will be activated.
 */
public class RFIDBehaviour extends Behaviour implements EventControllable {

    // what kind of context events are we interested in?
    private final static String[] SUPPORTED_EVENTS = { RFIDTagEvent.RFID_TAG_EVENT };

    private String mRfid = null;

    public void init() {
        // register at EventManager for RFID events
        WUIConfigurationManager.getEventManager().registerComponent(this, SUPPORTED_EVENTS);
    }

    // Set tag id that should be reacted upon
    public void setRfidTag(String tagid )
    {
        mRfid = tagid;
    }

    /****EventControllable interface implementation****/
```

```
public boolean isControllable(DeviceEvent event) {
   // ...
}

public void newLowLevelEvent(DeviceEvent event) {
   if (event instanceof RFIDTagEvent) {
      RFIDTagEvent rfidEvent = (RFIDTagEvent) event;

      // check scaned tag and finally activate
      // corresponding trigger

      activateTrigger();
   }
}
}
```

Listing 11.2: RFIDBehaviour implementation.

11.5.3   A Simple Abstract UI Modeling Example

For a better understanding of how an abstract model of an application may look like, this section illustrates the specification of a small abstract model for a login dialog.

User authentication in applications is usually done with a unique and personal key pair consisting of a user name and a password. Once a valid key pair is entered by the user, access to the application is granted. For the sake of simplicity it is assumed that the corresponding login dialog consists only of the following properties:

- A message requesting the user to enter a user/password key pair for authentication

- An input field to enter the user name as text

- Another input field to enter the user password as text

- A trigger that can be activated by the user once the key pair was entered

To additionally demonstrate the use of sensor based asynchronous context information, a user should also be able to pass the authentication dialog by scanning her personal RFID tag.

Abstract Model Specification of the Authentication Procedure

To specify the abstract model, the available Java API is used. It offers an easy integration of model specification and business logic of an application, because the entire Java API is available. For example, provided authentication data can be verified by dynamically querying a user account database.

Figure 11.11 shows an overview diagram encoding the tree structure of an abstract model that describes a small application requiring authentication. The example consists

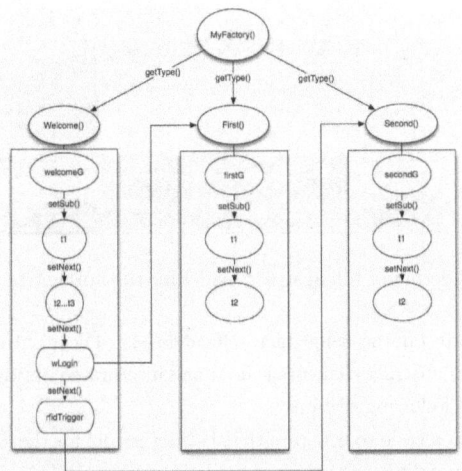

Figure 11.11: Example graph of the abstract model.

of three different dialogs. Based on the kind of authentication mechanism used, it will forward the user to either the *second* or *third* dialog of the application. Once a user decides to use the traditional login mechanism by providing user name and password as text, she will be forwarded to the second dialog after the ExplicitTrigger wLogin was activated (cf. arrow in figure 11.11). Alternatively, a user can scan her personal RFID tag and will be forwarded to the third dialog of the application.

As indicated in figure 11.11, the AbstractUIModel utilizes a Factory design pattern to instantiate a dialog. The MyFactory class manages all references to application dialogs and can be queried for a specific dialog. In particular for processing a model, the toolkit iteratively requests information fragments that contain single elements of the abstract model, until their specific rendering exceeds the capacity of information presentable to the user at a time.

In this example, the MyFactory handles only the three different dialogs mentioned above (Welcome, Second, Third). The elements used to describe the functionality of a dialog (specified by a *Group* element) are depicted inside the rectangle of figure 11.11. To link elements together and to form the hierarchical structure of the model, the methods setSub and setNext are used. Unlike setSub that is used to create a new level in the model hierarchy and declares elements as being sub parts of a particular structure, setNext links elements on the same level, i.e. inside a structure. Thus, setNext is used to sequentially

Figure 11.12: Rendering of the abstract model for the authentication Login dialog.

link different elements on the same hierarchical level. The resulting sequential order (temporal relation) of abstract elements is used and interpreted during the layout process. It is discussed in the following sections.

Listing 11.3 shows a code to generate the abstract model for the discussed authentication dialog. A corresponding user interface rendering for an HMD is shown in figure 11.12. To generate this interface, the DefaultRenderer of the toolkit was used (cf. section 11.6.3). Building the abstract model starts with instantiating abstract elements needed for the dialog (lines 15–36). In lines 30–35 a custom RFIDBehaviour (derived from Behaviour) is instantiated to handle implicit interaction. Users may provide login information with personal RFID tags. Using setTag, specific tags can be set to which RFIDBehaviour will react. After having instantiated needed abstract elements, the actual hierarchy of elements and their relation with each other is defined in lines 38–49. The remaining code glues application logic and the user interface together by implementing callback methods of interactive abstract elements such as triggers and input fields.

```
import org.tzi.abstractui.*;                                                    1
import org.tzi.abstractui.core.*;                                              2
                                                                               3
public class WelcomeScreen implements AbstractUIComponent{                     4
                                                                               5
  private Group welcomeG;                                                      6
  private Group login;                                                         7
  private ExplicitTrigger wLogin;                                             8
  private ExplicitTextInput wInput;                                          9
  private ExplicitTextInput wInput2;                                         10
  private ImplicitTrigger rfidTrigger;                                       11
  private RFIDBehaviour behaviour;                                           12
                                                                               13
  public WelcomeScreen(){                                                    14
  // creating abstract UI elements...                                       15
  Information t1 = new Information(new TextData("By using your username and password"),  16
  this);                                                                      17
                                                                               18
  Information t2 = new Information(new TextData("you can enter the application."),  19
  this);                                                                      20
                                                                               21
  Information t3 = new Information(new TextData("Also you can use your RFID chip."),  22
  this);                                                                      23
                                                                               24
  wInput  = new ExplicitTextInput(new TextData("User "), 35, this);          25
  wInput2 = new ExplicitTextInput(new TextData("Password "), 35, this);      26
                                                                               27
```

```
wLogin = new ExplicitTrigger(new TextData("Login"), this);                      28
                                                                                29
// defining custom behaviour, here, an implicit RFID trigger...                 30
myRFIDbehaviour = new RFIDBehaviour()                                           31
myRFIDbehaviour.setActionTag(("0102E461D4");                                    32
                                                                                33
rfidTrigger = new ImplicitTrigger(this, myRFIDbehaviour);                       34
                                                                                35
login = new Group(new TextData("Login by ID"), this);                          36
                                                                                37
  // linking elements together                                                  38
login.setSub(t1);                                                               39
t1.setNext(t2);                                                                 40
t2.setNext(t3);                                                                 41
t3.setNext(wInput);                                                            42
wInput.setNext(wInput2);                                                        43
wInput2.setNext(wLogin);                                                        44
wLogin.setNext(rfidTrigger);                                                    45
                                                                                46
welcomeG = new Group(new TextData("Login"), this);                             47
welcomeG.setSub(login);                                                         48
}                                                                               49
                                                                                50
// setting root element of the dialog                                           51
public Information getRoot() {                                                   52
  return welcomeG;                                                              53
}                                                                               54
                                                                                55
public Nav trigger(Trigger i) {                                                 56
  if(i==wLogin) {                                                               57
  // verify login data, forward to second dialog ...                            58
  return new NavPath("second", "");                                            59
  } if(i==rfidTrigger){                                                        60
  // verify login data, forward to third dialog ...                            61
  return new NavPath("third", "");                                             62
  }                                                                             63
}                                                                               64
                                                                                65
public void textInput(ExplicitTextInput inputItem, String input) {             66
  // Take and store the text representation of user name and password          67
  // once provided for later verification when wLogin is activated...          68
}                                                                               69
                                                                                70
}                                                                               71
```

Listing 11.3: Abstract model specification of a login dialog using the Java API.

11.6   Interface Rendering

The interpretation of an abstract model, and the rendering of a corresponding user interface is the actual core functionality of the WUI-Toolkit. As already indicated in figure 11.3 the WUI-Toolkit is a module of the core framework and utilizes all other modules available to provide its service. Besides the actual rendering, handled by the Rendering-Manager, there are two other components involved in the rendering process (cf. figure 11.13). The AppletManager serves as a managing component for the so-called *system applets*. A system applet can be any kind of process that informs or observes the user or the environment. System applets can either have a representation to be rendered or not. They are managed in a kind of system tray and provide an extensible plug-in infrastructure for custom functionalities, for example, implemented by application developers. System ap-

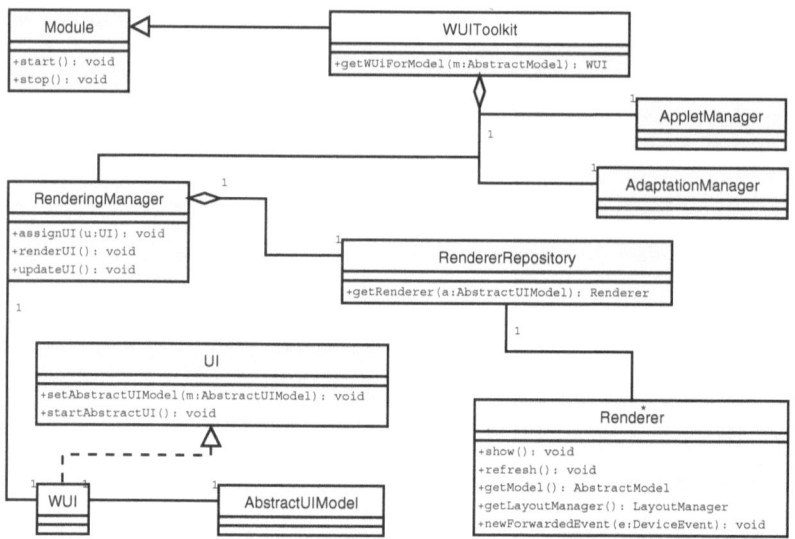

Figure 11.13: Overview of the WUIToolkit module including its main components.

plets are briefly described in section 11.6.3. Unlike the AppletManager that provides an interface to customize the behavior of the WUI-Toolkit, the AdaptationManager handles the adaptation procedure of generated user interfaces and queries context sources to adapt the interface at runtime. This is described in section 11.7.

11.6.1 Different Rendering Styles

Instead of defining the same fixed rendering style for all abstract models, the toolkit separates a particular rendering style in a Renderer. Renderers are stored in a repository that can be queried for a suitable renderer based on the abstract model that encodes the mayor constraints of the envisioned interface. With this, different renderings of the same abstract model are possible. Usually, such mechanisms are considered to implement output device adaptation of an adaptive or adaptable user interfaces (cf. e.g. [SRC01]). To implement a custom renderer that interprets and renders an abstract model in a certain way, it has to be derived from the abstract Renderer class.

Although the main focus of the toolkit is on wearable user interfaces, there may arise application requirements that call for a seamless change between the mobile and the wearable computing paradigm. For instance, Nicolai et al. [NSKW05] report on a case

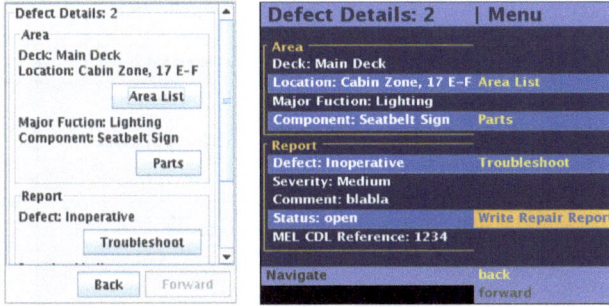

(a) Handheld rendering   (b) Wearable rendering

Figure 11.14: Different interface renderings for the same abstract model.

study where aircraft technicians wanted to seamlessly switch from a wearable interaction mode using an HMD to a handheld mode using a stylus at runtime without restarting the application. For these purposes, the toolkit can be reconfigured (on- or offline) to use different renderers depending on the I/O used. To demonstrate this, a HandheldRenderer, utilizing the Java Swing API to map elements of the abstract model to Swing widgets, was implemented for handheld devices. Figure 11.14(a) shows an example rendering of an abstract model with the HandheldRenderer. The same abstract model was used to render the interface depicted in figure 11.14(b) with the DefaultRenderer that is tailored to render interfaces for monocular HMDs.

Even though the currently available HandheldRenderer is sufficient to produce a plain user interface needed in simpler applications, the rendering of complex interfaces, that make use of a wide range and combination of sophisticated widgets, is difficult to achieve without considerable effort. Work from Nichols et al. [Nic06] on high-quality interface generation for mobile devices has, however, shown that it is generally possible to achieve this.

11.6.2   User Interaction

Rendering typically involves only the presentation of information on an output device. To generate a complete user interface, however, the possibility for the user to interact with the system is essential. Due to the model driven approach of the toolkit that gives only few basic constraints on how the actual interface has to be rendered, a resulting representation may contain elements that are not directly mapped onto an element in the abstract model. For instance, if an abstract model specifies a set of information elements

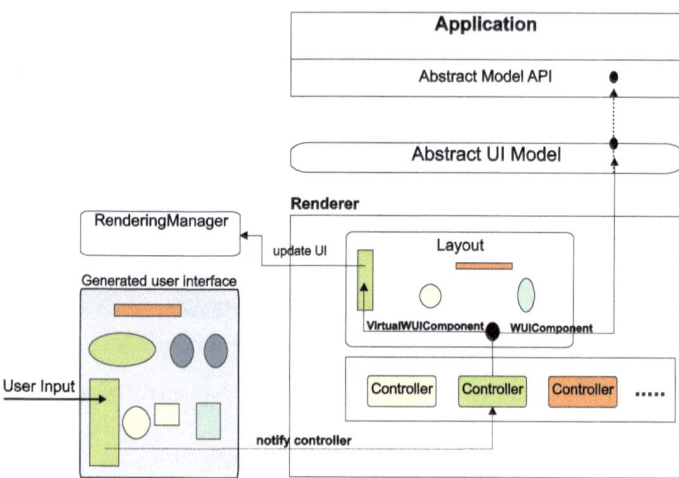

Figure 11.15: Communication flow for user interaction.

to be presented at a certain time, its graphical representation may exceed the available screen estate. To overcome this, the rendering process can split sets of information into different "pages". To allow the user to navigate to the next page, interactive elements need to be added to the representation that have no counterpart in the abstract model. For this, two different components that either directly represent an abstract element in the model (WUIComponent) or do not represent such an element in the model (VirtualWUIComponent) are available.

Interfaces generated by the toolkit support multiple focuses, i.e. different components of the interface can be controlled by different interaction devices. Each focus is maintained by a Controller that manages different interface components. Once an interaction was initiated by the user on an interactive component of the user interface, an event is received by its controller. Because interaction and rendering, which usually also includes layouting, are typically closely related to each other, it is the LayoutManager that hosts different Controllers dependent of the provided interacting style. If user activities on the interface directly belong to an element that has its counterpart in the abstract model (WUIComponent), the user activity is directly forwarded via the abstract model API to the application as an event. If, however, a VirtualWUIComponent is affected by a user activity, the event is internally handled by the Renderer, or more specifically by the LayoutManager (cf. figure 11.15). This may result in arbitrary complex changes on the generated interfaces that the application is not aware of, unless a state change occurred in the abstract model. This implies that, unlike ordinary GUI development, the state of the user interface cannot to be maintained by the application, but by the toolkit. This concept provides the toolkit with the opportunity to equip generated interfaces with many different functionalities developers do not have to take care of. For example, using Virtu-alWUIComponents each application can be enriched with a kind of "history function" that provides the service of back and forth navigation between already passed steps (screens) of an application similar to a web browser.

11.6.3   Default Layout and Interaction Style

The toolkit has been designed to host an arbitrary number of Renderers that provide user interface generation for an application. Apart from the mentioned HandheldRenderer that has mainly been implemented for the purpose of proof of concept, an DefaultRenderer is available that targets the generation of multi-modal user interfaces for wearable computers.

Together with the actual layout and interaction management, interface components are available that can render interfaces based on the expressiveness of the current abstract user interface modeling language. The design of interface components reflects various guidelines that were discussed in the first part of this thesis as well as the results of user experiments conducted by applying the interface component development process discussed in chapter 6, and previously gained experiences from former and current projects such as WINSPECT [BNSS01] and wearIT@work [Wea04].

So far, the primary focus of the designed interface components was set on graphical interfaces that can be used in conjunction with a head-mounted display device. However, because the abstract model may request the rendering of audio information, user interaction design was tailored to render multi-modal interfaces. The combination of gesture and speech interaction is supported by the DefaultRenderer as well as the rendering of text, images, audio, and video.

Interface Design and Layout

The graphical components, generated by the DefaultRenderer, are optimized for the MicroOptical SV-6 monocular "see-around" head-mounted display[4]. With a few changes, the renderer can be adopted to HMDs that have different resolutions, color depths, or are of the "see-through" type. The MicroOptical SV-6 is expected to be worn away from the visual center, i.e. on the right side in front of the right eye or on the left side in

---

[4]see http://www.microopticalcorp.com for further details

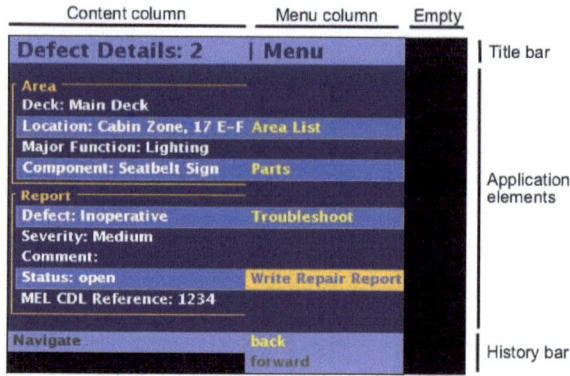

Figure 11.16: Layout used by the DefaultRenderer to align interface elements.

front of the left eye, respectively. This warrants that a user wearing the display can still maintain primary focus on the real world. The particular design and choices made for the DefaultRenderer were influenced by the wearIT@work project [Wea04], which called for graphical user interfaces in industrial applications that can be used with monocular HMDs.

When a monocular display is placed in front of the right eye, then there are areas on the display, that are more in the visual center and others being more in the periphery, where images become blurry (cf. section 3.2.1). Considering such a wearing situation, then, the left part of the screen is more in the visual center than the right part and thus more comfortable and clear to see. Rather than using the entire screen estate for rendering the interface, the overall layout concept adds a spacer on the right margin of the interface (cf. figure 11.16). This spacer causes the whole interface to be perceived as moved more to the left and thus more to the visual center of the user's eye. For left-eye usage, the situation is reversed.

The remaining screen space is used to render the actual interface. The two-column layout follows the same idea as the spacer and is based on findings in [WNK06, RaHPK04, BNSS01]. The important content is placed in the left column, where it is easy to perceive for the users, because the eye can focus objects that fall on the fovea best (cf. section 3.2.2). The standard interaction is reduced to a one-dimensional process, where a menu selection style is applied. The graphical interface reflects this by interactive items in a vertical list in the second column on the right side of the screen. This was done because we considered interaction to be secondary compared to content perception (cf. figure 11.16).

Additionally, the menu is kept as narrow and simple as possible for easy perception in dual-task situations like suggested by Rauch et. al. [RaHPK04].

The content column on the left is arranged vertically. The concept of borders and lines is used to create groups of elements and to visually align content and corresponding actions to each other. For example, the information "Location: Cabin Zone, 17 E-F" is clearly perceived as being connected to the menu action "Area List" by using colored lines (cf. section 3.2.4 for details on methods for graphical arrangement).

Because the DefaultRenderer observes different constraints regarding the available screen type and its screen estate, content is automatically arranged and rendered on multiple pages. For this, it fits blocks belonging together on a separate screen. Virtual-WUIComponents are used to add "paging" actions to the interface.

Besides these content related layout issues, the DefaultRenderer also offers some generic functionalities. For this, a small part at the bottom of the screen is reserved. A history function provides the possibility of a navigation to *next* and *previous* pages similar to a web browser. Because an internal cache is used, even previously entered text or decisions made are kept. Furthermore, the black area depicted in figure 11.16 at the bottom of the screen is used for the *system tray*. Applets that reside in this area can be used to provide the user, for example, with visual feedback on whether speech recognition is active or not (cf. appendix B.1) . The system tray provides a plug-in architecture that offers application developers an open interface to integrate custom applets.

The color design of the interface is inspired by work from Boronowsky et al. [BNSS01], but mainly by user suggestion from wearIT@work end users and the considerations described in [WNK06]. In contrast to desktop screen design, a dark background color is chosen with bright foreground colors by default. Dark colors tend to be perceived as being transparent on an HMD. A bright background might blind the user. Large fonts are chosen for comfortable reading on the small display for users with normal visual acuity (20/20). Independent of the default color setting, colors as well as font and size properties can be automatically adapted to a particular user profile and a certain context of use.

Interaction Style

Since menu selection is the preferred interaction style of the DefaultRenderer, all input devices that deliver interaction information in form of NavigationDeviceEvents are supported by the DefaultRenderer. The information that can be retrieved from a NavigationDeviceEvent contains three different navigation types that are sufficient for navigation in a menu: *Cursor up*, *cursor down*, and *select item*.

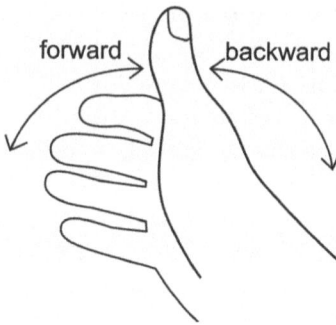

Figure 11.17: Intuitive and low visual attention requiring rotation gesture used for menu navigation.

Compared to direct manipulation techniques, gestures require comparatively lower visual attention due to kinesthetic feedback while gesturing (cf. chapter 10). If gestures are rather simple, they can be performed even without any kind of visual feedback if kinematic feedback is sufficient. Speech interaction, besides being probably the most natural way for interaction for most humans, requires neither visual feedback nor occupies the user's hands (cf. chapter 9). Both techniques can thus be used by the DefaultRenderer to achieve the overall goal of an easy to operate interface that only needs minimal visual attention.

For gesture interaction, three hand gestures that are simple and relatively easy to perform were implemented using the data glove device described in [LWK+06]. Each gesture is mapped onto the event structure needed to control the cursor: To navigate *forward* and *backward* through the menu, hand-based rotation gestures that were found intuitive to use and easy to learn [WJ07, WNK06], were implemented (cf. figure 11.17). Navigating back in the menu is done by rotating the hand to the right and back to the starting position (thumb up). To navigate forward in the menu structure, the starting motion is a left rotation. A third "trigger" gesture was used for *selecting* items. It was implemented by touching the middle finger with the thumb.

Speech interaction is supported in two slightly different ways. Firstly, the obvious approach of mapping speech commands such as "up", "down", and "select" to corresponding properties of a NavigationDeviceEvent object to manipulate the cursor position was implemented. This method is completely transparent for the DefaultRenderer that does not care about the actual source of an event, i.e. whether it may be originated by a gesture device, a joystick, a speech input device, or any other wearable computing input device. The second method supports direct speech navigation for precise and quick navigation. Here, users can say the text that is displayed in the menu list to directly jump to the corresponding point in the menu and to trigger it. This functionality is, however, not possible to build with a NavigationDeviceEvent, because a speech device driver has no information about the current position of the cursor in the menu which would be needed to translate a speech command to a sequence of NavigationDeviceEvents to stepwise move the cursor and to finally send an event with the *select item* property set. Therefore, the DefaultRenderer supports special SpeechInputDeviceEvents that offer the possibility to hand over a recognized string to the DefaultRenderer that in turn can then directly select a menu item by comparing strings. In [WK07] we, however, discovered that non-English native speakers with mid-level education may not be the best kind of users for direct speech command interaction. A conducted user study showed that this is due to pronunciation problems that decreased speech recognition accuracy which in turn decreased user performance and caused frustration.

11.7 Interface Adaptation System

Interfaces to available context frameworks such as the Context-Toolkit (cf. section 5.3) and other systems like those described in [BKLA06, ST06] provide the WUI-Toolkit with access to context information about the users current environment or activities. This information is essential to generate context-aware user interfaces that adapt themselves when the context changes.

Since the implementation of context-aware applications that react, for example, on activities a user performs without requiring explicit interaction, can become complex, the WUI-Toolkit features a component for basic user interface adaptations. The Interface Adaptation System observes available context sources and ensures the compliance of a given set of user interface related constraints. Thus, a basic reusable adaptation capability that lets generated interfaces automatically adapt themselves according to a number of constraints is available.

11.7.1 Interface Constraint Modification

For interface adaptation a rating approach is used that tries to satisfy existing adaptation constraints to an optimal level similar to approaches described in section 5.2. Values of different properties that influence interface generation outcomes of the toolkit are optimized in a continuously ongoing process. Such properties can range from simple color settings to complex layout or interaction settings. For instance, the design of an interface

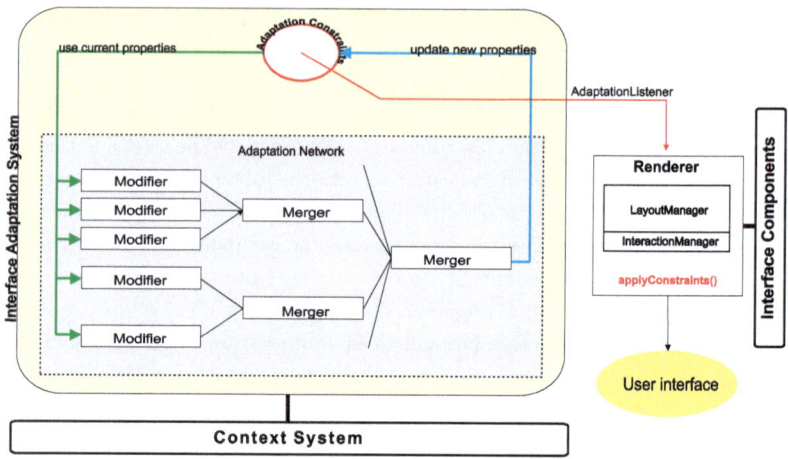

Figure 11.18: The constraint modification process of the interface adaptation system.

layout, encapsulated in a Renderer, is never static, i.e. it does not rely on a static fixed color setting, but on a dynamically changing set of properties assigned to a certain value at runtime. To assign or alter values of user interface related properties, two different constructs are known by the Adaptation System:

1. Modifier

   A modifier is an unary function. It takes a single property as an argument and computes a (new) optimized value based on its internal rules. Additionally, a "subjective" *local confidence value* is computed for the new value of that property, defining a kind of quality indicator for the correctness of the computed value. This indicator does not consider any *global* effect of the new property value, though.

2. Merger

   Mergers are responsible for a set of properties, which they take as input. They merge different values of the same property by evaluating their assigned *local* confidence values. While doing so, properties are merged to a single property by computing a *global* value that adheres to a set of constraints and prevents from *hunting* by stabilizing adaptation properties (cf. section 5.2).

By connecting the output and input of different modifiers and mergers, a propagation network is formed that continuously changes interface related properties during rendering.

Figure 11.18 shows the general structure of the adaptation system as well as some interfaces to other subsystems. Adaptation constraints are hosted by the adaptation system in a central repository. Interested entities register themselves as listeners for a set of constraints needed to provide their own adaptive services. For example, a Renderer may register for certain constraints used by a LayoutManager to layout interface components based on the wearing position of an output device. To alter adaptation constraints, an *adaptation network* composed of *modifiers* and *mergers* is used. In an iterative process currently valid constraints are provided to the first layer of the adaptation network, which processes these and propagates them to a next layer. Once having passed all layers, the adaptation constraint repository is updated. Modifiers and mergers usually make use of different context information. This context information, obtained from the *context system*, can either be of static or dynamic nature. A user's context (accessed through the UserProfileManager) is rather static than dynamic, with only sporadic changes. Each constraint alteration cycle is triggered and coordinated by the adaptation system that may consider context information to decide a suitable update rate. If a wearable system with comparatively low computational capabilities is used, update rates can be decreased.

11.7.2 Adaptation Network Model

Due to limited knowledge on how to design and adapt wearable user interfaces properly, only basic adaptation capabilities were implemented as proof of concept so far.

Figure 11.19 shows a section of an adaptation network to compute "look & feel" related properties of generated wearable user interfaces. Because established knowledge on look and feel related aspects of wearable user interfaces perceived over an HMD is still limited, the current adaptation network can be easily rearranged or extended to change adaptation behavior according to latest findings. This mechanism makes rapid prototyping and testing possible. New adaptation behaviors are immediately applicable during interface generation. Because configuration of the adaptation network is offloaded to XML files, there is no need to recompile the toolkit.

So far we approached the look & feel adaptation of interfaces by implementing algorithms in the following areas:

Font Adaptation According to what is known about visual acuity (cf. section 3.1), we implemented a visual acuity algorithm to calculate the minimum size of letters perceivable by humans having certain visual acuity. Visual acuity information is gathered from user profiles.

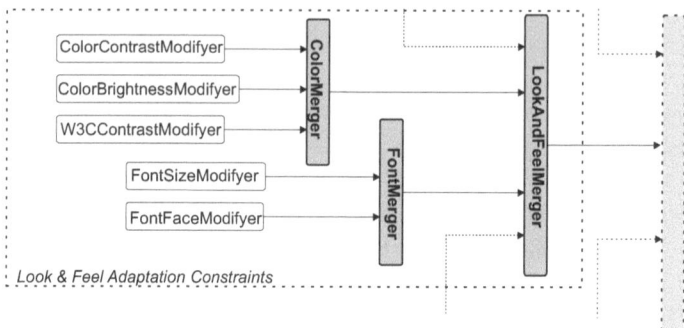

Figure 11.19: Look & Feel adaptation network.

Brightness Adaptation Brightness adaptation will try to optimize brightness of the interface to compensate changing illuminations that aversely affect perception of presented interfaces on HMDs. Different algorithms are known to adjust brightness. Illumination information is gathered from light sensors.

Contrast Adaptation Similar to brightness, contrast can also influence the perception of an interface under different illuminations. There is more than one algorithm available for contrast adjustment. Needed illumination information can be gathered from light sensors as well.

Although we implemented different algorithms from the areas above, like those described, for example, in [BBI07, VL05, Fos03, Bra03], it is not clear yet which combination of algorithms will yield best results and user acceptance. Because we need more insight on how wearable user interfaces have to be designed in general, the implementation and evaluation of adaptive interfaces is beyond the scope of this thesis. Preliminary experiments have, however, shown that font adaptation using the visual acuity algorithm gives reasonable results. For brightness and contrast adaptation, the right combination of algorithms is more complex and still an open question. First experiences have shown that changing brightness and contrast can improve the perception of information on an HMD. However, further experiments are needed to determine dependencies between brightness, contrast, illumination, and a certain HMD device in more detail. Figure 11.20 shows an example rendering of a light adaptive interface that automatically adapts brightness and contrast of colors according to illumination.

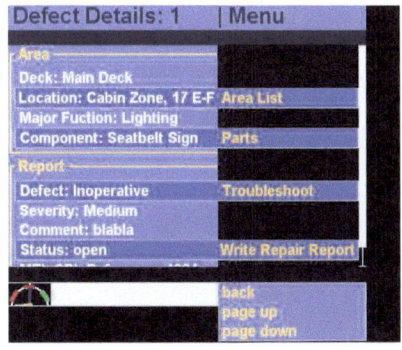
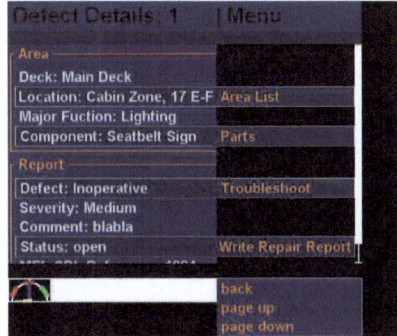

(a) Bright light conditions.   (b) Very dark light conditons.

Figure 11.20: Brightness and contrast adaptation based on illumination of the environment gathered from a light sensor.

11.8   Conclusion

This chapter has discussed the software architecture of a prototypical implementation of a WUI-Toolkit that is proposed to facilitate user interface implementation within the wearable user interface development process described in chapter 6.

The current implementation is based on a modular core infrastructure that provides a low-level abstraction of relevant operating system functionalities for the development of wearable user interfaces. This includes device and driver management, event queuing, and software module configuration management. The WUI-Toolkit is implemented as a module of the core infrastructure. With its abstract user interface description layer, it offers the opportunity to specify an envisioned user interface in an abstract and I/O device independent way. The abstract interface modeling approach allows application developers to develop user interfaces for their wearable computing applications, even though they do not have a detailed understanding of the various challenges in wearable computing.

Although the WUI-Toolkit is not limited to wearable user interface generation, the available DefaultRenderer allows generating optimized user interfaces for wearable computing application that rely on monocular HMDs. Interaction with generated user interfaces is not limited to a single or specific interaction device. Basic multi-modal interaction with interaction devices such as gesture and speech devices is supported.

To enrich wearable user interfaces with context-awareness, an interface adaptation system is available. Based on a combination of different adaptation constraints modeled on a network of modifiers and mergers, user interfaces can be equipped with context-awareness. As a reasonable adaptation of user interfaces requires in-depth understanding of adaptation effects, currently implemented adaptation capabilities are proof of concepts.

The next chapter will demonstrate the applicability of the implemented WUI-Toolkit to generate user interfaces for different applications where wearable computing technology is used to provide instant information delivery during physical work processes.

Chapter 12

Applications

The previous chapter presented the architecture and prototypical implementation of the WUI-Toolkit including its capabilities. This chapter reports on a number of applications that were successfully built and deployed using the current implementation of the WUI-Toolkit. Presented applications were developed according to the wearable application development process proposed in chapter 6. They are considered a first informal evaluation of the WUI-Toolkit, particularly with regards to its technical abilities and first experiences of application developers.

All presented applications target the professional environment in the domain of maintenance and assembly. They support the handling of complex maintenance or assembly procedures and are designed to empower a mobile worker with instant information access in regard to a currently performed activity.

12.1 KATO Aircraft Maintenance Assistant

A goal for aircraft industry is the enhancement of aircraft operation by optimizing ground procedures efficiency. The objective of the "KATO Maintenance Assistance" project was the support of technicians with the right information at the right time during maintenance and repair tasks. For this, location-based information retrieval as well as structural and expert knowledge were combined in a wearable computing application driven by knowledge management.

12.1.1 Main Functionalities

Detailed descriptions of the project, its use case, the software architecture, and crucial application requirements are discussed in [NSK+06, NSKW05]. To give an impression

(a) Details defect details.   (b) Interactive help and search system.

Figure 12.1: Wearable user interface of the KATO maintenance assistant.

of the complexity of the application, only main functionalities are described here. Using the KATO maintenance assistant, technicians can access defect lists and supplemental material of system failures to be fixed during a maintenance session. Single defect reports can be examined in detail. By browsing maintenance and troubleshooting manuals in the HMD using a gesture interface, technicians access information corresponding to maintenance procedures. At relevant locations within the cabin of an aircraft, a list of all technical components in the vicinity can be displayed. The recognition of these parts is done with a RFID reader. By navigating through an aircraft's technical component structure, experience knowledge of colleagues can be accessed via an interactive help system, too. Finally, repair reports are collected by the system once problems were resolved. Figure 12.1 shows two screen shots of the wearable user interface perceived through a monocular HMD.

For interaction with the system, a Bluetooth keyboard and a data glove with gesture recognition and an integrated RFID reader were used. According to the requirements of the KATO project, technicians should be able to seamlessly change the output device for the user interface dependent on the actual task and its characteristics. Because the hardware platform includes an OQO ultra mobile computer[1], which features a digitizer display and additional VGA output, technicians can select between a pen-based hand-held interface and a wearable user interface presented on a monocular HMD. Based on a single abstract model, both user interfaces were generated with the WUI-Toolkit. The output device adaptive rendering approach is depicted in figure 12.2.

---

[1]http://www.oqo.com

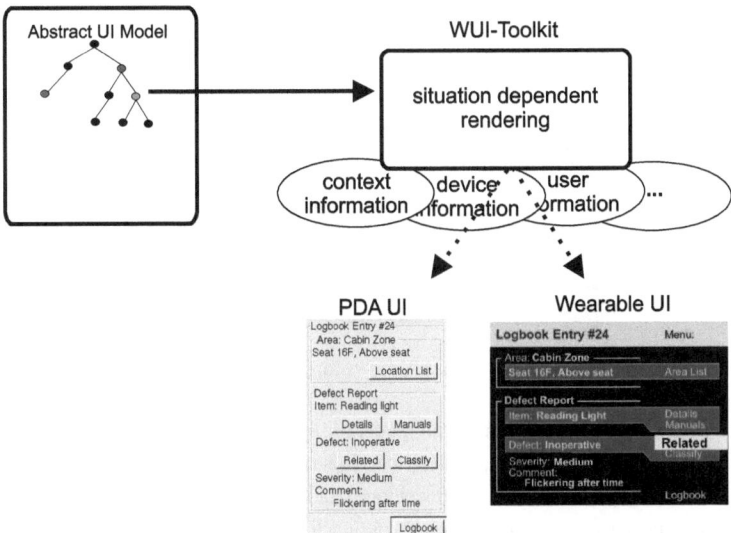

Figure 12.2: Output device dependent user interface rendering.

A special sensor, integrated in a special maintenance vest that carries the wearable equipment, recognizes whenever the wearable computer is held in hand and seamlessly changes between the two interface rendering modes on-line. Both user interfaces are different interpretations of the same abstract user interface model that specifies the functional requirements of the envisioned interface. For wearable user interface rendering, the default setup with the DefaultRenderer of the WUI-Toolkit was used. The hand-held interface was rendered using the toolkit's HandHeldRenderer.

To support all needed interface functionalities required by the KATO maintenance assistant, existing widget mappings of the toolkit were extended. New widgets were added to the component repository of the toolkit, which made them available for later reuse in other projects.

12.1.2 Application Developer's Experiences

Because the KATO maintenance assistant was the first extensive application built with the WUI-Toolkit, application developers had no experiences with the toolkit beforehand. However, the development team mainly consisted of students of our research group, which gave them the opportunity to directly talk to toolkit developers whenever needed. Based

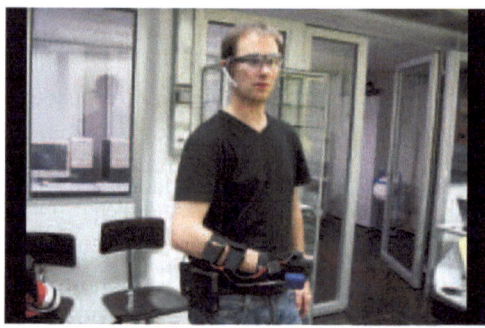

Figure 12.3: Person wearing the hardware components of the application [MKS+07].

on an introductory presentation of the model-based approach of the toolkit and abstract interface elements available, application developers started to work with the toolkit. In the beginning we experienced that developers had problems to understand the abstract model idea and particularly that there is only a limited number of elements available to model interface functionalities. But after a short time developers enjoyed the reduced complexity of resulting code, which gave developers with less experiences in interface programming the opportunity to build interfaces. Developers also expressed that they liked the low-level abstraction of hardware related issues and had not to deal with device drivers etc. for novel devices such as a data glove. Because it was their first time using the toolkit, naturally there were many situations, where toolkit developers had to extend or bug fix the toolkit's infrastructure to make the system more robust and stable.

In conclusion, the WUI-Toolkit was able to implement the requirements of the KATO maintenance assistant. It was able to generate a user interface based on context information for either an HMD or a digitizer display, i.e. it allowed implementing on-line user interface adaptation. Also, gesture based interaction provided by the toolkit was usable. Besides initial problems with understanding the model-based approach of the toolkit, application developers were able to implement the application rather quickly compared to a situation where the entire user interface has to be manually implemented from scratch. In line with this, developers enjoyed the low-level hardware abstractions provided.

12.2   Assembly Line Trainer for Car Production

Automotive production inhibits an industrial environment where variant products of high complexity and short life-cycles are manufactured. Hence, many situations exist where work is performed in a mobile manner. In order to cope with these conditions, concerted high quality training of personnel is a crucial issue [MKS$^+$07]. For this, the wearIT@work project implemented a wearable computing solution capable to support training procedures of Skoda's blue collar assembly line workers. The wearable application offers a mobile semi-autonomous training by utilizing context information. Trainees are provided with necessary (digital) information to successfully perform individual production tasks. At the same time, the performed tasks are tracked via mobile context sensors mounted on the body and in the environment. The application supports the trainees by detecting errors in their performance and presents context sensitive help and suggestions. The trainee can interact with the system through voice or an HMD if needed. Due to context-awareness features, the application automatically presents information in most cases. A more lengthy discussion of the background, current training approaches, challenges, and pre-study results for this scenario is given in [MKS$^+$07].

12.2.1   Hardware Architecture

The application is based on a distributed architecture. As wearable computer an OQO, worn by the user, was used. It features WLAN, Bluetooth, and external VGA output. A binocular look-around head mounted display and a Sony Ericson HBH-300 Bluetooth headset are used for interaction via speech commands. The tracking of user activities is done by sensors mounted on a special data glove (cf. figure 12.3). It comprises an inertial sensor package for motion detection and an RFID reader to identify tools. In addition, a set of force resistive sensors and magnetic switches are attached to the car body at the training island for monitoring interactions between tools, assembly parts, and the car body itself.

12.2.2   Software Architecture

The software architecture is shown in figure 12.4. The application including its business logic was written in Java. Sensor data processing is done by the Context Toolbox [BKLA06] and hooked up to the JContext API (an extension of the consideration presented in [ST06]) to access context events in the Java environment.

The application's business logic was implemented as a finite state machine: Each state corresponds to a specific task of the assembly procedure on which a worker is being trained. Transitions are triggered either by explicit user interaction, for example, speech commands, or implicit interaction. For the latter, the context system recognizes a certain activity and forwards it as an event to the application through the WUI-Toolkit's core framework context service wrapper.

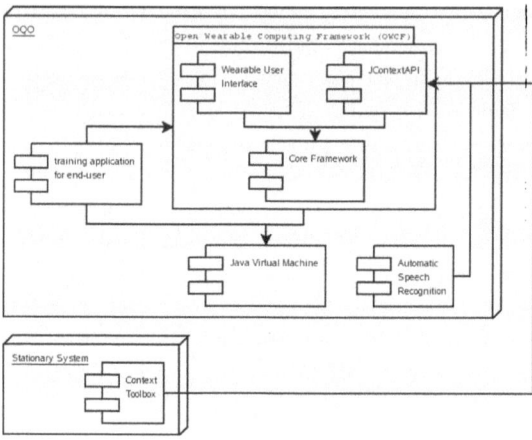

Figure 12.4: Software component structure of the Skoda application [MKS⁺07].

The user interface and interaction handling was implemented with the WUI-Toolkit. It presents the trainee the information needed during an assembly procedure in an appropriate manner on the HMD (cf. figure 12.5). The sequential characteristics of the training procedures and the implementation of the business logic as a finite state machine, directly maps to the hierarchical abstract model concept of the WUI-Toolkit. Application developers were able to directly structure their model by associating single procedure steps with abstract Group elements. Then, information to be presented in a certain step was modeled as a sub element of a Group. Because assembly procedures are dominated by text and image information, corresponding abstract elements for these media types were mainly used. Because in some special situations, videos are used to provide trainees with additional information of some complex procedures that are difficult to describe with words, video data was also modeled.

To implement the implicit interaction capabilities of the user interface, ImplicitTrigger elements were used. To let the interface react to context changes, custom Behaviors were implemented that registered themselves as a listener for certain context changes at the JContextAPI. If context information changes, a Behavior may activate a corresponding ImplicitTrigger.

In conclusion, the WUI-Toolkit was able to implement the requirements of the Skoda assembly line training system. Also, it could generate a context-aware user interface that reacted on both explicit and implicit user actions. It is worth to note that non of the application developers of this application were part of the group developing the toolkit

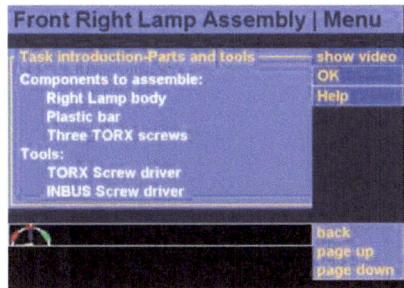 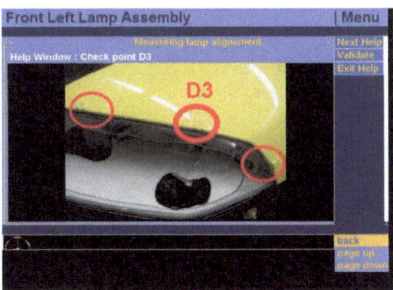

(a) Interface with textual instructions.   (b) Interface presenting image based instructions.

Figure 12.5: Wearable user interface of the assembly line trainer application.

infrastructure, but other partners of the wearIT@work project. Additionally to a Javadoc API documentation, developers were given a short written tutorial document explaining the model-based concept, available interface elements, toolkit configuration files, and some source code examples. Except for very few and specific questions, provided material was sufficient to let them implement the application. This suggests that the current abstract model approach has a complexity that does not need extensive training before being used, while still requiring some introductory instructions to understand it.

12.3   Aircraft Disassembly Assistant

The disassembly of old aircrafts is a special branch in the aircraft industry. Although airlines replace old aircrafts from time to time with new once, parts of discarded aircrafts can still be reused as spares to repair aircrafts of the same type still in use. A wearable application was developed that supports engineers during disassembly of aircrafts within the wearIT@work project .

As a first scenario to demonstrate the possibilities of wearable computer systems in that field, a cabin scenario was chosen. The subtask of passenger seat removal procedures was selected as content for the actual application. On the one hand this subtask offered the potential to demonstrate the benefit of wearable computers and on the other hand the possibility to equip aircraft engineers with additional knowledge to carry out procedures they were not able or allowed to carry out beforehand.

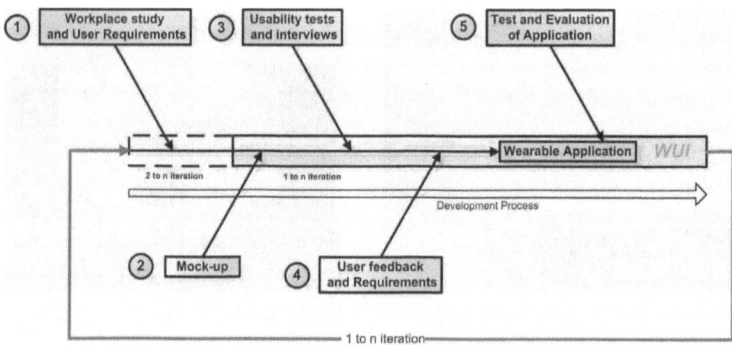

Figure 12.6: Application development process applied.

12.3.1 Development Process of the Application

The development process applied for the implementation of the envisioned wearable computing application closely followed the wearable application development process described in chapter 6. The specific instance of that process to design the maintenance disassembly assistant is depicted in figure 12.6.

First, initial requirements were gathered by utilizing classical workplace studies and interviews with end-users. Because the analyzed requirements yielded the need for further fundamental tests to determine user interface related issues, such as preferred input and output modalities by workers, usability tests with accompanied interviews were conduced with a mock application [WK07]. Based on experiment results, initial requirements were refined as a basis for the actual development of the wearable application, including its user interface and the abstract model specification. For a detailed description of the process including major requirements and findings we refer to [MW07].

12.3.2 Hardware and Software Architecture

The hardware platform selected for the disassembly assistant was an OQO computer. As physical input devices a USB microphone (speech navigation) and a data glove were connected to the system. The data glove provided gesture-based navigation through menus as well as the identification of RFID chips used to tag items or persons. A monocular HMD was used to display the visual part of the user interface generated by the WUI-Toolkit. Figure 12.7 shows an engineer wearing the hardware together with an excerpt of the user interface he sees on the HMD. In this case, the interface presents image-based information

Figure 12.7: Maintainer wearing the wearable system.

to indicate the position of a certain circuit breaker on a panel, because this media type has gained most acceptance by engineers to present location related information [MW07].

The functionalities implemented by the disassembly assistant include both, workflow and context-aware related features as well as presentation related features of the user interface. Because workflow and context related functionalities target mainly implicit interaction, for example, system login procedures based on personal digital keys or the automatic recognition of task steps, complex interface navigation can be omitted. If this is not possible, engineers can interact with the application by two modalities (hand gestures and speech commands). Based on the WUI-Toolkit's I/O device support, interaction can either be accomplished modal, with only one device, or multimodal by combining them.

Because working conditions in aircrafts strongly vary, engineers can explicitly switch between input modalities to particularly ensure their freedom to have a hands-free operation, if wanted. Visual feedback on the currently active input modality is given with a special plug-in for the system tray infrastructure of the WUI-Toolkit. Figure 12.8 shows two renderings generated by the WUI-Toolkit based on the abstract model of the application.

In conclusion, the WUI-Toolkit was able to implement the requirements of the aircraft disassembly assistant. It could generate a context-aware user interface that reacted on both explicit and implicit user actions. Moreover, the plug-in infrastructure of the WUI-Toolkit was successfully used to integrate custom visual feedback on interaction modalities currently in use. Besides the successful use of the WUI-Toolkit, the approach taken to develop the application, which was a concrete instance of the systematic user interface

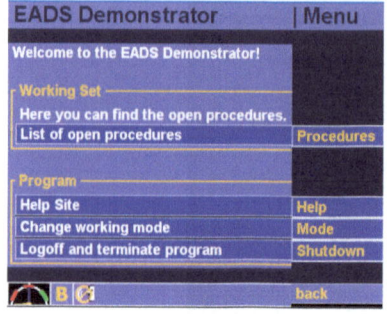

(a) Start screen with scheduled jobs.

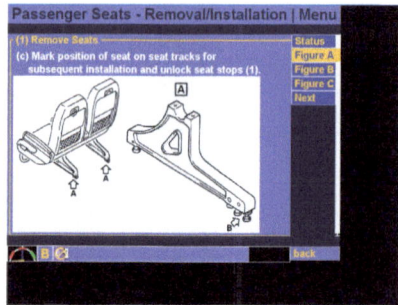

(b) Presentation of graphical information.

Figure 12.8: Application user interface generated by the WUI-Toolkit.

development process proposed in chapter 6, was shown to be applicable also. Similar to the previously discussed assembly line training application, application developers consisted of wearIT@work partners. Based on our experiences from past application developments with the toolkit, application developers were given, in addition to Javadoc and the written tutorial, a short presentation highlighting the model based idea and the benefits of that concept for developers. With the opportunity for developers to ask questions and to get instant answers, we had the feeling that this provided developers with an easier start with the toolkit. At least it resulted in less questions regarding the principles behind the toolkit throughout the implementation phase.

12.4 Conclusion

The three applications presented show that it is possible to integrate the concept of a WUI-Toolkit into application development processes. Moreover, the current prototypical implementation of the toolkit was shown to be able to implement and render different context-aware applications. Even though it can be argued that the discussed applications are instances of similar problems, those simple solutions are, however, already sufficient to increase productivity and to ease existing work processes in aircraft maintenance and assembly using wearable computers.

The process used to develop the applications discussed was based on the general wearable user interface development process proposed earlier in this thesis. Presented applications can be treated as working examples indicating both, the possibility to deploy the process in real application developments and its ability to systematize the implementation of wearable user interfaces by introducing special software tools like the WUI-Toolkit.

The presented applications provided a first attempt to evaluate the toolkit from a technical perspective. They cannot be easily used to evaluate the usability of the toolkit from an application developer's perspective. For this, a dedicated evaluation is needed. Such an evaluation would require examining the effort spent by application developers on specifying an abstract model for a given problem and then comparing results against findings obtained from standard interface building techniques. An evaluation with this focus is beyond the scope of the thesis. However, our first experiences with application developers using the toolkit are promising and suggest that the initial hurdle may not be too high, as it would require extensive training and support to start implementing even simpler applications. However, this cannot be stated with certainty, since long term experiences are missing due to the toolkit still being under development. This has to be left for the end of the wearIT@work project.

Part V

Conclusion

Chapter 13

Conclusions and Final Remarks

The main goal of every user interface should be the support of an easy communication and interaction between people and computer applications. In this thesis we have presented a systematic way to develop user interfaces for wearable computing applications. The systematic approach proposed mainly consists of a new evaluation method to evaluate wearable user interfaces or their artifacts in a controlled environment, as well as a special model-based software tool that facilitates the implementation of such interfaces with reusable components.

The research presented in this thesis was concerned with the development of a new evaluation method for wearable user interfaces. The new method allows realistically abstracting primary physical tasks in a controlled laboratory environment that involve manual work to a certain extend. Then, this new method was used to study, in three different user experiments, a user's interruptibility in wearable computing dual-task environments depending on the interaction device used. The obtained research results on the one hand provide general guidelines for the design of wearable user interfaces in respect to a proper interruption management and interaction design. On the other hand, they validated the applicability and appropriateness of the HotWire apparatus for user studies in the area of wearable computing. Obtained experiment results were integrated in the design of the WUI-Toolkit to make findings available as reusable components for interface development of forthcoming user interfaces.

Finally, the proposed user interface development process was successfully applied in different projects that developed three wearable computing applications for the domains of aircraft maintenance and disassembly, as well as the training of assembly line workers in car production. Here, the systematic development process and the prototypical implementation of the WUI-Toolkit were used by application developers. The toolkit provided the opportunity to generate usable and appropriate graphical user interfaces for industrial wearable computing applications based on abstract model specifications that did not require knowledge on wearable user interfaces from their developers. Preliminary investigations in user acceptance of the WUI-Toolkit (by application developers) found no general usability problems with the toolkit or with its model-based approach.

13.1 Contributions

This thesis presented several research contributions in the area of human-wearable-computer interaction. More specifically it answered the following research questions.

The main research question was concerned with how user interfaces and their components can be evaluated for wearable computers. The HotWire evaluation method developed allows for realistically simulating primary manual tasks in a controlled laboratory environment. A controlled environment is particularly of advantage to evaluate isolated interface components, such as interruption methods. The HotWire apparatus is reconfigurable and allows for easily abstracting primary manual tasks, while retaining their basic characteristics with an easy technical setup.

An inappropriate handling of interruptions can become a safety critical issue in dual-task environments. The three user studies conducted contribute to the question of the proper design of interruption handling dependent on a used interaction method. The experiments have shown a dependency between a preferred interruption method and the interaction device used. Although speech interaction showed least interference with a primary manual task and gave good interaction performance, it cannot be easily deployed in noisy environments. The use of audio notifications when using speech interaction was found to have most advantages, particularly exhibiting the best user acceptance. Additionally, hands-freeness offered the freedom to easier compensate physically challenging situations and allowed increasing task accuracy.

Basic gesture interaction with a data glove can be implemented as a robust system, but it can interfere more often with manual work than speech input. Unlike speech interaction, gesture interaction should not be used with negotiated interruption handling. The second gesture needed was found to impair performance and increase errors. Instead, scheduled, immediate, or mediated handling methods are preferred. Although arbitrary complex mediated interruption handling methods are possible, user studies showed that even very simple algorithms can improve user performance compared to scheduled or immediate treatments unless algorithms are reliable and selected properly.

Providing visual feedback for a more accurate gesture interaction was shown to have a diametrical effect. In our experiments, the tested continuous visual feedback decreased performance even though users tried to ignore it and visual feedback was not needed for interaction. The findings suggest that continuous visual feedback should be avoided in gesture interaction design for wearable computers, once used gestures are easy to perform.

The research question of whether mobility and different body postures impact gesture interaction could not be clearly answered in the thesis. Although we found that mobility apparently impaired gesture interaction, because users lost orientation with respect to the fixed frame of reference used by gesture recognition algorithms, a consecutively conducted experiment that compared gesture recognition algorithms with absolute and relative frame of reference approaches, was not able to give a clear answer. More specifically, study results suggested the opposite of observations being made beforehand. That is, a relative frame of reference for gesture recognition does not pay off and is also more difficult for users to understand and use. One evadable reason for this was found in an unrelaxed and "robot-like" behavior of users when controlling an application with novel data glove interaction devices, which impaired used algorithms. Here, more research is needed. Especially, a long term evaluation may provide more insight because users could become accustomed to the new interaction device, which in turn would reduce errors due to misunderstanding or misusing the device.

In respect to the more practical research questions that were concerned with a systematic development approach for wearable user interfaces and a model-based software tool, the thesis's contribution is the design and prototypical implementation of the WUI-Toolkit. Based on an abstract model, which can be specified even with limited knowledge on wearable user interfaces, the toolkit is able to automatically generate usable wearable user interfaces based on reusable components. The WUI-Toolkit guides the systematic development of wearable user interfaces and can be seamlessly integrated into existing application development processes. The model-based approach provides an extensible infrastructure to implement different renderers even for other or future interface technologies such as pure audio or augmented reality interfaces.

13.2 Future Work

This thesis has developed a comprehensive approach towards a systematic design, implementation, and evaluation of wearable user interfaces. Although the newly developed HotWire evaluation method and the WUI-Toolkit have been shown to be successfully applicable throughout the process of user interface development for wearable computers, there remains future work in several areas.

13.2.1   HotWire Evaluation

The HotWire evaluation method can be used to evaluate wearable user interface aspects in dual-task situations. Although the current technical setup is sufficient to conduct experiments, it can still be improved.

To provide users with maximum mobility during the experiment, different possibilities that can make the hand-held tool wireless should be investigated in future. In general, Bluetooth or similar techniques are suitable. The challenge, though, is to find an unobtrusive, miniaturized, and robust solution. A wrist mounted wireless transmitter is probably the most reliable solution.

Section 7.4 presented a first approach to track the user's hand including the location of occurred errors on the metallic wire track of the HotWire. However, the currently needed size of markers for the visual tracking is not sufficient for hand-held tool sizes like those used in experiments discussed in this thesis. Although high-quality video cameras allow decreasing the size of markers, different questions on the robustness and accuracy of tracking under different illuminations still remain. An approach based on resistance measurements at the time an error was recognized may be worth to be investigated as an alternative as well.

The HotWire apparatus can realistically abstract a physical manual task that requires visual attention. The secondary computer task used throughout the experiments in this thesis was considered to be always abstract enough not to interfere with the primary task. Although this was done to ensure the validity of obtained quantitative measurements, a secondary task that is more related to the primary HotWire task could make the entire experiment setup even more realistic. A secondary task that, for example, helps the user to successfully pass tricky sections of the HotWire would make the setup to be felt more like an integrated real world application, where the wearable computer would provide related information to carry out the primary task more easily.

The so-called *steering law*, proposed by Accot and Zhai [AZ97], is a predictive model of human movement, regarding speed and total time needed by users to navigate or "steer" through a 2D tunnel with a pointing device. The tunnel can be thought of as a trajectory on a plane, similar to driving a car down a road that has twists and turns with high speed. For future work it might be very appropriate to apply and/or compare the steering law to the HotWire apparatus. An investigation should be done on the extend to which the steering law could be also used as a predictive model for the real world and 3D HotWire task.

13.2.2   User Interface Development

Chapter 12 presented successful application developments with the WUI-Toolkit for industrial applications. Although the current implementation of the toolkit allows the development of sequential task-based applications found in maintenance or assembly domains, there are different aspects that should be extended and improved for future application development with the toolkit.

Abstract User Interface Modeling

The model-based approach of the WUI-Toolkit already features a fundamental set of abstract elements to build abstract user interface models for various applications. Besides the extension of available abstract interface elements or temporal relations for specific applications, a software tool facilitating the building process of abstract models is the most important future enhancement of the toolkit. A graphical modeling tool would significantly ease the abstract model design which in turn would reduce the acceptance threshold of the toolkit. As there are already graphical tools available that were developed to facilitate model design for other model-based description languages, an investigation of a possible adaptation of those for the WUI-Toolkit seems to be reasonable.

Additional Modalities

Although the toolkit features multi-modal information presentation, the current version was designed with visual user interfaces in focus. Wearable computing, however, might also make use of pure audio or haptic interfaces. In particular, the possibility to provide users with unobtrusive tactile feedback may overcome certain challenges and limitations of graphical or audio interfaces. An extension of existing graphical interface renderers is, therefore, among the possible next steps to be carried out to further optimize the usability of generated user interfaces. However, this again requires basic research first.

Interface Adaptation

The use of context information in wearable computing to automatically do something for the user is one of its major strengths. Although the WUI-Toolkit already features an infrastructure to implement adaptive user interface behaviors, currently there are only a few examples integrated. This was, however, not due to an insufficient design of the adaptation module, but because knowledge on how reasonable interface adaptation should be done is still limited. Understanding how to use available context information for interface adaptation is essential, though. Therefore, more user experiments on specific aspects, like those presented in this thesis, are needed as a prerequisite to establish more knowledge on how adaptive wearable user interfaces should be designed to not confuse their users.

Text Input

Some form of text input is required in almost every application. The WUI-Toolkit features the possibility to let users enter text when needed. Although the toolkit accepts any form of text input, no matter how it was produced, the possibility to efficiently enter text while being on the move is a challenging research issue. The KATO maintenance assistant application, presented in chapter 12, used a mini QWERTY keyboard for text input in repair reports. The Twiddler chording keyboard, especially designed for wearable computing, offers another possibility for text input. Both methods, however, require holding an interaction device during operation. Another part of future work could be, therefore, the exploration of gesture interaction with a data glove to input text. This would not require holding any additional devices. In [WJ07] we recently reported on a first attempt to implement text input with a combination of hand gestures and the chording principle. Although first results are promising, more research is still needed.

Bibliography

[AAR72]   D. A. Allport, B. Antonis, and P. Raynolds. On the division of attention: A disproof of the single channel hypothesis. *Experimental Psychology*, 24(25–235), 1972.

[AB04]   Piotr D. Adamczyk and Brian P. Bailey. If not now, when?: The effects of interruption at different moments within task execution. In *CHI '04: Proceedings of the SIGCHI conference on Human factors in computing systems*, pages 271–278, New York, NY, USA, 2004. ACM Press.

[ADB⁺99]   Gregory D. Abowd, Anind K. Dey, Peter J. Brown, Nigel Davies, Mark Smith, and Pete Steggles. Towards a better understanding of context and context-awareness. In *HUC '99: Proceedings of the 1st international symposium on Handheld and Ubiquitous Computing*, pages 304–307, London, UK, 1999. Springer-Verlag.

[AM90]   P. L. Alfano and G. F. Michel. Restricting the field of view: Perceptual and performance effects. *Perceptual and Motor Skills*, 70:35–45, 1990.

[APB⁺99]   Marc Abrams, Constantinos Phanouriou, Alan L. Batongbacal, Stephen M. Williams, and Jonathan E. Shuster. UTML: An appliance-independent XML user interface language. *Comput. Networks*, 31(11-16):1695–1708, 1999.

[ART07]   ARToolkit: Building augmented realtity software, 2007. http://www.hitl.washington.edu/artoolkit, Last access: 06-27-2007.

[AS03]   Daniel Ashbrook and Thad Starner. Using GPS to learn significant locations and predict movement across multiple users. *Personal Ubiquitous Computing*, 7(5):275–286, 2003.

[AZ97]   Johnny Accot and Shumin Zhai. Beyond fitts' law: models for trajectory-based hci tasks. In *CHI '97: Proceedings of the SIGCHI conference on*

Human factors in computing systems, pages 295–302, New York, NY, USA, 1997. ACM Press.

[Bab01] Chris Baber. Wearable computers: A human factors review. *International Journal on Human Computer Interaction*, 13(2):123–145, 2001.

[BAB06] Jacob T. Biehl, Piotr D. Adamczyk, and Brian P. Bailey. Djogger: a mobile dynamic music device. In *CHI '06: CHI '06 extended abstracts on Human factors in computing systems*, pages 556–561, New York, NY, USA, 2006. ACM Press.

[BB97] P. Bruce and M.D. Bernard. *Musculoskeletal Disorders Workplace Factors: A Critical Review of Epidemiologic Evidence for Work-Related Musculoskeletal Disorders of the Neck, Upper Extremity, and Low Back.* U.S. Department of health and Human Services, 1997.

[BB02] Guruduth Banavar and Abraham Bernstein. Software infrastructure and design challenges for ubiquitous computing applications. *Communications of the ACM*, 45(12):92–96, 2002.

[BBC97] P. J. Brown, J. D. Bovey, and X. Chen. Context-aware applications: from the laboratory to the marketplace. *IEEE Personal Communications*, 4(5):58–64, October 1997.

[BBI07] Sergey Bezryadin, Pavel Bourov, and Dmitry Ilin. Brightness calculation in digital image processing. KWE International, Inc. Article., March 2007. http://www.kweii.com/site/color_theory/2007_LV/ BrightnessCalculation.pdf, Last access: 10-01-2007.

[BC05] Joanna Berzowska and Marcelo Coelho. Kinetic electronic garments. In *ISWC '05: Proceedings of the 9th IEEE International Symposium on Wearable Computers*, pages 82–85, Osaka, Japan, 2005. IEEE Computer Society.

[BCK+03] E. Beck, M. Christiansen, J. Kjeldskov, N. Kolve, and H. Stage. Experimental evaluation of techniques for usability testing of mobile systems in a laboratory setting. In *Proceedings of OZCHI*, pages 106–115, 2003.

[BCPK02] Mark Billinghurst, Adrian Cheok, Simon Prince, and Hirokazu Kato. Real world teleconferencing. *IEEE Computer Graphics and Applications*, 22(6):11–13, 2002.

[BDS07]   Christof Breckenfelder, Christian Dils, and Hans Werner Seliger. Electrical
            properties of metal coated polyamide yarns. In *Proceedings of the 4th Inter-
            national Forum for Applied Wearable Computing (IFAWC)*, pages 117–124,
            Tel Aviv, Israel, March, 12–13 2007. VDE/ITG.

[Bec82]   J. Beck. Textural segmentation. In J. Beck, editor, *Organization and rep-
            resentation in perception*, pages 285–317. NJ:Erlbaum, Hillsdale, 1982.

[BFC05]   Gábor Blaskó, Steven Feiner, and Franz Coriand. Exploring interaction with
            a simulated wrist-worn projection display. In *ISWC'05: Proceedings of the
            9th International Conference on Wearable Computers*, pages 2–9, Osaka,
            Japan, 2005.

[BGA56]   J. S. Bruner, J. J. Goodnow, and G. A. Austin. *A study of thinking*. John
            Wiley, New York, 1956.

[BGB91]   W. Buxton, W. Gaver, and S. Bly. Tutorial number 8: The use of non-
            speech audio at the interface. In *Computer Human Interaction '91*, New
            Orleans, Louisiana., 1991. ACM.

[BH96]   D. I. Barmwell and A. Hurlbert. Measurements of color constancy by using
            a forced-choice matching technique. *Perception*, 25(229–241), 1996.

[BH99]   Ravin Balakrishnan and Ken Hinckley. The role of kinesthetic reference
            frames in two-handed input performance. In *UIST '99: Proceedings of the
            12th annual ACM symposium on User interface software and technology*,
            pages 171–178, New York, NY, USA, 1999. ACM Press.

[BH05]   Vincent Buil and Gerard Hollemans. Acceptable operating force for but-
            tons on in-ear type headphones. In *International Conference on Wearable
            Computers*, pages 186–191, Osaka, Japan, 2005.

[BHH+02]   Jochen Burkhardt, Horst Henn, Stefan Hepper, Klaus Rintdorff, and
            Thomas Schäck. *Pervasive Computing - Technology and Architecture of
            Mobile Internet Applications*. Pearson Education, Edinburgh, 2002.

[BKC00]   B. Bailey, J. Konstan, and J. Carlis. Measuring the effects of interruptions
            on task performance in the user interface. In *Proceedings of IEEE Confer-
            ence on Systems, Man, and Cybernetics (SMC 2000)*, pages 757–762. IEEE,
            2000.

[BKLA06]   David Bannach, Kai S. Kunze, Paul Lukowicz, and Oliver Amft. Distributed modular toolbox for multi-modal context recognition. In *Proceedings of the 19th International Conference on Architecture of Computing Systems (ARCS)*, pages 99–113, Frankfurt/Main, Germany, March 13-16 2006. Springer.

[BKLP05]   Doug A. Bowman, Ernst Kruijff, Joseph J. LaViola, and Ivan Poupyrev. *3D User Interfaces: Theory and Practice*. Addison-Wesley, Boston, MA, USA, 1st edition, 2005.

[BKM⁺97]   Len Bass, Chris Kasabach, Richard Martin, Dan Siewiorek, Asim Smailagic, and John Stivoric. The design of a wearable computer. In *CHI '97: Proceedings of the SIGCHI conference on Human factors in computing systems*, pages 139–146, New York, NY, USA, 1997. ACM Press.

[BLB⁺03]   Stephen Brewster, Joanna Lumsden, Marek Bell, Malcolm Hall, and Stuart Tasker. Multimodal 'eyes-free' interaction techniques for wearable devices. In *CHI '03: Proceedings of the SIGCHI conference on Human factors in computing systems*, pages 473–480, New York, NY, USA, 2003. ACM Press.

[BLC98]   S. Brewster, G. Leplatre, and M. Crease. Using non-speech sounds in mobile computing devices. In *Proceedings of the First Workshop on HCI for Mobile Devices*, pages 26–29, Glasgow, U.K., 1998.

[BLU06]   Martin R.K. Baumann, Sandro Leuchter, and Leon Urbas, editors. *MMI-Interaktiv: Aufmerksamkeit und Situation Awareness im Fahrzeug*, volume 11 of *Mensch-Maschine Interaktion und Human Factors*. Online-Jounal (http://useworld.net/mmiij/driving), December 2006.

[BM93]   David Benyon and Dianne Murray. Developing adaptive systems to fit individual aptitudes. In *IUI '93: Proceedings of the 1st international conference on Intelligent user interfaces*, pages 115–121, New York, NY, USA, 1993. ACM Press.

[BM00]   Stephen A. Brewster and Robin Murray. Presenting dynamic information on mobile computers. *Personal and Ubiquitous Computing*, 4(4):209–212, 2000.

[BM04]   B. Balentine and D. Morgan. *How to Build a Speech Recognition Application: A Style Guide for Telephony Dialogues*. Enterprise Integration Group, San Ramon, CA, 2004.

[BMM06]   Stephen Brewster, David McGookin, and Christopher Miller. Olfoto: designing a smell-based interaction. In *CHI '06: Proceedings of the SIGCHI conference on Human Factors in computing systems*, pages 653–662, New York, NY, USA, 2006. ACM Press.

[BNSS01]   Michael Boronowsky, Tom Nicolai, Christoph Schlieder, and Ansgar Schmidt. Winspect: A case study for wearable computing-supported inspection tasks. In *ISWC'01: Proceedings of the 5th International Symposium on Wearable Computers*, volume 5, pages 163–164, Zürich, 8–9 October 2001. IEEE Computer Society.

[BPG+06]   Jennifer L. Burke, Matthew S. Prewett, Ashley A. Gray, Liuquin Yang, Frederick R. B. Stilson, Michael D. Coovert, Linda R. Elliot, and Elizabeth Redden. Comparing the effects of visual-auditory and visual-tactile feedback on user performance: a meta-analysis. In *ICMI '06: Proceedings of the 8th international conference on Multimodal interfaces*, pages 108–117, New York, NY, USA, 2006. ACM Press.

[Bra03]   David H. Brainard. Color constancy. *The Visual Neurosciences*, 2003.

[Bre02]   Stephen Brewster. Overcoming the lack of screen space on mobile computers. *Personal Ubiquitous Computing*, 6(3):188–205, 2002.

[Bre03]   Stephen Brewster. Nonspeech auditory output. In Julie A. Jacko and Andrew Sears, editors, *The Human-Computer Interaction Handbook: Fundamentals, Evolving Technologies and Emerging Applications*, chapter 10, pages 220–244. Lawrence Erlbaum Associates, 2003.

[BS98]   Birgit Bomsdorf and Gerd Szwillus. From task to dialogue: task-based user interface design. *SIGCHI Bull.*, 30(4):40–42, 1998.

[BSG89]   Meera M. Blattner, Denise A. Sumikawa, and Robert M. Greenberg. Earcons and icons: Their structure and common design principles. *SIGCHI Bull.*, 21(1):123–124, 1989.

[BTN90]   D. Browne, P. Totterdel, and M. Norman, editors. *Adaptive User Interfaces*. Academic Press, London, 1990.

[BTT05]   David Benyon, Phil Turner, and Susan Turner. *Designing Interactive Systems: People, Activities, Contexts, Technologies*. Addison-Wesley, Boston, MA, USA, 1st edition, 2005.

[Bue06]   Leah Buechley. A construction kit for electronic textiles. In *ISWC'06: Proceedings of the 10th IEEE International Symposium on Wearable Computers*, pages 83–90, Montreux, Switzerland, October 11-14 2006. IEEE.

[Bux83]   William Buxton. Lexical and pragmatic considerations of input structures. *SIGGRAPH Computer Graphics*, 17(1):31–37, 1983.

[Bux90]   W. Buxton. The pragmatics of haptic input. In *Proceedings of Computer-Human Interaction (CHI'90). Tutorial 26 Notes*, New York, 1990. ACM.

[BVE05]   Abraham Bernstein, Peter Vorburger, and Patrice Egger. Direct interruptablity prediction and scenario-based evaluation of wearable devices: Towards reliable interruptability predictions. In *First International Workshop on Managing Context Information in Mobile and Pervasive Environments MCMP-05*, 2005.

[BWCL01]   Doug A. Bowman, Chadwick A. Wingrave, Joshua M. Campbell, and Vinh Q. Ly. Using pinch gloves for both natural and abstract interaction techniques in virtual environments. In *Proceedings of HCI International*, pages 629–633, 2001.

[Car03]   John M. Carroll. *HCI models, theories, and frameworks: Toward a multidisciplinary science*. Morgan Kaufmann Publishers, San Francisco, 2003.

[CCH01]   E. Cutrell, M. Czerwinski, and E. Horvitz. Notification, disruption, and memory: Effects of messaging interruptions on memory and performance. In *Proceedings of the IFIP TC.13 International Conference on Human-Computer Interaction (INTERACT '01)*, pages 263–269. IOS Press, 2001.

[CK60]   Manfred Clynes and Nathan Kline. Cyborgs and space. *Astronautics*, 14:26–27, September 1960.

[Cla00]   A. F. Clark. What do we want from a wearable user interface? In *Workshop on Software Engineering for Wearable and Pervasive Computing*, pages 3–5, Limerick, Ireland, June 2000.

[CLSC05]   James Clawson, Kent Lyons, Thad Starner, and Edward Clarkson. The impacts of limited visual feedback on mobile text entry for the twiddler and mini-qwerty keyboards. In *Ninth IEEE International Symposium on Wearable Computers (ISWC'05)*, pages 170–177. IEEE, 2005.

[CMR91]   Stuart K. Card, Jock D. Mackinlay, and George G. Robertson. A morpho-
          logical analysis of the design space of input devices. *ACM Trans. Inf. Syst.*,
          9(2):99–122, 1991.

[CNPQ02] Keith C. Clarke, Andrea Nuernberger, Thomas Pingel, and Du Qingyun.
          User interface design for a wearable field computer. In *dg.o '02: Proceed-
          ings of the 2002 annual national conference on Digital government research*,
          pages 1–5. Digital Government Research Center, 2002.

[Coc87]   G. Cockton. Some critical remarks on abstractions for adaptable dialogue
          managers. In *People and Computers III: Prceedings of the 3rd Conference on
          the British Computer Society*, pages 325–343. Human-Computer Interaction
          Specialist Group, University of Exeter, 1987.

[Cut97]   J. E. Cutting. How the eye measures reality and virtual reality. *Behaviour
          Research Methods, Instruments & Computers*, 29(1):27–36, 1997.

[CWH03]   Wousheng Chou, Tianmiao Wang, and Le Hu. Design of data glove and arm
          type haptic interface. In *11th International Symposium on Haptic Interfaces
          for Virtual Environment and Teleoperator Systems (HAPTICS 2003)*, pages
          422–427, 2003.

[DA04]   Anind K. Dey and Gregory D. Abowd. Support for the adapting applications
          and interfaces to context. In Ahmed Seffah and Homa Javahery, editors,
          Multiple User Interfaces, pages 261–296. John Wiley & Sons Inc., 2004.

[Dah06]   Markus Dahm. *Grundlagen der Mensch-Computer-Interaction*. Pearson,
          München, Germany, 2006.

[Dav01]   Lisa Louise Davis. 2-d pointing while walking. In *CHI '01: CHI '01 ex-
          tended abstracts on Human factors in computing systems*, pages 125–126,
          New York, NY, USA, 2001. ACM Press.

[DDA+95] M. D'Esposito, J. A. Detre, D.C. Alsop, R.K. Shin, S. Atlas, and M. Gross-
          mann. The natural basis of the central executive of working memory. *Nature*,
          378:279–281, 1995.

[DEMA01] Elizabeth Dykstra-Erickson, Wendy MacKay, and Jonathan Arnowitz. Per-
          spectives: trialogue on design (of). *Interactions*, 8(2):109–117, 2001.

[Der06]   Nigel Derrett. Is automation automatically a good thing? *Personal Ubiq-
          uitous Computing*, 10(2):56–59, 2006.

234 Bibliography

[Dey98]   Anind K. Dey. Context aware computing: The cyberdesk project. In *AAAI Springer Symposium on Intelligent Environments*, pages 51–54, 1998.

[DL04]   Norman K. Denzin and Yvonna S. Lincoln. *Handbook of Qualitative Research*. SAGE Publications, 3rd edition, March 2004.

[DMKSH93]   H. Dieterich, U. Malinowski, T. Kühme, and M. Schneider-Hufschmidt. State of the art in adaptive user interfaces. In M. Schneider-Hufschmidt, T. Kühme, and U. Malinowski, editors, *Adaptive User Interfaces: Principles and Practice*, pages 13–48. North-Holland, Amsterdam, 1993.

[DNL+04]   Mikael Drugge, Marcus Nilsson, Urban Liljedahl, Kare Synnes, and Peter Parnes. Methods for interrupting a wearable computer user. In *ISWC '04: Proceedings of the Eighth International Symposium on Wearable Computers*, pages 150–157, Washington, DC, USA, 2004. IEEE Computer Society.

[Dri98]   J. Driver. The neuropsychology of spatial attention. In H. Paschler, editor, *Attention*, pages 297–340. UK: Psychology Press, Hove, 1998.

[DS98]   J. Driver and C. Spence. Crossmodal links in the crossmodal construction of space. In *The royal society london series B*, pages 1–13, 1998.

[DSA01]   Anind Dey, Daniel Salber, and Gregory Abowd. A conceptual framework and a toolkit for supporting the rapid prototyping of context-aware applications. *Human-Computer Interaction (HCI) Journal*, 16(2-4):97–166, October 2001.

[DT06]   Patrick De La Hamette and Gerhard Tröster. Fingermouse - a button size visual hand tracking and segmentation device. In *Architecture of Computing Systems - ARCS 2006, 19th International Conference*, pages 31–41, Frankfurt/Main, Germany, May 2006. Springer.

[DThC06]   Henry Been-Lirn Duh, Gerald C. B. Tan, and Vivian Hsueh hua Chen. Usability evaluation for mobile device: A comparison of laboratory and field tests. In *MobileHCI '06: Proceedings of the 8th conference on Human-computer interaction with mobile devices and services*, pages 181–186, New York, NY, USA, 2006. ACM Press.

[Duk06]   Tania Dukic. *Visual demand in manual task performance - Towards a virtual evaluation*. PhD thesis, Chalmers University of Technology, Department of Product and Production Development Production Systems, Göteborg, Sweden, 2006.

[Dum03]   Joseph S. Dumas. User-based evaluations. pages 1093–1117, 2003.

[DWPS06]   Mikael Drugge, Hendrik Witt, Peter Parnes, and Kåre Synnes. Using the HotWire to study interruptions in wearable computing primary tasks. In *ISWC'06: Proceedings of the 10th International Symposium for Wearable Computers*, pages 37–44, Montreux, Switzerland, October 11–14 2006. IEEE.

[EC00]   H. Eyrolle and C. Cellier. The effects of interruptions in work activity: field and laboratory results. *Applied Ergonomics*, 31:537–543, 2000.

[EEB67]   William K. English, Douglas C. Engelbart, and Melvyn L. Berman. Display-selection techniques for text manipulation. *IEEE Transactions on Human Factors in Electronics*, HFE-8(1):5–15, March 1967.

[EK05]   Michael W. Eysenck and Mark T. Keane. *Cognitive Psychology: A Student's Handbook*. Psychology Press (UK), 5th edition, 2005.

[EMW+03]   G. O. Einstein, M. A. McDaniel, C. L. Williford, J. L. Pagan, and R. K. Dismukes. Forgetting of intentions in demanding situations is rapid. *Journal of Experimental Psychology: Applied*, 9(3):147–162., 2003.

[Esp97]   Chris Esposito. Wearable computers: Field test observations and system design guidelines. *Personal and Ubiquitous Computing*, 1(2):81–87, 1997.

[FB97]   George W. Fitzmaurice and William Buxton. An empirical evaluation of graspable user interfaces: towards specialized, space-multiplexed input. In *CHI '97: Proceedings of the SIGCHI conference on Human factors in computing systems*, pages 43–50, New York, NY, USA, 1997. ACM Press.

[FDM04]   Peter Forbig, Anke Dittmar, and Andreas Müller. Adaptive task modelling: From formal methods to XML representations. In Ahmed Seffah and Homa Javahery, editors, *Multiple User Interfaces*, pages 171–192. John Wiley & Sons Inc., 2004.

[Fos03]   David H. Foster. Does colour constancy exist? *Trends in Cognitive Science*, 1:439–443, 2003.

[Fow03]   M. Fowler. Inversion of control containers and the dependency injection pattern., 2003. http://martinfowler.com/articles/injection.html, Last access: 06-27-2007.

[FWC84]   James D. Foley, Victor L. Wallace, and Peggy Chan. The human factors of computer graphics interaction techniques. *IEEE Comput. Graph. Appl.*, 4(11):13–48, 1984.

[Gav89]   William W. Gaver. The sonicfinder: An interface that uses auditory icons. *SIGCHI Bull.*, 21(1):124, 1989.

[GCH+05]   Krzysztof Gajos, David B. Christianson, Raphael Hoffmann, Tal Shaked, Kiera Henning, Jing Jing Long, and Daniel S. Weld. Fast and robust interface generation for ubiquitous applications. In Michael Beigl, Stephen S. Intille, Jun Rekimoto, and Hideyuki Tokuda, editors, *Ubicomp*, volume 3660 of *Lecture Notes in Computer Science*, pages 37–55. Springer, 2005.

[GCTW06]   Krzysztof Z. Gajos, Mary Czerwinski, Desney S. Tan, and Daniel S. Weld. Exploring the design space for adaptive graphical user interfaces. In *AVI '06: Proceedings of the working conference on Advanced visual interfaces*, pages 201–208, New York, NY, USA, 2006. ACM Press.

[GHJV95]   Erich Gamma, Richard Helm, Ralph Johnson, and John Vlissides. *Design patterns: elements of reusable object-oriented software*. Addison-Wesley Longman Publishing Co., Inc., Boston, MA, USA, 1995.

[Gol02]   Bruce E. Goldstein. *Sensation and Perception*. Wadsworth Group, Pacific Grove, California, 6th edition, 2002.

[GOS01]   Francine Gemperle, Nathan Ota, and Daniel P. Siewiorek. Design of a wearable tactile display. In *5th International Symposium on Wearable Computers (ISWC 2001)*, pages 5–12, Zürich, Switzerland, 8-9 October 2001.

[GPZGB05]   Ilenia Graziola, Fabio Pianesi, Massimo Zancanaro, and Dina Goren-Bar. Dimensions of adaptivity in mobile systems: personality and people's attitudes. In *IUI '05: Proceedings of the 10th international conference on Intelligent user interfaces*, pages 223–230, New York, NY, USA, 2005. ACM Press.

[Gra97]   Winfried H. Graf. *Intentionsgesteuertes Layout-Design multimedialer Präsentationen mit Constraints*. PhD thesis, Technische Universität des Saarlandes, Saarbrücken, 1997.

[Gre96]   Saul Greenberg. Teaching human computer interaction to programmers. *interactions*, 3(4):62–76, 1996.

[GW04]   Krzysztof Gajos and Daniel S. Weld. Supple: automatically generating user interfaces. In *IUI '04: Proceedings of the 9th international conference on Intelligent user interface*, pages 93–100, New York, NY, USA, 2004. ACM Press.

[Ham89]   P. J. Hampson. Aspects of attention and cognitive science. *The Irish Journal of Psychology*, 10:261–275, 1989.

[HB99]   David J. Haniff and Chris Baber. Wearable computers for the fire service and police force: Technological and human factors. In *ISWC '99: Proceedings of the 3rd IEEE International Symposium on Wearable Computers*, page 185, Washington, DC, USA, 1999. IEEE Computer Society.

[Her05]   Ewald Hering. *Grundzüge der Lehre vom Lichtsinn*, volume 5 of *Handbuch der gesamten Augenheilkunde*, chapter 13. Berlin, 1905.

[HGK+04]   Lars Erik Holmquist, Hans-Werner Gellersen, Gerd Kortuem, Albrecht Schmidt, Martin Strohbach, Stavros Antifakos, Florian Michahelles, Bernt Schiele, Michael Beigl, and Ramia Mazé. Building intelligent environments with smart-its. *IEEE Computer Graphics and Applications*, 24(1):56–64, 2004.

[HH93]   Deborah Hix and H. Rex Hartson. *Developing user interfaces: ensuring usability through product & process*. John Wiley & Sons, Inc., New York, NY, USA, 1993.

[HI05]   Joyce Ho and Stephen S. Intille. Using context-aware computing to reduce the perceived burden of interruptions from mobile devices. In *CHI '05: Proceedings of the SIGCHI conference on Human factors in computing systems*, pages 909–918, New York, NY, USA, 2005. ACM Press.

[HJ07]   Helen Hodgetts and Dylan Jones. Reminders, allerts and pop-ups: The cost of computer-initiated interruption. In *Proceedings of the 12th International Conference on Human-Computer Interaction (HCII 2007)*, Beijing, P.R. China, July 22–27 2007. Springer.

[HLJ+05]   Sunyu Hwang, Geehyuk Lee, Buyong Jeong, Woohun Lee, and Ilyeon Cho. Feeltip: tactile input device for small wearable information appliances. In

CHI '05: CHI '05 extended abstracts on Human factors in computing systems, pages 1475–1478, Portland, OR, USA, 2005. ACM Press.

[HMNS01]   Uwe Hansmann, Lothar Merk, Martin Nicklous, and Thomas Stober. *Pervasive Computing Handbook*. Springer Verlag, Heidelberg, 2001.

[HPGK94]   Ken Hinckley, Randy Pausch, John C. Goble, and Neal F. Kassell. A survey of design issues in spatial input. In *UIST '94: Proceedings of the 7th annual ACM symposium on User interface software and technology*, pages 213–222, New York, NY, USA, 1994. ACM Press.

[HPHS05]   Ken Hinckley, Jeff Pierce, Eric Horvitz, and Mike Sinclair. Foreground and background interaction with sensor-enhanced mobile devices. *ACM Transactions on Computer-Human Interaction*, 12(1):31–52, 2005.

[HS88]   S.G. Hart and L. Staveland. Development of nasa-tlx (task load index): Results of empirical and theoretical research. In *Human mental workload*, pages 139–183. P.A. Hancock and N. Meshkati (Eds.), Amsterdam: Elsevier, 1988.

[HSR+80]   W. Hirst, E. S. Spelke, C. C. Reaves, G. Caharack, and U. Neisser. Dividing attention without alternation or automaticity. *Journal of Experimental Psychology*, 109:98–117, 1980.

[Hur81]   L. Hurvich. *Color Vision*. MA: Sinauer Associates, Sunderland, 1981.

[Hur99]   A. C. Hurlbert. Colour vision: Is colour constancy real? *Current Biology*, 9:R558–R561, 1999.

[Iwa03]   Hiroo Iwata. Haptic interfaces. In Julie A. Jacko and Andrew Sears, editors, *The Human-Computer Interaction Handbook: Fundamentals, Evolving Technologies and Emerging Applications*, chapter 10, pages 206–219. Lawrence Erlbaum Associates, 2003.

[JHA+05]   Rod Johnson, Juergen Hoeller, Alef Arendsen, Thomas Risberg, and Dmitriy Kopylenko. *Professional Java Development with the Spring Framework*. Wrox Press Ltd., Birmingham, UK, UK, 2005.

[JLT04]   Holger Junker, Paul Lukowicz, and Gerhard Tröster. Sampling frequency, signal resolution and the accuracy of wearable context recognition systems. In *8th International Symposium on Wearable Computers (ISWC)*, pages 176–177. IEEE Computer Society, 2004.

[JM06]   Matt Jones and Gary Marsden. *Mobile Interaction Design*. John Wiley &
            Sons, February 2006.

[Joh00]   Jeff Johnson, editor. *GUI bloopers: don'ts and do's for software developers
            and Web designers*. Morgan Kaufmann Publishers Inc., San Francisco, CA,
            USA, 2000.

[KASS04]   Nicky Kern, Stavros Antifakos, Bernt Schiele, and Adrian Schwaninger. A
            model for human interruptability: Experimental evaluation and automatic
            estimation from wearable sensors. In *ISWC '04: Proceedings of the Eighth
            International Symposium on Wearable Computers (ISWC'04)*, pages 158–
            165, Washington, DC, USA, 2004. IEEE Computer Society.

[KC06]   Ashraf Khalil and Kay Connelly. Context-aware telephony: privacy pref-
            erences and sharing patterns. In *CSCW '06: Proceedings of the 2006 20th
            anniversary conference on Computer supported cooperative work*, pages 469–
            478, New York, NY, USA, 2006. ACM Press.

[KG03]   Jesper Kjeldskov and Connor Graham. A review of mobile HCI research
            methods. In *Mobile HCI*, pages 317–335, 2003.

[Kha06]   Ashraf Khalil. *Context-Aware Telephony and Its Users: Methods to Im-
            prove the Accuracy of Mobile Device Interruptions*. PhD thesis, Indiana
            University, April 2006.

[KKMP06]   Sanna Kallio, Juha Kela, Jani Mäntyjärvi, and Johan Plomp. Visualiza-
            tion of hand gestures for pervasive computing environments. In *AVI '06:
            Proceedings of the working conference on Advanced visual interfaces*, pages
            480–483, New York, NY, USA, 2006. ACM Press.

[KNW+07]   Holger Kenn, Tom Nicolai, Hendrik Witt, Stéphane Beauregard, Michael
            Lawo, Michael Boronowsky, and Otthein Herzog. Artificial intelligence in
            wearable computing - perspectives and challenges. *Künstliche Intelligenz*,
            2:17–23, 2007.

[Kob93]   A. Kobsa. User modeling: Recent work, prospects and hazards. In
            M. Schneider-Hufschmidt, T. Kühme, and U. Malinowski, editors, *Adaptive
            User Interfaces: Principles and Practice*, pages 111–128. North-Holland,
            1993.

[Kra94]   G. Kramer. An introduction to auditory display. In Santa Fe Institute Stud-
             ies in the Sciences of Complexity, editor, *Auditory Display: Sonification,
             Audification, and Auditory Interfaces*, pages 1–77. Addison-Wesley, 1994.

[KS03]   Nicky Kern and Bernt Schiele. Context-aware notification for wearable com-
             puting. In *ISWC '03: Proceedings of the 7th IEEE International Sympo-
             sium on Wearable Computers*, page 223, Washington, DC, USA, 2003. IEEE
             Computer Society.

[KSB98]   Gerd Kortuem, Zary Segall, and Martin Bauer. Context-aware, adaptive
             wearable computers as remote interfaces to 'intelligent' environments. In
             *ISWC '98: Proceedings of the 2nd IEEE International Symposium on Wear-
             able Computers*, page 58, Washington, DC, USA, 1998. IEEE Computer
             Society.

[KX05]   Rakesh B. Katragadda and Yong Xu. A novel intelligent textile technol-
             ogy based on silicon flexible skins. In *ISWC '05: Proceedings of the 9nd
             IEEE International Symposium on Wearable Computers*, pages 78–81, Os-
             aka, Japan, 2005. IEEE Computer Society.

[LB00]   G. Leplatre and S. Brewster. Designing non-speech sounds to support navi-
             gation in mobile phone menus. In *Proceedings of ICAD2000*, pages 190–199,
             Atlanta, USA, 2000. Academic Press.

[LBW+07]   Kent Lyons, Helene Brashear, Tracy Westeyn, Jung Soo Kim, and Thad
             Starner. GART: The gesture and activity recognition toolkit. In *Proceedings
             of HCI International 2007*, Beijing, China, July 2007. Springer.

[LG04]   Kristof Van Laerhoven and Hans-Werner Gellersen. Spine versus porcupine:
             A study in distributed wearable activity recognition. In *ISWC '04: Pro-
             ceedings of the 8th IEEE International Symposium on Wearable Computers*,
             pages 142–149, 2004.

[LGSC05]   Kent Lyons, Brian Gane, Thad Starner, and Richard Catrambone. Improv-
             ing novice performance on the twiddler one-handed chording keyboard. In
             Proceedings of the International Forum on Applied Wearable Computing,
             pages 145–159, Zurich, Switzerland, 2005. IEEE Computer Society.

[LH99]   G. Li and C. M. Haslegrave. Seated work postures for manual, visual and
             combined tasks. ergonomics. *Ergonomics*, 42(8):1060–1086, 1999.

[LJS+04]   Paul Lukowicz, Jamie A. Wardand Holger Junker, Mathias Stäger, Gerhard Tröster, Amin Atrash, and Thad Starner. Recognizing workshop activity using body worn microphones and accelerometers. In *Pervasive Computing: Proceedings of the 2nd International Conference*, pages 18–22. Springer-Verlag Heidelberg: Lecture Notes in Computer Science, 2004.

[LK93]   James A. Landay and Todd R. Kaufmann. User interface issues in mobile computing. In *Proceedings of the Fourth Workshop on Workstation Operating Systems*, pages 40–47, Napa, Canada, October 1993.

[LKAR05]   Torsten Linz, Christine Kallmayer, Rolf Aschenbrenner, and Herbert Reichl. Embroidering electrical interconnects with conductive yarn for the integration of flexible electronic modules into fabric. In *ISWC '05: Proceedings of the 9th IEEE International Symposium on Wearable Computers*, pages 86–91, Osaka, Japan, 2005. IEEE Computer Society.

[LM90]   S. J. Liebowitz and Stephen E. Margolis. The fable of the keys. *Journal of Law and Economics*, 33(1):1–25, April 1990.

[LPL+06]   Joseph Luk, Jerome Pasquero, Shannon Little, Karon MacLean, Vincent Levesque, and Vincent Hayward. A role for haptics in mobile interaction: initial design using a handheld tactile display prototype. In *CHI '06: Proceedings of the SIGCHI conference on Human Factors in computing systems*, pages 171–180, Montreal, Quebec, Canada, 2006. ACM Press.

[LPS04]   Kent Lyons, Daniel Plaisted, and Thad Starner. Expert chording text entry on the twiddler one-handed keyboard. In *ISWC '04: Proceedings of the Eighth International Symposium on Wearable Computers (ISWC'04)*, pages 94–101, Washington, DC, USA, 2004. IEEE Computer Society.

[LRO03]   Holger Luczak, Matthias Roetting, and Olaf Oehme. Visual displays. In *The Human-Computer Interaction Handbook: Fundamentals, Evolving Technologies and Emerging Applications*, pages 187–205. Lawrence Erlbaum Associates, Inc., Mahwah, NJ, USA, 2003.

[LS01]   Kent Lyons and Thad Starner. Mobile capture for wearable computer usability testing. In *Proceedings of IEEE International Symposium on Wearable Computing (ISWC 2001)*, pages 69–76, Zurich, Switzerland, 2001.

[LSP+04]   Kent Lyons, Thad Starner, Daniel Plaisted, James Fusia, Amanda Lyons, Aaron Drew, and E. W. Looney. Twiddler typing: One-handed chording text entry for mobile phones. In *CHI '04: Proceedings of the SIGCHI conference on Human factors in computing systems*, pages 671–678, New York, NY, USA, 2004. ACM Press.

[Lun01]   Nick Lund. *Attention and Pattern Recognition*. Routledge, East Sussex, UK, 2001.

[LWK+06]   Michael Lawo, Hendrik Witt, Holger Kenn, Tom Nicolai, and Rüdiger Leibrand. A glove for seamless computer interaction - understand the winspect. Proceedings of the Smart Glove Workshop 33, TZI, University of Bremen, 2006.

[Man97]   Steve Mann. An historical account of 'wearcomp' and 'wearcam' inventions developed for applications in 'personal imaging'. In *ISWC '97: Proceedings of the 1st IEEE International Symposium on Wearable Computers*, pages 66–73, 1997.

[Man01a]   Steve Mann. Guest editor's introduction: Wearable computing-toward humanistic intelligence. *IEEE Intelligent Systems*, 16(3):10–15, 2001.

[Man01b]   Steve Mann. *Intelligent Image Processing*. John Wiley and Sons, November 2 2001. ISBN: 0-471-40637-6.

[MAS04]   Christian Metzger, Matt Anderson, and Thad Starner. Freedigiter: A contact-free device for gesture control. In *ISWC '04: Proceedings of the Eighth International Symposium on Wearable Computers (ISWC'04)*, pages 18–21, Washington, DC, USA, 2004. IEEE Computer Society.

[MB06]   Georgios N. Marentakis and Stephen A. Brewster. Effects of feedback, mobility and index of difficulty on deictic spatial audio target acquisition in the horizontal plane. In *CHI '06: Proceedings of the SIGCHI conference on Human Factors in computing systems*, pages 359–368, New York, NY, USA, 2006. ACM Press.

[McF99]   Daniel C. McFarlane. Coordinating the interruption of people in human-computer interaction. In *Human-Computer Interaction - INTERACT'99*, pages 295–303. IOS Press, Inc., 1999.

[McF02a]   D. C. McFarlane. Comparison of four primary methods for co-ordinating the interruption of people in human-computer interaction design. *Human-Computer Interaction*, 17(1):63–139, 2002.

[McF02b]   Daniel C. McFarlane. Comparison of four primary methods for coordinating the interruption of people in human-computer interaction. *Human-Computer Interaction*, 17(1):63–139, 2002.

[McL77]   P. McLeod. A dual-task response modality effect: Support for multiprocessor models of attention. *Quarterly Journal of Experimental Psychology*, 29:651–667, 1977.

[MFPBS97]   Mark R. Mine, Jr. Frederick P. Brooks, and Carlo H. Sequin. Moving objects in space: exploiting proprioception in virtual-environment interaction. In *SIGGRAPH '97: Proceedings of the 24th annual conference on Computer graphics and interactive techniques*, pages 19–26, New York, NY, USA, 1997. ACM Press/Addison-Wesley Publishing Co.

[MHM05]   Jane McCann, Richard Hurford, and Adam Martin. A design process for the development of innovative smart clothing that addresses end-user needs from technical, functional, aesthetic and cultural view points. In *ISWC '05: Proceedings of the 9th IEEE International Symposium on Wearable Computers*, pages 70–77, Osaka, Japan, 2005. IEEE Computer Society.

[Mil56]   G. A. Miller. The magic number seven, plus or minus two: Some limits on our capacity for processing information. *Psychological Review*, 63:81–93, 1956.

[MKS+07]   Iñaki Maurtua, Pierre T. Kirisci, Thomas Stiefmeier, Marco Luca Sbodio, and Hendrik Witt. A wearable computing prototype for supporting training activities in automotive production. In *4th International Forum for Applied Wearable Computing (IFAWC)*, pages 45–55, Tel Aviv, Israel, March 12–13 2007. VDE Verlag.

[ML02]   D. C. McFarlane and K. A. Latorella. The scope and importance of human interruption in human-computer interaction design. *Human-Computer Interaction*, 17(1):1–61, 2002.

[MM76]   H. McGurk and T. MacDonald. Hearing lips and seeing voices. *Nature*, 264:746–748, 1976.

[MM97]   James E. Melzer and Kirk Moffitt. *Head-Mounted Displays: Designing for the User*. McGraw-Hill Professional, 1997.

[MP06]   Gerard McAtamney and Caroline Parker. An examination of the effects
            of a wearable display on informal face-to-face communication. In *CHI '06:
            Proceedings of the SIGCHI conference on Human Factors in computing sys-
            tems*, pages 45–54, New York, NY, USA, 2006. ACM Press.

[MPS04]   Giulio Mori, Fabio Paterno, and Carmen Santoro. Design and development
            of multidevice user interfaces through multiple logical descriptions. *IEEE
            Trans. Softw. Eng.*, 30(8):507–520, 2004.

[Mur87a]   D. Murray. Embedded user models. In B. Shackel and H-J. Bullinger, edi-
            tors, *Proc. INTERACT '87, Second IFIP Conference on Human-Computer
            Interaction*, pages 229–235. Elsevier Science Publishers, Amsterdamm,
            1987.

[Mur87b]   D. Murray. A survey of user modelling definitions and techniques. Technical
            Report 92/87, NPL DITC Report, Teddington, U.K., 1987.

[MW98]   Mark T. Maybury and Wolfgang Wahlster, editors. *Readings in intelligent
            user interfaces*. Morgan Kaufmann Publishers Inc., San Francisco, CA,
            USA, 1998.

[MW07]   Ernesto Morales Kluge and Hendrik Witt. Developing applications for wear-
            able computers: A process driven example. In *Proceedings of the 4th In-
            ternational Forum on Applied Wearable Computing (IFAWC)*, pages 23–33.
            VDE/ITG, 2007.

[Myn94]   Elizabeth D. Mynatt. Designing with auditory icons: how well do we identify
            auditory cues? In *CHI '94: Conference companion on Human factors in
            computing systems*, pages 269–270, New York, NY, USA, 1994. ACM Press.

[NCM07]   Jeffrey Nichols, Duen Horng Chau, and Brad A. Myers. Demonstrating the
            viability of automatically generated user interfaces. In *CHI '07: Proceedings
            of the SIGCHI conference on Human factors in computing systems*, pages
            1283–1292, New York, NY, USA, 2007. ACM Press.

[NDL+05]   Marcus Nilsson, Mikael Drugge, Urban Liljedahl, Kåre Synnes, and Peter
            Parnes. A study on users' preference on interruption when using wearable
            computers and head mounted displays. In *PerCom'05: Proceedings of the
            4th annual IEEE International Conference on Pervasive Computing and
            Communications*, pages 149–158, 2005.

[Nic06]   Jeffrey Nichols. *Automatically Generating High-Quality User Interfaces for Appliances*. PhD thesis, Carnegie Mellon University, December 2006.

[Nie94]   Jakob Nielsen. Enhancing the explanatory power of usability heuristics. In *CHI '94: Proceedings of the SIGCHI conference on Human factors in computing systems*, pages 152–158, New York, NY, USA, 1994. ACM Press.

[NMH⁺02] Jeffrey Nichols, Brad A. Myers, Michael Higgins, Joseph Hughes, Thomas K. Harris, Roni Rosenfeld, and Mathilde Pignol. Generating remote control interfaces for complex appliances. In *UIST '02: Proceedings of the 15th annual ACM symposium on User interface software and technology*, pages 161–170, New York, NY, USA, 2002. ACM Press.

[Noy83]   J. Noyes. Chording keyboards. *Applied Ergonomics*, 14:55–59, 1983.

[NRC97]   NRC. Tactical display for soldiers: Human factors considerations. National Academy Press, Washington, DC 1997.

[NRCM06] Jeffrey Nichols, Brandon Rothrock, Duen Horng Chau, and Brad A. Myers. Huddle: automatically generating interfaces for systems of multiple connected appliances. In *UIST '06: Proceedings of the 19th annual ACM symposium on User interface software and technology*, pages 279–288, New York, NY, USA, 2006. ACM Press.

[NS72]   B. R. Newell and H. A. Simon. *Human problem solving*. NJ: Prantice Hall, Englewood Cliffs, 1972.

[NSK⁺06] Tom Nicolai, Thomas Sindt, Holger Kenn, Jörn Reimerders, and Hendrik Witt. Wearable computing for aircraft maintenance: Simplifying the user interface. In *Proceedings of the 3rd International Forum on Applied Wearable Computing (IFAWC)*, pages 21–31, Bremen, Germany, March 15-16 2006.

[NSKW05] Tom Nicolai, Thomas Sindt, Holger Kenn, and Hendrik Witt. Case study of wearable computing for aircraft maintenance. In *Proceedings of the 2nd International Forum on Applied Wearable Computing (IFAWC)*, pages 97–109, Zürich, Switzerland, 2005.

[OS04]   Antti Oulasvirta and Pertti Saariluoma. Long-term working memory and interrupting messages in human-computer interaction. *Behaviour and Information Technology*, 23(1):53–64, 2004.

[OS06]   Zeljko Obrenovic and Dusan Starcevic. Adapting the unified software development process for user interface development. *The international journal on computer science and information systems*, 3(1):33–52, 2006.

[Pal99]   S.E. Palmer. *Vision science: Photons to Phenomenology*. MA: MIT Press, Cambridge, 1999.

[Pat99]   Fabio Paternò. *Model-Based Design and Evaluation of Interactive Applications*. Springer Verlag, 1999.

[PBH02]   Antti Pirhonen, Stephen Brewster, and Christopher Holguin. Gestural and audio metaphors as a means of control for mobile devices. In *CHI '02: Proceedings of the SIGCHI conference on Human factors in computing systems*, pages 291–298, New York, NY, USA, 2002. ACM Press.

[PE02]   Angel Puerta and Jacob Eisenstein. XIML: a common representation for interaction data. In *IUI '02: Proceedings of the 7th international conference on Intelligent user interfaces*, pages 214–215, New York, NY, USA, 2002. ACM Press.

[Pel98]   Eli Peli. The visual effects of head-mounted display (HMD) are not distinguishable from those of desk-top computer display. *Vision Research*, 38:2053–2066, 1998.

[PLN04]   Tim F. Paymans, Jasper Lindenberg, and Mark Neerincx. Usability tradeoffs for adaptive user interfaces: ease of use and learnability. In *IUI '04: Proceedings of the 9th international conference on Intelligent user interface*, pages 301–303, New York, NY, USA, 2004. ACM Press.

[PPRS06]   Jennifer Preece, Jenny Preece, Yvonne Rogers, and Helen Sharp. *Beyond Interaction Design: Beyond Human-Computer Interaction*. John Wiley & Sons, Inc., New York, NY, USA, 2nd edition, 2006.

[PR94]   S. E. Palmer and I. Rock. Rethinking perceptual organization: the role of uniform connectedness. *Psychonomic Bulletin & Review*, 1(1):29–55, 1994.

[Pue97]   Angel R. Puerta. A model-based interface development environment. *IEEE Software*, 14(4):40–47, 1997.

[RaHPK04] N. Rauch and I. Totzke amd H.-P. Krüger. Kompetenzerwerb für fahrerinformationssysteme: Bedeutung von bedienkontext und menüstruktur. *VDI-*

Berichte: Integrierte Sicherheit und Fahrerassistenzsysteme, 1864:303–323, 2004.

[RB00]   David A. Ross and Bruce B. Blasch. Evaluation of orientation interfaces for wearable computers. In *ISWC '00: Proceedings of the 4th IEEE International Symposium on Wearable Computers*, page 51, Washington, DC, USA, 2000. IEEE Computer Society.

[RBF03]   Davide Rocchesso, Roberto Bresin, and Mikael Fernstrom. Sounding objects. *IEEE MultiMedia*, 10(2):42–52, 2003.

[Ree79]   Trygve Reenskaug. Thing-model-view-editor: An example from a planning system. Technical report, Xerox PARC, May 1979.

[Rek01]   Jun Rekimoto. Gesturewrist and gesturepad: Unobtrusive wearable interaction devices. In *5th International Symposium on Wearable Computers (ISWC 2001)*, page 21. IEEE Computer Society, 2001.

[Rho97]   Bradly Rhodes. The wearable remembrance agent. *Personal Technologies*, 1(4):218–225, March 1997.

[RLF06]   Peter H. Rossi, Mark W. Lipsey, and Howard E. Freeman. *Evaluation: A Systematic Approach*. B & T, 7 edition, 2006.

[Rou88]   W. B. Rouse. Adaptive aiding for human-computer control. *Human Factors*, 30(4):431–443, 1988.

[RPB07]   Emma Russell, Lynne Millward Purvis, and Adrian Banks. Describing the strategies used for dealing with email interruptions according to different situational parameters. *Computer Human Behaviour*, 23(4):1820–1837, 2007.

[RS99]   R. Rosenberg and M. Slater. The chording glove: a glove-based text input device. *IEEE Transactions on Systems, Man, and Cybernetics, Part C*, 29(2):186–191, 1999.

[RV95]   Paul Resnick and Robert A. Virzi. Relief from the audio interface blues: expanding the spectrum of menu, list, and form styles. *ACM Transactions on Computer-Human Interaction*, 2(2):145–176, 1995.

[RW03]   Janice Redish and Dennis Wixon. Task analysis. In J. A. Jacko and A. Sears, editors, *The Human-Computer Interaction Handbook*, pages 922–940. Lawrence Erlbaum Associates, Inc., Mahwah, NJ, USA, 2003.

[SAAG00]   Thad Starner, Jake Auxier, Daniel Ashbrook, and Maribeth Gandy. The
            gesture pendant: A self-illuminating, wearable, infrared computer vision
            system for home automation control and medical monitoring. In *ISWC
            '00: Proceedings of the 4th IEEE International Symposium on Wearable
            Computers*, pages 87–94, Washington, DC, USA, 2000. IEEE Computer
            Society.

[Sam93]   J. B. Sampson. Cognitive performance of individuals using head-mounted
            displays while walking. In *Proceedings of the Human Factors and Er-
            gonomics Society 37th Annual Meeting*, pages 338–342, Santa Monica, CA,
            1993. Human Factors and Ergonomics Society.

[Sat01]   Mahadev Satyanarayanan. Pervasive computing: Vision and challenges.
            IEEE Personal Communications, pages 10–17, August 2001.

[SB97]   Jane Siegel and Malcolm Bauer. A field usability evaluation of a wearable
            system. In *ISWC '97: Proceedings of the 1st IEEE International Sympo-
            sium on Wearable Computers*, page 18, Washington, DC, USA, 1997. IEEE
            Computer Society.

[SB06]   Heike Sacher and Heiner Bubb. Was bedient der fahrer? feldversuche zu
            erfassung der fahrer-fahrzeug-interaktion. *MMI-Interaktiv*, 11:18–29, De-
            cember 2006.

[SC03]   William R. Sherman and Alan B. Craig. *Understanding Virtual Reality.
            Interface, Application, and Design*. Morgan Kaufmann Publishers Inc., San
            Francisco, CA, USA, 2003.

[Sch94]   Christopher Schmandt. *Voice communication with computers: conversa-
            tional systems*. Van Nostrand Reinhold Co., New York, NY, USA, 1994.

[Sch00]   Albrecht Schmidt. Implicit human computer interaction through context.
            Personal and Ubiquitous Computing, 4(2/3):191–199, 2000.

[Sch02]   Albrecht Schmidt. *Ubiquitous Computing - Computing in Context*. PhD
            thesis, Lancaster University, Lancaster, UK, November 2002.

[SG97]   F. J. Seagull and D. Gopher. Training head movement in visual scan-
            ning:anembedded approach to the development of piloting skills with
            helmet-mounted displays. *Journal of Experimental Psychology: Applied*,
            3:163–180, 1997.

[SGBT00]   A. Schmidt, H. Gellersen, M. Beigl, and O. Thate. Developing user interfaces for wearable computers: Don't stop to point and click. In *International
Workshop on Interactive Applications of Mobile Computing (IMC2000)*,
2000.

[She06]   Lauralee Sherwood. *Human Physiology : From Cells to Systems*. Brooks/-
Cole, Thomson Learning, 6 edition, 2006.

[SHMK93]   Matthias Schneider-Hufschmidt, Uwe Malinowski, and Thomas Kuhme, editors. *Adaptive User Interfaces: Principles and Practice*. Elsevier Science
Inc., New York, NY, USA, 1993.

[SHN76]   E. S. Spelke, W. Hirst, and U. Neisser. Skills of divided attention. *Cognition*,
4:215–230, 1976.

[Shn83]   Ben Shneiderman. Direct manipulation: A step beyond programming languages. *IEEE Computer*, 16(8):57–69, 1983.

[SJ01]   D. L. Strayer and W. A. Johnston. Driven to distraction: Dual-task studies
of simulated driving and conversing on a cellular telephone. *Psychological
Science*, 12(462–466), 2001.

[SJ04]   A. Seffah and H. Javahery. *Multiple User Interfaces Cross-Platform Applications and Context-Aware Interfaces*. John Wiley & Sons, West Sussex,
UK, 2004.

[SJWM05]   Debbie Stone, Caroline Jarrett, Mark Woodroffe, and Shailey Minocha.
User Interface Design and Evaluation. Morgan Kaufmann, March 2005.

[SOJ+06]   T. Stiefmeier, G. Ogris, H. Junker, P. Lukowicz, and G. Tröster. Combining motion sensors and ultrasonic hands tracking for continuous activity
recognition in a maintenance scenario. In *ISWC'06: Proceedings of the
10th Intnational Symposium on Wearable Computers*, pages 97–104. IEEE
Computer Society, October 2006.

[Som04]   Ian Sommerville. *Software Engineering*. Pearson Addison Wesley, 7th edition, 2004.

[SP05]   Ben Shneiderman and Catherine Plaisant. *Designing the User Interface:
Strategies for Effective Human-Computer Interaction*. Addison-Wesley,
Boston, MA, USA, 4th edition, 2005.

[Spr06]   The Spring Framework:a layered Java/J2EE application framework, 2006.
           http://www.springframework.org/, Last access: 06-27-2007.

[SRC01]   A. Seffah, T. Radhakrishan, and G. Canals. Multiple user interfaces over
           the internet: Engineering and applications trends. In *Workshop at the IHM-
           HCI: French/British Conference on Human-Computer Interaction*, Lille,
           France, September 10–14 2001.

[SS98]   N. Sawhney and C. Schmandt. Speaking and listening on the run: Design
           for wearable audio computing. In *ISWC '98: Proceedings of the 2nd IEEE
           International Symposium on Wearable Computers*, page 108, Washington,
           DC, USA, 1998. IEEE Computer Society.

[SS00]   Nitin "Nick" Sawhney and Chris Schmandt. Nomadic radio: speech and
           audio interaction for contextual messaging in nomadic environments. *ACM
           Trans. Comput.-Hum. Interact.*, 7(3):353–383, 2000.

[SSF+03]   Daniel Siewiorek, Asim Smailagic, Junichi Furukawa, Andreas Krause,
           Neema Moraveji, Kathryn Reiger, Jeremy Shaffer, and Fei L. Wong. Sensay:
           A context-aware mobile phone. In *ISWC '03: Proceedings of the 7th IEEE
           International Symposium on Wearable Computers*, Washington, DC, USA,
           2003. IEEE Computer Society.

[ST94]   Bill Schilit and M. Theimer. Disseminating active map information to mo-
           bile hosts. *IEEE Network*, 8(5):22–32, 1994.

[ST06]   Marco Luca Sbodio and Wolfgang Thronicke. Context processing within
           an open, componentoriented, software framework. In *Proceedings of the 3rd
           International Forum on Applied Wearable Computing (IFAWC)*, Bremen,
           Germany, March 15-16 2006.

[Sta95]   Thad Starner. The cyborgs are comming. Perceptual Computing 318, MIT
           Media Laboratory, November 1995.

[Sta99]   Thad Starner. *Wearable Computing and Contextual Awareness*. PhD thesis,
           Massachusetts Institute of Technology, June 1999.

[Sta01a]   Thad Starner. The challenges of wearable computing: Part 1. *IEEE Micro*,
           21(4):44–52, 2001.

[Sta01b]   Thad Starner. The challenges of wearable computing: Part 2. *IEEE Micro*,
           21(4):54–67, 2001.

[Sta02a]   Thad Starner. Attention, memory, and wearable interfaces. *IEEE Pervasive Computing*, 1(4):88–91, 2002.

[Sta02b]   Thad Starner. Thick clients for personal wireless devices. *IEEE Computer*, 35(1):133–135, January 2002.

[Sta02c]   Thad E. Starner. The role of speech input in wearable computing. *IEEE Pervasive Computing*, 1(3):89–93, 2002.

[STM00]   Albrecht Schmidt, Antti Takaluoma, and Jani Mäntyjärvi. Context-aware telephony over wap. *Personal Ubiquitous Computing*, 4(4):225–229, 2000.

[Stu01]   Rory Stuart. *The Design of Virtual Environments*. McGraw-Hill, New York, 2001.

[Sul76]   L. Sullivan. Selective attention and secondary message analysis: A reconsideration of broadbent's filter model of selective attention. *Quarterly Journal of Experimental Psychology*, 28:167–178, 1976.

[SZ94]   David J. Sturman and David Zeltzer. A survey of glove-based input. *IEEE Computer Graphics ands Applications*, 14(1):30 – 39, January 1994.

[TCC04]   David Thevenin, Joelle Coutaz, and Gaelle Calvary. A reference framework for the development of plastic user interfaces. In Ahmed Seffah and Homa Javahery, editors, *Multiple User Interfaces: Cross-Plattform Applications and Context-Aware Interfaces*, chapter 3, pages 29–51. John Wiley and Sons Ltd., West Sussex, UK, 2004.

[TD73]   A. M. Teisman and A. Davies. Divided attention to ear and eye. In S. Kornblum, editor, *Attention and performance, Vol. 4*, pages 101–117. London: Academic Press, 1973.

[TP97]   Hong Z. Tan and Alex Pentland. Tactual displays for wearable computing. In *Proceedings of the 1st International Symposium on Wearable Computers*, page 84, Los Alamitos, CA, USA, 1997. IEEE Computer Society.

[TP02]   Bruce H. Thomas and Wayne Piekarski. Glove based user interaction techniques for augmented reality in an outdoor environment. *Virtual Reality*, 6(3):167–180, 2002.

[Tre86]   A. Treisman. Features and objects in visual processing. *Scientific America*, 255:114B–125B, 1986.

[Tre98]   A. Treisman. The perception of features and objects. In R. D. Wright, editor, *Visual attention*, pages 26–54. Oxford University Press, New York, 1998.

[TTM06]   Aaron P. Toney, Bruce H. Thomas, and Wynand Marais. Managing smart garments. In *ISWC'06: Proceedings of the 10th International Symposium on Wearable Computers*, pages 91–94, Montreux, Switzerland, Oktober 11–14 2006. IEEE.

[TY04]   Koji Tsukada and Michiaki Yasumura. Activebelt: Belt-type wearable tactile display for directional navigation. In *UbiComp 2004: Proceedings of the 6th International Conference on Ubiquitous Computing*, pages 384–399, Nottingham, UK, September 7-10 2004.

[vdBRZK96]   P. van den Berg, R. A. Roe, F. R. H. Zijlstra, and I. Krediet. Temperamental factors in the execution of interrupted editing tasks. *European Journal of Personality*, 10:233–248, 1996.

[VIR01]   Karel Vredenburg, Scott Isensee, and Carol Righi. *User-Centered Design: An Integrated Approach*. Prentice Hall PTR, 2001.

[VL05]   James Verges-Llahi. *Color Constancy and Image Segmentation Techniques for Applications to Mobile Robotics*. PhD thesis, Universitat Politecnica de Catalunya, 2005.

[VPL+06]   Kristin Vadas, Nirmal Patel, Kent Lyons, Thad Starner, and Julie Jacko. Reading on-the-go: a comparison of audio and hand-held displays. In *MobileHCI '06: Proceedings of the 8th conference on Human-computer interaction with mobile devices and services*, pages 219–226, New York, NY, USA, 2006. ACM Press.

[War04]   Colin Ware. *Information Visualization: Perception for Design*. Morgan Kaufmann Publishers Inc., San Francisco, CA, USA, 2004.

[WBAS03]   Tracy Westeyn, Helene Brashear, Amin Atrash, and Thad Starner. Georgia tech gesture toolkit: supporting experiments in gesture recognition. In *ICMI '03: Proceedings of the 5th international conference on Multimodal interfaces*, pages 85–92, New York, NY, USA, 2003. ACM Press.

[WD06]   Hendrik Witt and Mikael Drugge. Hotwire: an apparatus for simulating primary tasks in wearable computing. In *CHI '06: CHI '06 extended abstracts on Human factors in computing systems*, pages 1535–1540, New York, NY, USA, 2006. ACM Press.

[Wea04] WearIT@Work. The wearit@work project: Empowering the mobile worker with wearable computing. IST Project (No. IP 004216-2004), 2004. http://www.wearitatwork.com, Last access: 06-27-2007.

[Wei91] Mark Weiser. The computer for the 21th century. *Scientific America*, 265:94–104, 1991.

[Wes98] Leonard J. West. The standard and Dvorak keyboards revisited: Direct measures of speed. Research in Economics 98-05-041e, Santa Fe Institute, Santa Fe, May 1998.

[WFVMP02] R. L. Woods, I. Fetchenheuer, F. Vargas-Martín, and E. Peli. The impact of non-immersive HMDs on the visual field. *Journal on Social Information Display*, 11:191–198, 2002.

[Wit05] Hendrik Witt. A toolkit for context-aware wearable user interface development for wearable computers. In *ISWC'05: The 9th International Symposium on Wearable Computing. Doctoral Colloquium*, pages 15–17. IEEE, 2005. ISBN 3-902376-05-8.

[Wit07a] Hendrik Witt. Design, Entwicklung und Evaluation von Benutzerschnittstellen für Wearable Computer. *I-com*, 2:4–10, 2007.

[Wit07b] Hendrik Witt. Evaluation of five interruption methods for speech interaction in wearable computing dual-task environments. In *ISWC'07: Proceedings of the 11th International Symposium for Wearable Computers*, pages 63–66, Boston, MA, USA, October 11–13 2007. IEEE.

[WJ07] Hendrik Witt and Torben Janssen. Comparing two methods for gesture based short text input using chording. In *CHI '07: CHI '07 extended abstracts on Human factors in computing systems*, pages 2759–2764, New York, NY, USA, 2007. ACM Press.

[WK07] Hendrik Witt and Ernesto Morales Kluge. Domain expert vs. layman: Exploring the effect of subject selection in user studies for industrial wearable applications. In *Proceedings of the 4th ACM International Conference on Mobile Technology, Applications and Systems (MC'07)*, Singapore, September 10-12th 2007. ACM.

[WL06]   B. N. Walker and J. Lindsay. Navigation performance with a virtual audi-
           tory display: Effects of beacon sound, capture radius, and practice. *Human
           Factors*, 48(2):286–299, 2006.

[WLKK06]   Hendrik Witt, Rüdiger Leibrandt, Andreas Kemnade, and Holger Kenn.
           Scipio: A miniaturized building block for wearable interaction devices. In
           *Proceedings of the 3rd International Forum on Applied Wearable Computing
           (IFAWC)*, pages 103–108, Bremen, Germany, March 15-16 2006.

[WNK06]   Hendrik Witt, Tom Nicolai, and Holger Kenn. Designing a wearable user
           interface for hands-free interaction in maintenance applications. In *Per-
           Com'06: Proceedings of the 4th annual IEEE International Conference
           on Pervasive Computing and Communications Workshops*, pages 652–655,
           Pisa, Italy, 2006. IEEE Computer Society.

[WNK07]   Hendrik Witt, Tom Nicolai, and Holger Kenn. The WUI-Toolkit: A model-
           driven UI development framework for wearable user interfaces. In *Proceed-
           ings of the 7th International Workshop on Smart Appliances and Wearable
           Computing (IWSAWC)*, pages 43–48. IEEE, 2007.

[YAM+05]   Yasuyuki Yanagida, Takuya Adachi, Tsutomu Miyasato, Akira Tomono,
           Shinjiro Kawato, Haruo Noma, and Kenichi Hosaka. Integrating a
           projection-based olfactory display with interactive audio-visual contents.
           In *Proceedings of HCI International 2005*, Las Vegas, USA, July 2005.

[YLM95]   Nicole Yankelovich, Gina-Anne Levow, and Matt Marx. Designing
           speechacts: issues in speech user interfaces. In *CHI '95: Proceedings of the
           SIGCHI conference on Human factors in computing systems*, pages 369–
           376, New York, NY, USA, 1995. ACM Press/Addison-Wesley Publishing
           Co.

[ZSH02]   S. Zhai, B. A. Smith, and M. Hunter. Performance optimization of virtual
           keyboards. *Human-Computer Interaction*, 17:89–129., 2002.

[ZTG05]   Joanne Zucco, Bruce H. Thomas, and Karen Grimmer. Evaluation of three
           wearable computer pointing devices for selection tasks. In *9th International
           Symposium on Wearable Computers (ISWC 2005)*, pages 178–185, Osaka,
           Japan, 18-21 October 2005.

Appendix

Appendix A

User Studies

A.1 Questionnaires

The following documents were given to participants of the three user studies presented in this thesis. When assigning participants to a certain time slot in the schedule of the user study, the *participants instructions*, containing general information about the experiment, were given to them. On arrival at the facility where the user study was conducted, participants were given the same instruction document once again together with an *inquiry* that collected mainly demographical data. When a post experiment inquiry was available, participants were ask to fill out a *post-experiment inquiry* after they completed the experiment.

Inquiry #1 – Fill in *before* the study
(Gesture Experiment)

(This box is filled in by the test leader)

Subject ID: _____   Place: _____

Date: ___ : ___ / ___   Notes: _____

Time: ___ : ___

Privacy note

All answers you provide will be kept strictly confidential. In all results, e.g. articles or conference papers and presentations, derived from this study, we will exclude any information that can be used to identify you as a participant. You will remain anonymous and only be identified by the subject ID above. Please do *not* write your name anywhere on this paper.

Questions

1. Age _____ years
2. Gender   □ Female   □ Male
3. Dominant hand   □ Left   □ Right
4. Dominant eye   □ Left   □ Right
5. Colour blindness   □ Yes   □ No

For the remaining questions on the next page, please mark (by making a circle around one of the numbers) on the scale between 0 and 10 your answer to the question. Since the questions are based on your own experiences, there is no "right" or "wrong" answer. Do not attempt to answer how you think we may "expect" or "want" you to answer – please just answer sincerely.

6. How much computer experience do you have?

0	1	2	3	4	5	6	7	8	9	10

None   Substantial

7. How good are you at using computers in general?

0	1	2	3	4	5	6	7	8	9	10

No skills   Expert

8. What experience do you have of doing more than one thing at the same time?

0	1	2	3	4	5	6	7	8	9	10

None   Substantial

9. How skilled are you of doing more than one thing at the same time?

0	1	2	3	4	5	6	7	8	9	10

No skill   Expert

10. How much do interruptions affect your ability to perform a task?

0	1	2	3	4	5	6	7	8	9	10

Not at all   Significantly

11. How much do distractions affect your ability to perform a task?

0	1	2	3	4	5	6	7	8	9	10

Not at all   Significantly

12. How skilled are you at visual puzzling / matching games?

0	1	2	3	4	5	6	7	8	9	10

No skill   Expert

Thank you for filling in this form,
now continue with the experiment!

Inquiry #1 – Fill in *before* the study

(Audio Experiment)

(This box is filled in by the test leader)

Subject ID: _____   Place: _____

Date: _____ - _____ - _____   Notes: _____

Time: _____ : _____

Privacy note

All answers you provide will be kept strictly confidential. In all results, e.g. articles or conference papers and presentations, derived from this study, we will exclude any information that can be used to identify you as a participant. You will remain anonymous and only be identified by the subject ID above. Please do *not* write your name anywhere on this paper.

Questions

1. Age   _____ years
2. Gender   □ Female   □ Male
3. Dominant hand   □ Left   □ Right
4. Dominant eye   □ Left   □ Right
5. Colour blindness   □ Yes   □ No

For the remaining questions on the next page, please mark (by making a circle around one of the numbers) on the scale between 0 and 10 your answer to the question. Since the questions are based on your own experiences, there is no "right" or "wrong" answer. Do not attempt to answer how you think we may "expect" or "want" you to answer – please just answer sincerely.

6. How much computer experience do you have?

0	1	2	3	4	5	6	7	8	9	10

None   Substantial

7. How good are you at using computers in general?

0	1	2	3	4	5	6	7	8	9	10

No skills   Expert

8. What experience do you have of doing more than one thing at the same time?

0	1	2	3	4	5	6	7	8	9	10

None   Substantial

9. How skilled are you of doing more than one thing at the same time?

0	1	2	3	4	5	6	7	8	9	10

No skill   Expert

10. How much do interruptions affect your ability to perform a task?

0	1	2	3	4	5	6	7	8	9	10

Not at all   Significantly

11. How much do distractions affect your ability to perform a task?

0	1	2	3	4	5	6	7	8	9	10

Not at all   Significantly

12. How skilled are you at visual puzzling / matching games?

0	1	2	3	4	5	6	7	8	9	10

No skill   Expert

13. How good is your **spoken** English?

0	1	2	3	4	5	6	7	8	9	10

Can't speak   Accent free

Thank you for filling in this form,
now continue with the experiment!

Inquiry #2 – Fill in *after* the study
(Audio Experiment)

(This box is filled in by the test leader)

Subject ID: _____ — — — — Notes: _____

Privacy note

All answers you provide will be kept strictly confidential. In all results, derived from this study, we will exclude any information that can be used to identify you as a participant. You will remain anonymous and only be identified by the subject ID above. Please do *not* write your name anywhere on this paper.

Questions

For the following questions, please mark (by making a circle around one of the numbers) on the scale between 0 and 10 your answer to the question. Since the questions are based on your own experiences, there is no "right" or "wrong" answer. Do not attempt to answer how you think we may "expect" or "want" you to answer – please just answer sincerely.

1. How much anxiety did you feel during the experiment?

0	1	2	3	4	5	6	7	8	9	10

None   Substantial

2. How motivated did you feel during the experiment?

0	1	2	3	4	5	6	7	8	9	10

Not motivated   Very motivated

3. How easy/difficult was it to use the speech recognition?

0	1	2	3	4	5	6	7	8	9	10

Very easy   Very difficult

Why? Please motivate if possible

For the treatments that involved *both* the Hotwire game and the matching task at the same time, please answer the questions below by ranking the treatments from 1 to 5.

δ λ ψ ξ ω

a) Rank how well you liked them.	—	—	—	—	—	1-most ... 5-least
b) Ease of performing both of the tasks.	—	—	—	—	—	1-easy... 5-hard
c) Ease of performing the matching task.	—	—	—	—	—	1-easy ... 5-hard
d) Ease of performing the Hotwire game.	—	—	—	—	—	1-easy ... 5-hard
e) Stress caused	—	—	—	—	—	1-most ... 5-least
f) Feeling interrupted	—	—	—	—	—	1-most ... 5-least
g) Feeling distracted.	—	—	—	—	—	1-most ... 5-least
h) Ease of predicting the interruptions.	—	—	—	—	—	1-easy ... 5-hard
i) How busy did you feel when interrupted?	—	—	—	—	—	1-very ... 5-little
j) Ease of continuing after an interruption.	—	—	—	—	—	1-easy ... 5-hard

Treatment ψ

4. How easy was it to predict the next interruptions?

0	1	2	3	4	5	6	7	8	9	10

Unpredictable   Easy to predict

Treatment δ

5. How did you like the ability to choose when to present the matching task?

0	1	2	3	4	5	6	7	8	9	10

Not at all   Very much

6. How much extra effort did it take to choose when to present the matching task?

0	1	2	3	4	5	6	7	8	9	10

No extra effort   Substantial

7. How distracting were the visual notifications?

0	1	2	3	4	5	6	7	8	9	10

Not distracting   Very distracting

8. How stressful were the visual notifications?

0	1	2	3	4	5	6	7	8	9	10

Not stressful   Very stressful

Treatment λ

9. How did you like the ability to choose when to present the matching task?

0	1	2	3	4	5	6	7	8	9	10

Not at all   Very much

10. How much extra effort did it take to choose when to present the matching task?

0	1	2	3	4	5	6	7	8	9	10

No extra effort   Substantial

11. How distracting were the audio notifications?

0	1	2	3	4	5	6	7	8	9	10

Not distracting   Very distracting

12. How stressful were the audio notifications?

0	1	2	3	4	5	6	7	8	9	10

Not stressful   Very stressful

Treatment ω

13. How much more easy/difficult was this compared to ξ?

0	1	2	3	4	5	6	7	8	9	10

Easier   More difficult

All treatments

14. Comments?

Thank you for having participated in our experiment!

Inquiry #1 – Fill in *before* the study
(Feedback and Frame of Reference Experiment)

(This box is filled in by the test leader)

Subject ID: _____   Place: _____

Date: _____   Notes: _____

Time: _____

Privacy note

All answers you provide will be kept strictly confidential. In all results, e.g. articles or conference papers and presentations, derived from this study, we will exclude any information that can be used to identify you as a participant. You will remain anonymous and only be identified by the subject ID above. Please do *not* write your name anywhere on this paper.

Questions

1. Age   _____ years

2. Gender   ☐ Female   ☐ Male

3. Dominant hand   ☐ Left   ☐ Right

4. Dominant eye   ☐ Left   ☐ Right

5. Colour blindness   ☐ Yes   ☐ No

For the remaining questions on the next page, please mark (by making a circle around one of the numbers) on the scale between 0 and 10 your answer to the question. Since the questions are based on your own experiences, there is no "right" or "wrong" answer. Do not attempt to answer how you think we may "expect" or "want" you to answer – please just answer sincerely.

6. How much computer experience do you have?

| 0 | 1 | 2 | 3 | 4 | 5 | 6 | 7 | 8 | 9 | 10 |
None   Substantial

7. How good are you at using computers in general?

| 0 | 1 | 2 | 3 | 4 | 5 | 6 | 7 | 8 | 9 | 10 |
No skills   Expert

8. What experience do you have of doing more than one thing at the same time?

| 0 | 1 | 2 | 3 | 4 | 5 | 6 | 7 | 8 | 9 | 10 |
None   Substantial

9. How skilled are you of doing more than one thing at the same time?

| 0 | 1 | 2 | 3 | 4 | 5 | 6 | 7 | 8 | 9 | 10 |
No skill   Expert

10. How much do interruptions affect your ability to perform a task?

| 0 | 1 | 2 | 3 | 4 | 5 | 6 | 7 | 8 | 9 | 10 |
Not at all   Significantly

11. How much do different body positions affect your ability to perform a task?

| 0 | 1 | 2 | 3 | 4 | 5 | 6 | 7 | 8 | 9 | 10 |
Not at all   Significantly

12. How much do distractions affect your ability to perform a task?

| 0 | 1 | 2 | 3 | 4 | 5 | 6 | 7 | 8 | 9 | 10 |
Not at all   Significantly

13. How skilled are you at visual puzzling / matching games?

| 0 | 1 | 2 | 3 | 4 | 5 | 6 | 7 | 8 | 9 | 10 |
No skill   Expert

14. How skilled are you in mental arithmetic?

| 0 | 1 | 2 | 3 | 4 | 5 | 6 | 7 | 8 | 9 | 10 |
No skill   Expert

Thank you for filling in this form!

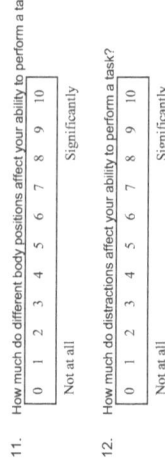
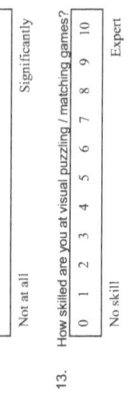

Inquiry #2 – Fill in *after* the study

(Feedback and Frame of Reference Experiment)

(This box is filled in by the test leader)

Subject ID: _ _ _ _   Notes: _____

Privacy note

All answers you provide will be kept strictly confidential. In all results, derived from this study, we will exclude any information that can be used to identify you as a participant. You will remain anonymous and only be identified by the subject ID above. Please do *not* write your name anywhere on this paper.

Questions

For the following questions, please mark (by making a circle around one of the numbers) on the scale between 0 and 10 your answer to the question. Since the questions are based on your own experiences, there is no "right" or "wrong" answer. Do not attempt to answer how you think we may "expect" or "want" you to answer – please just answer sincerely.

1. How much anxiety did you feel during the experiment?

| 0 | 1 | 2 | 3 | 4 | 5 | 6 | 7 | 8 | 9 | 10 |

None   Substantial

2. How motivated did you feel during the experiment?

| 0 | 1 | 2 | 3 | 4 | 5 | 6 | 7 | 8 | 9 | 10 |

Not motivated   Very motivated

3. How easy/difficult was it to use the dataglove?

| 0 | 1 | 2 | 3 | 4 | 5 | 6 | 7 | 8 | 9 | 10 |

Very easy   Very difficult

Why? Please motivate if possible

For the treatments that involved *both* the Hotwire game and the matching task at the same time, please answer the questions below by ranking the treatments from 1 to 5.

	δ	λ	ψ	ξ	ω	
a) Rank how well you liked them.						1-most … 5-least
b) Ease of performing both of the tasks.						1-easy … 5-hard
c) Ease of performing the matching task.						1-easy … 5-hard
d) Ease of performing the Hotwire game.						1-easy … 5-hard
e) Stress caused						1-most … 5-least
f) Feeling interrupted						1-most … 5-least
g) Feeling distracted,						1-most … 5-least
h) Ease of predicting the interruptions.						1-easy … 5-hard
i) How busy did you feel when interrupted?						1-very … 5-little
j) Ease of continuing after an interruption?						1-easy … 5-hard

Treatment ψ

4. How easy was it to predict the next interruptions?

| 0 | 1 | 2 | 3 | 4 | 5 | 6 | 7 | 8 | 9 | 10 |

Unpredictable   Easy to predict

Treatment δ

5. How did you like the ability to choose when to present the matching task?

| 0 | 1 | 2 | 3 | 4 | 5 | 6 | 7 | 8 | 9 | 10 |

Not at all   Very much

6. How much extra effort did it take to choose when to present the matching task?

| 0 | 1 | 2 | 3 | 4 | 5 | 6 | 7 | 8 | 9 | 10 |

No extra effort   Substantial

7. How distracting were the visual notifications?

| 0 | 1 | 2 | 3 | 4 | 5 | 6 | 7 | 8 | 9 | 10 |

Not distracting   Very distracting

8. How stressful were the visual notifications?

| 0 | 1 | 2 | 3 | 4 | 5 | 6 | 7 | 8 | 9 | 10 |

Not stressful   Very stressful

Treatment λ

9. How did you like the ability to choose when to present the matching task?

| 0 | 1 | 2 | 3 | 4 | 5 | 6 | 7 | 8 | 9 | 10 |

Not at all   Very much

10. How much extra effort did it take to choose when to present the matching task?

| 0 | 1 | 2 | 3 | 4 | 5 | 6 | 7 | 8 | 9 | 10 |

No extra effort   Substantial

11. How distracting were the audio notifications?

| 0 | 1 | 2 | 3 | 4 | 5 | 6 | 7 | 8 | 9 | 10 |

Not distracting   Very distracting

12. How stressful were the audio notifications?

| 0 | 1 | 2 | 3 | 4 | 5 | 6 | 7 | 8 | 9 | 10 |

Not stressful   Very stressful

Treatment ω

13. How much more easy/difficult was this compared to ξ?

| 0 | 1 | 2 | 3 | 4 | 5 | 6 | 7 | 8 | 9 | 10 |

Easier   More difficult

All treatments

14. Comments?

Thank you for having participated in our experiment!

Appendix B

WUI-Toolkit

B.1 User Interface Screenshots

This section shows additional impressions of different user interface renderings generated with the DefaultRenderer.

(a) Demo application at ISWC 2006.

(b) Demo application for EADS.

Figure B.1: Text renderings.

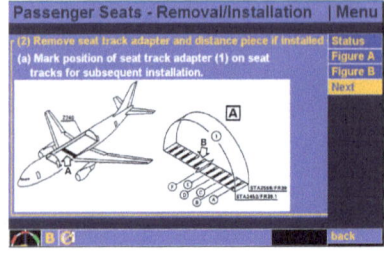

(a) Task instruction with image data.

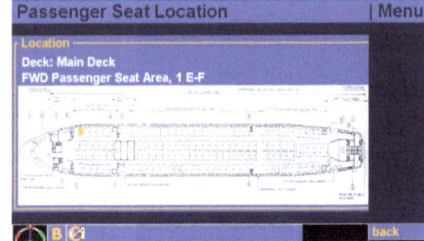

(b) Graphical location information.

(c) Graphical high resolution information.

(d) Image instruction in Skoda application.

Figure B.2: Image renderings.

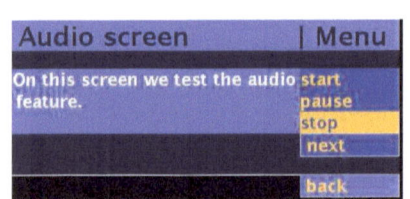

(a) Interface component to playback audio.

(b) Interface component to playback video.

Figure B.3: Multimedia renderings.

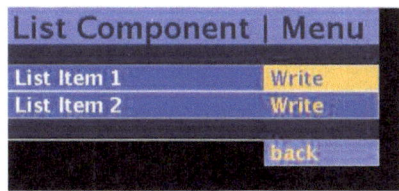
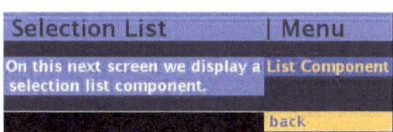

(a) SelectionList with different actions.   (b) SelectionList with common actions.

Figure B.4: List renderings.

(a) Property based emphasizing of content.   (b) Modal notification.

Figure B.5: Notification renderings.

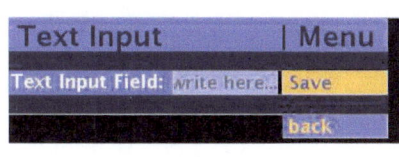

(a) Text input rendering.   (b) Visual feedback for Process elements.

Figure B.6: Miscellaneous renderings

B.2   Abstract User Interface Description Layer

B.2.1   Language Specification

The following description shows the general structure of the abstract user interface description language in a more formalized manner using Backus Naur notation (BNF).

```
<AbstractUIModel>  ::= Group(<Name>, <Elements>)

<Elements>    ::= (<Element>, <Elements>) | <Element>

<Element>     ::= Information(<Data>, <Properties>) |
                  Group(<Name>, <Elements> ) |
                  SelectionList( <Name>, <Elements>, <Common> ) |
                  ExplicitTextInput(<Name>) |
                  <Trigger>

<Trigger>     ::= ExplicitTrigger(<Name>, <ComputeTask>) |
                  ImplicitTrigger(<Behaviour>)


<Common>      ::= Information(<Data>, <Properties>)

<Data>        ::= ( <MediaType>, <Content> ) | CompositeData( <Data>, <Data>)

<MediaType>   ::= Text | Image | Audio | Video


<Properties>  ::= <Property> , <Property> | <Property>
<Property>    ::= <Key> = <Value>
<Key>         ::= Importance | Notification | InputNotification
<Value>       ::= High | Medium | Low


<ComputeTask> ::= Process | NULL
<Behaviour>   ::= Behaviour(RFID) | Behaviour(Timer) | Behaviour(<CustomBehaviour>)

<CustomBehaviour> ::= [reference executable source code]

<Name>            ::= [text]

<Content>         ::= [source URI] | [text]
```

Listing B.1: BNF description of the abstract user interface description language

B.3   WUI-Toolkit Configuration

Following examples show the structure of the most important configuration files used by the core framework to load modules with the Spring framework. Additionally, it shows examples of user profiles and renderings constrains used by the WUI-Toolkit itself.

B.3.1   Framework Configuration

```
<?xml version="1.0" encoding="UTF-8"?>
<!DOCTYPE beans PUBLIC "-//SPRING//DTD BEAN//EN"
"http://www.springframework.org/dtd/spring-beans.dtd">
<!--
```

```xml
Specification of the core framework configuration.

@author: Hendrik Witt (hwitt@tzi.de)
         TZI, Wearable Computing Lab.
         University of Bremen, Germany
-->

<beans>
  <!-- CORE MODULES -->
  <!-- Load Event Manager.-->
  <bean id="DeviceEventManager" class="org.tzi.device.event.DeviceEventManager" >
    <property name="name"><value>DeviceEventManagerModule</value></property>
  </bean>

  <!-- Load Bluetooth Device Manager.-->
  <bean id="CoreModule2" class="org.tzi.device.BluetoothDeviceManager" >
    <property name="name"><value>DeviceManagerModule</value></property>
    <property name="configFile"><value>deviceconfig.xml</value></property>
    <property name="eventManager"><ref bean="DeviceEventManager"/></property>
  </bean>

  <!--
  Load Context Module Connector to JContext API from wearIT@prok project.-->
  <bean id="ContextModule" class="org.tzi.context.ContextModule" >
    <property name="name"><value>ContextEventModule</value></property>
    <property name="configFile"><value>owcf.config.xml</value></property>
  </bean>

  <!-- Load WUI-Toolkit Module.-->
  <bean id="WUIToolkit" class="org.tzi.wui.WUIToolkit">
    <property name="name" value="WUIToolkitModule"/>
    <property name="renderingManager">
      <bean id="DefaultRenderingManager" class="org.tzi.wui.rendering.RenderingManager">
        <property name="rendererRepository">
          <!--Define Renderers in the Repository.-->
          <bean id="DefaultRendererRepository"
                class="org.tzi.wui.rendering.RendererRepository">
            <property name="renderer">
            <list>
              <bean id="DefaultRenderer" class="org.tzi.wui.rendering.RenderProfile">
                <property name="className"
                     value="org.tzi.wui.rendering.layout.DefaultRenderer"/>
              </bean>
              <bean id="HandHeldRenderer" class="org.tzi.wui.rendering.RenderProfile">
                <property name="className"
                     value="org.tzi.wui.rendering.layout.HendHeldRenderer"/>
              </bean>
            </list>
            </property>
          </bean>
        </property>
      </bean>
      <property name="sessionManagement" value="false"/>
      <property name="sessionPath" value=".tzi//session"/>
      <property name="scrollerEnabled" value="true"/>
      <property name="backForwardNavigationEnabled" value="true"/>
    </bean>

    <property>
    <!-- Enable System Tray.-->
    <property name="appletManager"><ref bean="AppletManager"/></property>
    </property>

    <property>
    <!-- Enable Adaptation System.-->
    <property name="adaptationManager"><ref bean="AdaptationManager"/></property>
    </property>
  </bean>

  <!-- CORE MODULES END -->

  <bean id="AppletManager" class="org.tzi.wui.rendering.systemapplets.AppletManager">
    <property name="applets">
    <list>
    <!-- Load Clock.-->
    <bean id="Time" class="org.tzi.wui.rendering.applets.Clock">
    <!-- Load Gesture-Feedback. -->
```

```xml
<bean id="GestureFeedback"
      class="org.tzi.wui.rendering.systemapplets.gesture.GestureFeedbackApplet">
  <!-- Add Properties Here.-->
</bean>
<!-- Load Speech On/Off Feedback.-->
<bean id="SpeechRecognizerFeedback"
      class="org.tzi.wui.rendering.systemapplets.speech.RecognizerFeedbackApplet">
  <property name="activeImage" value=".tzi/active.jpg"/>
  <property name="inactiveImage" value=".tzi//inactive.jpg"/>
</bean>
</list>
</property>
</bean>

<!-- Definition of Adaptation Network.-->
<bean id="AdaptationManager" class="org.tzi.wui.adaptation.AdaptationManager">
<!-- Reference to Context Module.-->
<property name="contextModule"><ref bean="ContextModule"/></property>
<!-- What are the default Constraints?-->
<property name="defaultAdaptationConstraints">
  <ref bean="DefaultAdaptationConstraints"/>
</property>
<!--
Create Network Tree.


           |—A
     |— C —|
Root —       |—B
     |— D


-->
<property name="adaptationNetworkRoot">
  <bean id="NetworkRoot" class="org.tzi.wui.adaptation.lookandfeel.LookAndFeelHandler">
    <property name="adaptationConstraintSources">
    <list>
      <bean id="Merger_C"
            class="org.tzi.wui.adaptation.lookandfeel.LookAndFeelHandler">
        <property name="adaptationConstraintSources">
        <list>
          <bean id="Modifier_A"
                class="org.tzi.wui.adaptation.lookandfeel.BrightnessContrast">
            <property name="adaptationConstraintsAsSource" value="true"/>
          </bean>
          <bean id="Modifier_B"
                class="org.tzi.wui.adaptation.lookandfeel.ColorBrightnessModifier">
            <property name="adaptationConstraintsAsSource" value="true"/>
            <property name="lightSensitivity" value="4.0"/>
          </bean>
        </list>
        </property>
      </bean>
      <bean id="Modifier_D"
            class="org.tzi.wui.adaptation.lookandfeel.BrightnessContrast">
        <property name="adaptationConstraintsAsSource" value="true"/>
      </bean>
    </list>
    </property>
  </bean>
</property>
</bean>
<!-- Define the Default Adaptation Constraints used.-->
<bean id="DefaultAdaptationConstraints"
      class="org.tzi.wui.adaptation.AdaptationConstraints"/>

</beans>
```

Listing B.2: Framework.xml

B.3.2 I/O Device Configuration

```xml
<?xml version="1.0" encoding="UTF-8"?>
```

```xml
<!DOCTYPE beans PUBLIC "-//SPRING//DTD BEAN//EN"
"http://www.springframework.org/dtd/spring-beans.dtd">

<!--
Maximum Device Configuration of the Wearable System.

@author: Hendrik Witt (hwitt@tzi.de)
         TZI, Wearable Computing Lab.
         University of Bremen, Germany
-->
<beans>
  <!-- Ponting Device may be present for Testing.-->
  <bean id="device1" class="org.tzi.device.DeviceProfile">
    <property name="deviceName"><value>Pointing Device</value></property>
    <property name="driverClass">
      <value>org.tzi.device.service.PointingDeviceDriver</value>
    </property>
    <property name="deviceType"><value>OSManaged</value></property>
    <property name="deviceAddress"><value>000000000</value></property>
    <property name="deviceChannel"><value>0</value></property>
  </bean>

  <!-- We may have a RFID Scanner.-->
  <bean id="rfid1" class="org.tzi.device.DeviceProfile">
    <property name="deviceName"><value>RFID Scanner</value></property>
    <property name="driverClass">
      <value>org.tzi.device.service.RFIDTagSensor</value>
    </property>
    <property name="deviceType"><value>Bluetooth</value></property>
    <property name="deviceAddress"><value>00a0960be732</value></property>
    <property name="deviceChannel"><value>1</value></property>
  </bean>

  <!-- We may have Speech Input -->
  <bean id="device12" class="org.tzi.device.DeviceProfile">
    <property name="deviceName"><value>SpeechInput</value></property>
    <property name="driverClass">
      <value>org.tzi.device.service.MultitelInputDeviceDriver</value>
    </property>
    <property name="deviceType"><value>OSManaged</value></property>
    <property name="deviceAddress"><value>000000000</value></property>
    <property name="deviceChannel"><value>0</value></property>
    <property name="configurationProperties">
      <props>
      <!-- Multitel's Recognizer requires Default Configuration.-->
      <prop key="mroLibName">mroWrapping</prop>
      <prop key="mroSampleRate">16000</prop>
      <prop key="mroSampleSizeInBits">16</prop>
      <prop key="mroSigned">true</prop>
      <prop key="mroBigEndian">false</prop>
      <prop key="mroBufferSize">1000</prop>
      <prop key="mroLanguageModelFileName">lng/enu16fdd_0204001.lng</prop>
      <prop key="mroDefaultGrammar">app/enudefault.app</prop>
      <prop key="mroNBest">10</prop>
      <prop key="mroGarbageEntrancePenalty">-500</prop>
      <prop key="mroVadMode">off</prop>
      <!-- Custom Settings for Direct Navigation.-->
      <prop key="grammar">navigation_grammar.fsg</prop>
      </props>
    </property>
  </bean>

  <!-- We may have a Data-Glove Gesture Device.-->
  <bean id="device2" class="org.tzi.device.DeviceProfile">
    <property name="deviceName"><value>WINSPECT</value></property>
    <property name="driverClass">
      <!-- Hardware is based on SCIPIO Sensor Beard.-->
      <value>org.tzi.device.service.DataGloveDriver3D</value>
    </property>
    <property name="deviceType"><value>Bluetooth</value></property>
    <property name="deviceAddress"><value>00b53132eb9</value></property>
    <property name="deviceChannel"><value>1</value></property>
    <property name="configurationProperties">
      <props>
        <!-- Define the Gesture Recognition Algorithm used.-->
        <prop key="sensor_purpose">interaction</prop>
```

```
<prop key="sensordata_preprocessor">
        org.tzi.device.service.TiltAnglePreprocessor
</prop>
<prop key="calibration_offset">85</prop>
</props>
</property>
</bean>


<!-- We may have a Textinput Device.-->
<bean id="device3" class="org.tzi.device.DeviceProfile">
<property name="deviceName"><value>Keyboard</value></property>
<property name="driverClass">
    <value>org.tzi.device.service.TextInputDeviceDriver</value>
</property>
<property name="deviceType"><value>OSManaged</value></property>
<property name="deviceAddress"><value>000000000</value></property>
<property name="deviceChannel"><value>0</value></property>
</bean>

</beans>
```

Listing B.3: DeviceConfig.xml

B.3.3   User Profile

```
<?xml version="1.0" encoding="UTF-8"?>
<!DOCTYPE beans PUBLIC "-//SPRING//DTD BEAN//EN"
"http://www.springframework.org/dtd/spring-beans.dtd">

<!--
    Declaration of user profiles for all system users.-->
<beans>
<bean id="user2" class="org.tzi.user.UserProfile">
<property name="username" value="Bob"/>
<property name="properties">
    <props>
    <prop key="visual-acuity">20/20</prop>
    <prop key="color-blindness">false</prop>
    <prop key="dominant-eye">left</prop>

    <prop key="screen-resolution">800x600</prop>
    <prop key="skill-level">novice</prop>
    ...
    </props>
</property>
</bean>

<!--
There may be also other users of the application.-->
<bean id="user1" class="org.tzi.user.UserProfile">
    <property name="username" value="Bob"/>
    ...
</bean>
</beans>
```

Listing B.4: UserProfile.xml

B.3.4   Adaptation Constraints (Excerpt)

```
#Holds the information to be used by Renderes and modified by the adaptation system.
#Excerpt shows color and font constraints.
...
text=true
text.color.fg.r=255
text.color.fg.g=255
```

```
text.color.fg.b=255
text.color.bg.r=113
text.color.bg.g=113
text.color.bg.b=185
text.color.hi.r=255
text.color.hi.g=255
text.color.hi.b=255
text.font.style=1
text.font.size=20
text.font.name=SansSerif
hightext=true
hightext.color.fg.r=255
hightext.color.fg.g=255
hightext.color.fg.b=255
hightext.color.bg.r=255
hightext.color.bg.g=0
hightext.color.bg.b=0
hightext.color.hi.r=255
hightext.color.hi.g=255
hightext.color.hi.b=255
hightext.font.style=1
hightext.font.size=30
hightext.font.name=SansSerif
mediumtext=true
mediumtext.color.fg.r=113
mediumtext.color.fg.g=113
mediumtext.color.fg.b=185
mediumtext.color.bg.r=255
mediumtext.color.bg.g=255
mediumtext.color.bg.b=255
mediumtext.color.hi.r=255
mediumtext.color.hi.g=255
mediumtext.color.hi.b=255
mediumtext.font.style=1
mediumtext.font.size=20
mediumtext.font.name=SansSerif
group=true
group.color.fg.r=246
group.color.fg.g=184
group.color.fg.b=25
group.color.bg.r=113
group.color.bg.g=113
group.color.bg.b=185
group.color.hi.r=255
group.color.hi.g=255
group.color.hi.b=255
group.font.style=1
group.font.size=20
group.font.name=SansSerif
title=true
...
```

Listing B.5: AdaptationConstraints.xml